Doomed Romance

DOOMED ROMANCE

Broken Hearts, Lost Souls,
and Sexual Tumult
in Nineteenth-Century America

CHRISTINE LEIGH HEYRMAN

ALFRED A. KNOPF   NEW YORK   2021

Library of Congress Cataloging-in-Publication Data
Names: Heyrman, Christine Leigh, author.
Title: Doomed romance : broken hearts, lost souls, and sexual tumult in
nineteenth-century America / Christine Leigh Heyrman.
Description: New York : Alfred A. Knopf, 2021. | "This is a Borzoi Book published
by Alfred A. Knopf." | Includes bibliographical references and index.
Identifiers: LCCN 2019036182 (print) | LCCN 2019036183 (ebook) |
ISBN 9780525655572 (hardcover) | ISBN 9780525655589 (ebook)
Subjects: LCSH: Tenney, Martha T. Parker, 1804–1876. | Tenney, Thomas, 1798–
1873. | Gridley, Elnathan, 1796–1827. | American Board of Commissioners for
Foreign Missions. | Christian women—United States—Biography. |
Women teachers—United States—Biography. | Missionaries' spouses—United
States—Biography. | Missionaries—United States—Biography. | Christian
biography—United States. | Evangelicalism—Social aspects—United States—
History—19th century. | Triangles (Interpersonal relations)—United States. |
Sex role—Religious aspects—Congregational Churches. | Sex role—United
States—History—19th century. | Women—United States—Social conditions—
19th century. | New England—Religious life and customs. |
United States—Social conditions—19th century.
Classification: LCC BR1725.T37 H49 2021 (print) | LCC BR1725.T37 (ebook) |
DDC 266/.023730092 [B]—dc23
LC record available at https://lccn.loc.gov/2019036182
LC ebook record available at https://lccn.loc.gov/2019036183

Jacket images: The Library Company of Philadelphia.
(watercolor) ami mataraj / Shutterstock
Jacket design by Emily Mahon

Manufactured in the United States of America
First Edition

For Annie

Contents

Dramatis Personae

THE TRIANGLE

Martha Parker, a teacher
Thomas Tenney, a teacher training for the ministry
Elnathan Gridley, a minister preparing for the mission field

THE PARKER FAMILY

Ann Parker Bird, the eldest sister, a teacher and, with her
    husband, Isaac Bird, a member of the Palestine mission in
    Ottoman Syria
Emily Parker Kimball, the second-eldest sister, a teacher and the
    wife of James Kimball, a minister in Vermont and friend of
    Elnathan Gridley
William Parker, their younger brother, a student at Dartmouth
    College
Martha Tenney Parker Mills, the family matriarch, widow of
    Captain William Parker, remarried to Lieutenant Thomas
    Mills

MARTHA PARKER'S OTHER CONNECTIONS

Abigail Hasseltine, the preceptress of Bradford Academy
William Gould and Charlotte Gage Gould, Martha's employers
    at a school in Fairhaven, Massachusetts
Walter Harris, the minister in Dunbarton, New Hampshire

THOMAS TENNEY'S CIRCLE

Sarah Tenney, Thomas's sister and fellow teacher at Moor's Charity School in Hanover, New Hampshire

Elisha Jenney, a student at Dartmouth College and the son of a Fairhaven, Massachusetts, merchant

Silas Aiken, a tutor at Dartmouth College and the son of a New Hampshire farmer

Bennet Tyler, the president of Dartmouth College

PROMINENT EVANGELICALS

Jeremiah Evarts, a lawyer who headed the American Board of Commissioners for Foreign Missions

Rufus Anderson, Evarts's subordinate and later his successor

Leonard Woods, a professor at Andover Theological Seminary and mentor to Elnathan Gridley

Catharine Beecher, an educator and author, the eldest daughter of Lyman Beecher, an evangelical leader in the early republic

Charles Finney, a famed evangelical revivalist who allowed women to take active roles at his worship services

OTHER AMERICAN MISSIONARIES IN THE OTTOMAN EMPIRE AND ON MALTA

Abigail Davis Goodell and William Goodell

Pliny Fisk and Levi Parsons

Eli Smith

Daniel Temple

Introduction

Years spent in the company of high-minded people have given me a taste for low gossip, and that's how this book began. Research for another project had me reading the letters of early-nineteenth-century missionaries scattered throughout the Ottoman Empire, a correspondence among pious Yankees set on saving the world. But into those earnest pages occasionally strayed bits of news about a romantic triangle back in New England. At its apex was a gifted young schoolteacher, Martha Parker; at its two other points were Thomas Tenney, an intense striver who kept school while studying for the ministry, and Elnathan Gridley, a clergyman and accomplished charmer who aspired to become a missionary. Both men hoped to marry her, and she, at different times, accepted proposals from each. My snooping turned up just enough to tantalize, but the possibility of finding out more about this story of love and loss, romance and rivalry in the early nineteenth century seemed slim to none.

That's what makes two-hundred-year-old tales of heartbreak so intriguing: private lives were much more private then. For centuries, stoicism served as the default mode for nearly everyone in the Western world, ordinary people especially. The harder life was, the more crucial to hold emotion in check: sometimes survival itself demanded restraint, even hiding the heart's desire. By the 1820s, when her suitors vied to win Martha Parker, some women and men had begun to give freer voice to their feelings, but most letters and diaries still withheld more than they revealed. The notable exception to that reticence was religion, a subject about which some could not divulge enough. By contrast, the intimate matters of flirtation, courtship, engagement, and above all sex received terse and even cryptic coverage.

That made missionaries' gossip stick in my mind. There it stayed until several years later when I came across a reference to an archival collection titled "Papers Relating to the Case of Martha T. Parker and Elnathan Gridley, 1825–1828." There they were again, that pretty pair of twentysomethings in pursuit of their dreams until, thanks to Thomas Tenney and his allies, the stars crossed. Most likely, I guessed, these so-called papers would amount to no more than a couple of letters—yet more testimony to the era's entrenched reserve. That expectation lasted until the moment that an archivist approached my table at the library and set down a very large box.

Within lay hundreds of loose pages, along with a bound volume containing a transcription of the whole lot in a neat clerk's hand. There were letters, firsthand accounts of events, and a long narrative summary, all setting forth the thoughts, feelings, and actions of Martha Parker, the men who courted her, and the wide circle of their friends and relatives. Here was a window onto the past that rarely opened, an intimate view of the inner lives of young Americans who were, like most of their white contemporaries in the North, rural in their origins, middling in their means, and deeply religious. The secrets kept close by most of their contemporaries spilled out of these pages, and the women and men making those disclosures—their personalities and the plots of their lives—staked a claim on my imagination. Perhaps most intriguing was the mix of desire and fear that this young woman aroused in many of her male admirers, a potent combination which, then as now, could produce explosive consequences.

For anyone curious about the lost emotional worlds of the past, this box was missing only a ribbon and a bow.

Who had made this gift to the present? That was the easy question to answer. The unlikely collector of all those documents as well as the author of the long narrative drawn from them was one Jeremiah Evarts, Esquire. Trained as a lawyer, he brought those skills to building the main organization sponsoring evangelical Protestant missions—the American Board of Commissioners for Foreign Missions—into the largest corporation in the early republic. An organizational dynamo, he managed agents throughout the United States who established local missionary societies and drummed up donations. A fund-raising genius, he invented the direct-mail campaign. He also kept up a correspondence with scores of missionaries scattered through India, Sri Lanka, Hawai'i, the Mediterranean, the Middle East, and the Indian nations of the American South. By the 1820s, he had thrown himself into a campaign protesting the forced removal of Native people west of the Mississippi River.

Harder questions followed. Why had Evarts compiled so full and careful an account of his findings about a romantic triangle? Consumed by business and travel, often hobbled by poor health, he devoted little time even to his own family. It seemed out of character, his prying into other people's love lives, conducting a long investigation, and then investing hours in composing a narrative. What made him so intent on mastering every detail about the progress of courtships, the promises made and broken, and the passions of the flesh and the spirit among these three? About his view of the inquiry's importance, Evarts left no doubt, declaring that "no case has occurred, respecting which we have been more desirous that every word which we write, and every feeling which we indulge, should be such as we shall have reason to approve . . . when the secrets of all hearts shall be revealed." Certain that he would answer on Judgment Day, Evarts took the precaution of preparing in this life for that tribunal in the next. His long lawyerly brief, he hoped, would vindicate him and his fellow members of the American Board in the here and now and the hereafter awaiting.

What made him believe that the stakes were so high? Reckoning with that question made me realize that this archival box held more, much more, than revelations about what people in this corner of the distant past kept most private. It also recounted a telling episode in a great and enduring struggle that first took shape between the American Revolution and the Civil War. As Evarts's record discloses—inadvertently, but powerfully—Martha Parker was at once the beneficiary of profound changes that were reshaping the lives of many American women and men and a casualty of the resistance to those changes. And yes, Jeremiah Evarts—and others—had a great deal to answer for.

Martha Parker was no Everywoman. The vast majority of wives and daughters, widows and single women, free and enslaved, in the early-nineteenth-century United States put in long hours of labor on family farms and plantations, in town dwellings and textile mills. But Martha Parker did typify a growing number of women in the white northern middle class. They were the fortunate among their sex, seizing on the opportunities created by the access to formal education offered in a growing number of academies and the informal learning afforded by a newly wide and diverse array of books and periodicals. And many, like Martha, sought a wider scope, venturing beyond the household to build meaningful lives. Imbued with a strong sense of their rights and obligations as citizens in a republic, they pioneered as educators, authors, and activists, joining associations dedicated to religious proselytizing, moral uplift, and social reform. They made their presence felt most profoundly in the places where her story unfolds, the rural hamlets and seaport towns of New England.

The most daring, Martha among them, dreamed of becoming foreign missionaries. It was one of the few careers open to women—and, at first, only to those who married men headed for the mission field. No matter that the American Board classified them as "assistant missionaries": wives saw themselves partnering as equals in a ministry abroad, educating women while their husbands proselytized among men. They hoped to serve God and grow in grace, but they also believed that foreign missions would afford them greater adventure, influence, and even fame than they would ever enjoy at home. Today the word "missionary" does not bring the word "superstar" to the minds of most Americans, but enlisting in the campaign to convert the world to Christianity started its long run two hundred years ago as a career that beckoned venturesome, ambitious women. (It was still going strong as late as 1959, when the reigning princess of the silver screen, Audrey Hepburn, starred as a nun committed to nursing work in the Belgian Congo.) Imagine, then, how thrilled Martha Parker felt—how lucky, even if a little daunted—to receive a proposal of marriage from Elnathan Gridley, whom the American Board had recruited and trained to join its mission in the Ottoman Empire.

Many of the new opportunities that made Martha Parker a young woman of uncommon promise—the formal schooling, the many books and newspapers, the benevolent and reform societies, and the foreign missions—she owed to evangelical Protestants. Thanks to successive waves of religious revivals, those believers made up a majority of American churchgoers in the first half of the nineteenth century, dominating the major denominations of Congregationalists and Presbyterians, Baptists and Methodists. Evangelicals strove to shape the nation as energetically then as they do now. Those in the North especially were eager liberators, intent on freeing individuals from the thrall of anything that got in the way of realizing their God-given potential—their true selves—whether drink, ignorance, disability, prostitution, slavery, or the wrong kinds of religions, particularly Catholicism and Islam. Some of the inequalities that had long narrowed women's horizons made their list, too, at least for a time. Under these religious auspices, significant numbers of white middle-class women like Martha Parker for the first time gained opportunities for a good education, intellectual fulfillment, and rewarding work outside the home. Indeed, nothing did more to transform women's lives in the nineteenth century than the encouragement offered and the institutions built by evangelicals.

But even by the 1820s, some in their movement, leaders as well as rank and file, had come to feel threatened by the energies they had done so much to cultivate among female believers. Fearing that their faith's empowerment of women diminished men, they entered the vanguard of those Americans, members of both sexes, who discouraged women from stepping outside the home and exercising influence in the churches and society at large. Theirs was a place in time that took male privilege for granted. Yet it was also one in which that privilege was coming under challenge. And when some began to suspect Martha Parker of being one of the challengers, her past became the stuff of scandal. Its reverberations quickly reached across the Atlantic and along the Mediterranean littoral as missionaries throughout that region became caught up in the controversy sparked by her fate. Their mounting resistance laid bare deep differences among evangelicals over womanhood, manhood, and sexuality, divisions that threatened the future of their movement in the United States.

That makes Martha Parker's story a signal chapter in the history of both American evangelicalism and sexual politics. It sharpens our sensitivity to the influences that encourage women in every era to strike out from shore as well as the riptides of resistance that threaten to drown their efforts. It deepens our understanding of the formal and, even more important and elusive, the informal means through which supporters of male prerogative sought to shame and punish women in quest of a wider world and the often surprising ways those bold spirits fought back. It discloses, too, the paradoxical role played by evangelicalism in what was a formative era for both that religious culture and women's rights by revealing its emergence as a hearth of opposition to the very changes this faith at first promoted. It raises the broader question of whether the resistance to vesting power and authority in women endures in the United States in part because evangelical Protestantism has thrived far longer there than anywhere else in the West. Finally, it offers a usable past to those in the present seeking to strengthen that faith's commitment to equality and justice. In the pages that follow, they will find like-minded believers who provided women with avenues of liberation and even strategies to counter the backlash against those who followed paths newly opened to wherever they led.

Martha Parker's world is not ours. If women in the United States today look through a glass ceiling, she and her sisters lifted their eyes to a roof thickly plastered and stoutly raftered. Yet in many ways their historical moment presages our own. As ever larger numbers of women assume influential positions in every sphere of the nation's life today, they find both allies and antagonists. Even as many cheer at the sound of glass shattering in the highest reaches of business, politics, and the professions, others resist entrusting women with power, equal opportunity, and control over their bodies. While some Americans welcome the new gender equality when it comes to power and pay, prestige and opportunity, others resent the competition and mourn the loss of those advantages that assisted earlier generations. To gain a deeper understanding of this contest as it continues to unfold in the present—a conflict that shows no signs of subsiding—listen to its historical echoes in this story of a doomed romance.

Doomed Romance

CHAPTER ONE

The World Before Her

She was perfection. That late spring day at Fairhaven, where he had preached a sermon, how the congregation wept as they sang the parting hymn. Then the pews emptied, and all in the church gathered around the young woman who had once taught their children. The devout in this southern Massachusetts seaport marveled, as did pious evangelicals everywhere, at her decision to marry him, a missionary bound for the Ottoman Empire that very summer. How brave she was, how selfless—and how soon would they all read of her exploits in popular religious monthlies like *The Missionary Herald*. It must have been a quarter of an hour before the crowd finally gave way and he could reclaim his prize. They were already almost famous.

Being the center of attention was nothing new to Martha Parker. She had drawn admirers long before these last several weeks as the engaged pair made their farewell visits to family and friends in Connecticut and Massachusetts. Some of the most heartfelt tributes came from young men at Dartmouth College, one of whom sighed that she was "possessed of many charms" and "these have secured for her an <u>abundant tribute</u> of flatteries, caresses and admiration." Her elders praised Martha, too. "Lovely" was the word that often came to mind among the teachers and ministers who extolled her Christian character and winning ways. She was pretty, it seems, though no portrait survives. She was accomplished, her lively intelligence cultivated by a year of schooling at a private academy. She was devout, a religious seriousness intensified by losses early in her life. Her eldest sibling, twelve-year-old Leonard, had drowned in a millpond when Martha was five; her father, William, sickened and died six years later. Through it all, her faith held firm.

And now, much to Elnathan Gridley's satisfaction, she was nearly his own. After traveling through New England in June, they would wed and shortly thereafter set sail for the island of Malta, then on to Beirut, part of Ottoman Syria. How providential, he reflected, that adulation had not spoiled his fiancée. Being so popular, as she confided to him, had made her "accustomed to caresses," but all that "tribute" was unwelcome, "beyond what she desired," because, as they both knew, the sin of pride feasted on a surfeit of praise.

Such sentiments reflected the evangelical Calvinist culture pervading rural New England, the milieu in which the two had been raised, one that deemed ambition suspect and self-regard among the worst of sins. From her earliest youth, Martha recalled, she had taken those teachings to heart and felt drawn to a life of sacrifice for others. No sooner had she received some assurance of saving grace and found "peace in believing" than she "desired to spend my life on heathen shores," converting the rest of the world. Modest and self-effacing as she was, when Elnathan first sounded her out on the subject of marriage, she had demurred and "looked in vain for an excuse from engaging in so great a work." It was only some six months later, after being encouraged by him and her family, that Martha at last saw "the finger of Providence point[ing] me plainly . . . to Western Asia." Somewhere in that part of the world, she would labor with him as an "assistant missionary." She would organize and teach in schools that boarded and educated local children. And she would reach out to their mothers, striving to challenge the customs that kept them subservient.

Other fingers had also pointed Martha Parker in the direction of foreign missions, most of them attached to mere mortals at Bradford Academy. Founded in 1803 by some forward-thinking inhabitants of Essex County, Massachusetts, it was one of many institutions springing up in the early republic, often under evangelical auspices, that offered sons—and a growing number of daughters—from elite and middling households an education more advanced than the rudiments taught in the common schools. When Martha attended Bradford Academy in the years around 1820, women considerably outnumbered men in a student body of nearly two hundred, and many, like her, came from some distance and boarded with local families. The academy reserved training in Latin and Greek for those young men headed toward college and instruction in navigation for the sons of merchants and master mariners, but male and female students alike received a firm grounding in English grammar and composition, arithmetic and geography. Bradford also offered its female students some of the "ornamentals"—drawing, embroidery, and painting—genteel accomplishments that reinforced geography lessons. Students drew maps on paper, embroidered them on silk, or painted them on velvet.

Their conservative religious beliefs did not keep these committed Calvinists from numbering among the new nation's staunchest proponents of formal education for young women. "It is pagan to keep the female sex in ignorance," one leading evan-

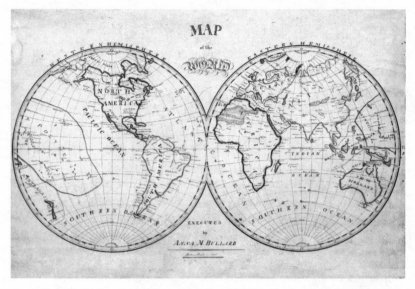

Anne Bullard was a student at a female academy in Boston when she made this map of the world with India ink and watercolors in 1836.

gelical periodical pronounced, so women must "illuminate their minds," to keep from being "compelled to think that their sphere is that of the butterfly, to flutter in useless gaiety and wandering thoughtlessness." (Hence the deliberate omission of dancing and French classes in Bradford's offering of "ornamentals.") A pious Middlebury College student and future missionary agreed, lecturing his sister that ignorance was "a mark disgrace" in women because of the essential role that they stood to play in promoting social progress and the spread of their evangelical faith. Such were the convictions that prompted Bradford's citizens to launch the town's academy and to take particular pride in its predominantly female clientele. According to Isaac Bird, one of Martha's brothers-in-law, she ranked among the school's most promising graduates. He cherished "higher hopes" for her than for anyone else within the Parker family circle and described her letters to him as "a treasure, an intellectual feast."

Evangelicals' prominent role in their founding fostered a deeply religious atmosphere at schools like Bradford Academy. Every day there began and ended with devotions led by the preceptor (or principal) of the young men's department or a local clergyman, and ministers in training from neighboring Andover Theological Seminary often conducted evening prayer meetings. Particular fervor seems to have prevailed among Bradford's female students, one of whom recalled the occasion on which her teacher singled out "all who loved the Saviour, to remain a few moments after the close of the school," and then pointed out to these young converts their "obligations and duties as Christians" to exert a good influence on their companions who had not yet experienced saving grace. The efforts of their elders combined with the zeal of adolescents ensured that religious revivals often set afire academies like Bradford, and students who had not yet received some inward assurance of salvation were pressed to strive toward that goal by both their teachers and their peers.

Some found that atmosphere oppressive. There was the poet Emily Dickinson, who kept her distance from a revival during her time at Mount Holyoke Female Seminary and avoided all organized religion for the rest of her life. But other young women welcomed the spiritual urgency that suffused academy life, and Martha Parker seems to have been among them. She spent her youth in an intensely pious household, her parents being pillars of the local Congregational church in the rural village of Dunbarton, New Hampshire. Martha, along with most of her siblings, came to join in that communion upon her "entertaining a hope in Christ"—experiencing the transformative "second birth" that, then as now, stands as the hallmark of evangelical spirituality.

In Dunbarton's meetinghouse, she would also have first heard the message that Christianity could offer a great deal to young women, a favorite theme of the village's longtime minister, Walter Harris. From his sermons Martha would have learned that women as well as the twelve apostles "followed Jesus and ministered unto him." Indeed, as Harris pointed out, those early female followers had proved more faithful than most of the men, staying with him throughout his crucifixion and burial, a loyalty that Jesus rewarded by appearing first to Mary Magdalene. Thereafter, committed believers like Phoebe and Dorcas "took a very active part" in the early Christian community, and even the apostle Paul—no fan of women who stepped too far forward in defense of the faith—commended their service to the church. Scripture itself thus showed to Harris's satisfaction "that it is the will of our Lord, to make use of the exertions of women . . . in support of his cause." They should not, of course, exert themselves unduly: allowing women to preach was as remote from the mind of Dunbarton's minister as he believed it was from that of the deity. Still, his including women in New Testament narratives on a basis of equality with men must have caught the attention and nurtured the piety of the village's young women.

Among them was one of Martha's friends, an earnest thirteen-year-old when she embroidered a sampler to read, "Lydia Hacket is my name / English is my nation / Dunbarton is my dwelling place / And Christ is my salvation." But the most locally renowned of the village's spiritual prodigies was Sally Ladd, a young woman only a few years older than Martha. After her death from tuberculosis in 1816, Sally became the subject of a pious memoir, one probably composed by Walter Harris himself. The little pamphlet did not circulate widely, but it celebrated Sally for recognizing "that she was in the hands of a God, who is 'angry with the wicked every day'" and for warning her friends of their peril. Such influences—to say nothing of the premature deaths of her father and eldest brother—would have disposed Martha toward religious seriousness even before her time at Bradford Academy.

They would have taught her, too, that piety could be empowering for women.

The prime mover when it came to putting a religious impress on education at Bradford Academy was the preceptress of its "female department," Abigail Hasseltine. The daughter of a prosperous local deacon, she ruled the lives of her pupils for several decades, a figure of Olympian dignity as one recalled, "moving about in our midst like a queen." As realms go, hers was not even a Monaco. Bradford's female department occupied half of a one-story brick structure topped by a belfry and consisted of a single large schoolroom with ascending rows of hard, double-plank seats. Yet within that small kingdom, Hasseltine exercised absolute rule and taught her subjects to honor and imitate inspiring role models.

Those most worthy of imitation were missionaries, among them Abigail's younger sister, Ann Hasseltine Judson. How gratifying for Bradford's preceptress, the stir it created among the students when Ann, after several years in the mission field of Burma (today's Myanmar), returned to visit her alma mater in 1823. Years later, one Bradford graduate remembered Ann as "a woman of much grace and beauty and of a refined and lady-like manner," and another could still recall her account of Burma as "thrilling in the extreme." Abigail could do more than bask in her sister's reflected glory, because by then she had made Bradford a veritable greenhouse for the forcing and flowering of missionary wives. It was an outcome fostered by the academy's proximity to Andover Theological Seminary, then the prime training ground for evangelical clergymen set on the conversion of the world. Hasseltine knew how to make the most of that advantage.

By the time that Martha Parker sat under her tutelage, two

Bradford alumnae numbered among the first missionary cohort sent to the Sandwich Islands (Hawai'i), and another had accompanied her husband to a mission at Bombay. Then there were the two other Bradford graduates who had served for a time as assistant teachers under Hasseltine's direction before following their missionary husbands abroad. The first, Mary Christie Spaulding, inspired so much affection that her Bradford students formed a group they called "the Sister Circle" to support two of the children who boarded at a mission school in Ceylon (now Sri Lanka) staffed by their former teacher and her husband. Donors won the privilege of giving their sponsored children new names—a popular fund-raising ploy—and the members of the Sister Circle decided on "Fanny Baker," in memory of a devout classmate who had died "hopeful" for her salvation "in the triumphs of faith," and "Parker Kimball Hasseltine," the surnames of three Bradford teachers.

Among the trio so honored was that second Bradford alumna and assistant teacher, Martha's eldest sister, Ann Parker Bird. Shortly after Ann married Isaac Bird at the end of 1822, they decamped to the newly established headquarters of the Palestine mission in Beirut. The examples set by Mary Christie Spaulding and Ann Parker Bird imparted a powerful lesson to Martha and the Sister Circle: they saw that women just like themselves could put their impress on the wider world, knowing it in ways that went well beyond mastering the globe and drawing maps.

Ensuring that her younger sister took that lesson to heart became Ann's cherished aim. Five years Martha's senior, she had forged a close connection with her in childhood, one that only strengthened over time. "From infancy, until I left America, I knew her whole heart, as far as it could be known by man," Ann recalled, and "perhaps, no other human being ever possessed that influence over her which I have." She could discern in her younger sister, having "read her character over and over" for all those years, the sort of woman who was "best qualified and most suitable for the wife of a missionary." What fitter judge than this veteran teacher, one who had spent several years at Bradford Academy "studying the character of hundreds of young ladies many of whom are now the ornament and glory of our land"? Proud of her sex, even prouder of her sister, Ann gave Martha the gift of her esteem—and possibly, the burden of her expectations. For her part, Martha admired her eldest sister, longed for her approval, and even stood a little in awe of her. She missed her, too. After Ann settled in Beirut, Martha wrote to her more often than did all their other relatives combined.

Even if her eldest sister had not come to number among them, missionary wives would still have loomed large in Martha's imagination. Everything that she read or heard about them—reports in religious newspapers and magazines, biographies and memoirs, and their widely circulated letters to family and friends—beckoned her admiration and imitation. Evangelicals touted these women as superior spirits who, not content with the usual round of benevolent activities, undertook more strenuous and courageous work to advance God's kingdom. There were, for example, the plucky wives of missionaries in Rangoon who—as breathlessly chronicled in the religious press—escaped the wrath of a Burmese mob by donning native dress, darkening their faces, and losing themselves in a milling crowd before being rescued by an invading British fleet. Such women would submit to any sacrifice, even the loss of their own lives or those of their spouses and children, for the great cause of converting the world. They would awaken the globe's inhabitants to the truth of Christianity and, beyond that, to the dignity of all humankind. They would play a pivotal role, as one New England minister expressed it, in bringing the women of other nations "to realize that they are not an inferior race of creatures; but stand upon a par with men." Today we might call these missionaries moral radicals, people whose consciences cannot bear the sufferings of others, even those a world away, and who subject themselves to risk and hardship in order to succor those in need. But most nineteenth-century evangelicals considered missionary wives something close to Protestant saints, spiritual models for men as well as women.

For members of Martha's generation, the most prominent figure in that pantheon was one of the first American missionaries to India and another Bradford alumna, Harriet Atwood Newell. Although she died before her missionary band managed to settle anywhere on the subcontinent, her zeal for the cause captured the imagination of the Reverend Leonard Woods, a professor at Andover Theological Seminary. In 1814 he produced a memoir by editing Harriet's journals and correspondence, adding his own commentary, and prefacing the whole with a sermon that pronounced her "the first martyr to the missionary cause from the American world." In Woods's judgment, missionary wives like her showed even greater self-denial than their husbands: they made the "more costly sacrifice" because of the stronger ties that bound women to their kin and their homes. And in Harriet's case, the reward for her forsaking all to follow Christ was immense: "the fair and exalted character" of "this lovely saint" had now been "exhibited upon the most extensive theatre, and excited the love and attention of the Christian nations."

If hers was not already a name on the lips of the devout, Woods's memoir made it so, endowing Harriet with an iconic status among evangelicals on both sides of the Atlantic. Its frontispiece featured her portrait: she stares directly at the viewer, serious and earnest. But what offsets the intensity of her gaze are the tendrils of curls framing her pretty face and the fashionable Empire-waisted dress with a frilly collar showing off her trim figure. That beckoning image made Harriet Newell, only nineteen at the time of her death, into someone whom many other young women could imagine themselves becoming, even longing to become. And, like Martha Parker, they might also have friends like Sally Ladd, who credited her religious conversion to reading the memoir.

If young women like Martha regarded the lives of missionary wives as inspiring, they also, more unexpectedly, envisioned them as adventurous and even glamorous. They did so with plenty of encouragement from the evangelical press. Particularly influential in promoting that message was Woods's memoir, which devoted many of its pages to chronicling Harriet's voyage from Boston to Calcutta in 1812 and her brief sojourn in and around that part of Bengal. She found sailing along the Ganges so picturesque and such fun that she joked in her letters home that it was "the most delightful *trial* I ever had." There followed a visit to the British Baptist mission in Serampore, an impressive spread that included large stone houses for each of the four missionary families as well as a sprawling common house complete with bedchambers, dining hall, two libraries, and a garden "larger and much more elegant, than any I ever saw in America." Besides being attended by a large staff of Hindu servants who ensured that the missionaries enjoyed "*all* the comforts of life," Newell rubbed shoulders with the mission's famous founder, the Reverend William Carey, who "is now advanced to a state of honour, with six thousand dollars a year." On those rare occasions when she ventured forth among the locals, servants either carried her on a palanquin or rowed her in a budgerow, a boat with a cushioned enclosure shaded by venetian blinds. From those perches Newell might easily have imagined a time when she and her husband would also enjoy a cushy life.

Reports from other missionary wives invited readers to imagine them ensconced in comfortable, if not luxurious, domestic settings. After being transplanted to the Sandwich Islands, Sybil Moseley Bingham favored her sisters back in New England with a detailed description of the room she shared with her husband in the missionary compound, one that quickly made

Harriet Atwood Newell and Ann Hasseltine Judson number among the first and most famous American women who served in Protestant foreign missions.

its way into the religious press. Colored straw mats, a present from one of the island kings, made the walls appear "neatly papered," and the furniture—a sofa, rocking chair, high bedstead with curtains, secretary, cupboard containing her best china, and even "my looking-glass"—completed the picture of middle-class comfort and respectability. Before the British war with Burma destroyed their mission home in 1825, Ann Judson and her husband resided for many years in what she described as a "large, convenient" dwelling surrounded by gardens and staffed with servants. On her way to Beirut, Abigail Davis Goodell reported sharing an airy villa on Malta with her husband and Isaac and Ann Bird and added that they all spoke Italian when gathered for dinner.

Just as they claimed to have suffered no lapse in their standard of living, missionary wives also boasted of their chummy relations

with native elites. Readers of the religious press could pore over
letters composed by a Sandwich Island queen to thank the mothers of two missionary wives. Another Bradford alumna, Lucy
Goodale Thurston, told tales about her cordial meeting with an
array of Hawaiian royals, the women among them sumptuously
dressed. In a similar vein, Abigail Davis Goodell informed her
sister back in Boston that the Turkish governor joined "a crowd
of 100 or more people" to watch as she and Ann Parker Bird dis-
embarked at Beirut and then took up temporary lodgings with
the English consul. Thereafter the company they kept included a
highborn Arab woman who set off her elegant dress by sporting
a turban encrusted with gold coins. Ann Judson, as usual, topped
the rest by relating how the wife of Burma's viceroy tried to cheer
up the missionary couple after the death of their infant son with
rides on an elephant outfitted with a howdah. Like that elephant
ride, such stories served as distractions from the grim realities of
deprivation, sickness, and death that stalked most men, women,
and children in the mission field.

What all accounts of missionary wives emphasized was the
wonder and excitement of exploring the wider world. Just as Harriet Newell professed to have the time of her life floating along the
Ganges, Elizabeth Shaw Nichols, en route to India, declared that
Ceylon had rightfully been dubbed "the paradise of the Indies,"
being "the most beautiful landscape I ever saw"—or it was until
her ship approached Bombay's harbor, which held twice the number of ships in Boston's and excelled "in beauty any thing I ever
saw." As for Abigail Davis Goodell, when the vessel bearing her
into Beirut "could proceed no farther" toward the shore, she and
Ann Parker Bird "were taken up by half naked Arabs . . . and carried to dry land." The message of such accounts was that stay-at-
homes were missing out. Evangelical editors who carefully shaped
these accounts before they went to press aimed to arouse curiosity and even to invite envy among their readers. They enjoyed

an especially receptive audience among young women like Martha Parker whose academy educations had already directed their fancy to geography's charms.

Whether for the trials they suffered or the perks they enjoyed, some women in the mission field attained fame. In fact, foreign missions offered one of the few avenues to celebrity open to a respectable woman at any time during the nineteenth century. To be sure, most who undertook that work, whether married or single, labored in obscurity. But even by the 1820s as Martha Parker came of age, two of them—Harriet Newell and Ann Judson—had not only won international renown but also enjoyed even greater acclaim among evangelicals than did most of their male counterparts. When a Vermont teenager lay dying in 1818, she spoke of her hopes for meeting Harriet—known to her only from Woods's memoir—in heaven. Another fan of that book, Rufus Anderson, a Bradford Academy alumnus, spent some of his time at Bowdoin College fantasizing about marrying one of Harriet's younger sisters and joining an American mission in India. ("If she be like her sister, God grant she may be mine.")

Missionary heroines found their way into their readers' imaginations because the religious press so effectively formatted their letters, reports from the field, and memoirs to resemble novels. Missionary chronicles abounded in tales of drama and romance, peril and courage, unfolding in exotic settings, and like novels they beckoned readers to imagine themselves as heroines having such adventures and inhabiting their own stories. The resemblance is a choice irony in view of the stout evangelical opposition to novels as frivolous and dangerous, particularly for their eager consumers among young women. It was exactly that readership, especially those in middling and elite families, who devoured the literature of women in missions, even as some also sneaked novels on the sly.

For at least one missionary wife, Ann Judson, that fame

translated into real power within evangelical circles. Leaving her husband behind in Burma on the trip that brought her back to Bradford Academy, she stopped in Britain long enough to impress a Baptist member of Parliament who introduced her to other moneyed and influential English evangelicals. Once in the United States, those connections opened doors for Ann among leading Baptist ministers and laymen, who solicited her suggestions about expanding their denomination's missionary outreach and formed "Judson Societies" to fund that expansion. Savvy about enlisting the press to enhance her authority within those all-male church councils, she also produced an account of the Burmese mission that made her its public face in both America and England. Had there been a guide explaining how missionary women could leverage their status to wield power within the churches, Ann Judson would have written it.

Not every evangelical believer in the early republic coveted her fame and influence. And some of the devout, female and male alike, disdained women who exercised authority beyond their households or who drew undue attention to themselves in any way. Those were the voices that filled Martha Parker's ears when she professed her mistrust of, even discomfort with, the admiration of others. Yet young women and men from her background also received no shortage of conflicting messages about ambition and achievement, with some of the most powerful, paradoxically, emanating from the evangelical movement itself. Even as sermons and the religious press celebrated missionaries as exemplars of self-denial, no one paying attention could have missed noticing that some of those paragons enjoyed the good life and glory in the here and now. Lucky young folks like Martha who attended academies had the opportunity to become even more confused, because such institutions accustomed women as well as men to compete for public notice and applause. "Exhibitions" staged at the end of every term called on students to deliver orations or compositions and to perform in dialogues or plays for an audience of relatives, trustees, and townspeople. Standing out, garnering praise, even striving to influence public opinion, became goals to attain rather than temptations to shun.

Ambition allured all the more because early-nineteenth-century New England offered so little to most young women, even those with some formal education like the Parker sisters. Parents of meager or even ordinary means expected that their grown daughters, at least until marriage, would contribute to family income, whether through working on farms or earning wages in textile mills or teaching in the common schools. For Martha Parker and her two elder sisters, that obligation became all the more pressing because of their father's early death. Sometime during the first decade of the nineteenth century, Captain William Parker—the honorific signifying his service in the militia—had moved his young family up the Merrimack River from the town of Bradford in Essex County, Massachusetts, to settle fresh acreage in a crossroads carved from the forest several miles west of Concord. There in Dunbarton he established a profitable grain farm and a tannery on more than two hundred acres of land, operations that yielded a respectable estate by the time of his death in 1815. But he was then in his mid-forties, leaving behind eight children, the eldest fifteen years old.

Fortunately, his widow knew how to shift for herself. Martha Tenney Parker maintained the family farm with the help of growing sons and at least one hired man, and she supplemented that income by taking in boarders. She also called on family and friends back in Bradford to help look after her three eldest daughters, possibly even to house them, as they acquired enough education at the town's academy to support themselves as teachers. Ann

Parker entered Bradford Academy in 1816, spent a year in classes, and then taught at the school until her marriage to Isaac Bird and their departure for Beirut. During Ann's time at Bradford, her younger sisters Emily and Martha also attended, each entering at the age of eighteen, to prepare themselves for teaching positions. While launching her three eldest daughters, the widow Parker also sought to secure her own future by marrying into Dunbarton's leading family: in 1821 she became the second wife of a widower, Lieutenant Thomas Mills.

Heir to her mother and namesake's resourcefulness, Martha spent only a year at Bradford Academy before landing her first job at a newly established "female seminary" in Fairhaven, a coastal town of neat clapboard houses hugging Buzzards Bay, just south of Cape Cod. The seminary's founders, the Reverend William Gould and his wife—the former Charlotte Gage, who had preceded Abigail Hasseltine as Bradford's preceptress—opened their doors in the spring of 1823. Their curriculum included "solid" academic subjects, even instruction in astronomy and "use of the globe," but an advertisement for the school in the local newspaper also touted Charlotte's specialty, "Painting in Water and Oil Colours, and in Crayons, on paper, wood, canvass, silk and velvet." Doubtless the Goulds called on their Bradford connection to recruit teachers, and there was Martha, eager for a position. What an eye-opener for her, moving from sedate farming villages like Dunbarton and Bradford to this hub of the whaling industry and the China trade. Fairhaven was booming along with its twin town on the opposite side of the Acushnet River, New Bedford, and both had become home to veterans of far-flung voyages. Her new acquaintances among merchants, supercargoes, and mariners coupled with her sister's departure for Beirut could only have drawn Martha's imagination to a wide world of places that she never expected to see except as points on a globe.

This novice teacher's prospects for adventure in distant spots seemed dim by the spring of 1825, but challenges of a different sort came her way. It was then that Martha began to teach at the "school for young ladies" over which her sister Emily had presided a year earlier, an academy organized by some aspiring townspeople in Boscawen, New Hampshire. Located several miles north of Concord, this small, prosperous village of grain farmers and millers supported an array of institutions inspired by their evangelical convictions. There was a society to promote upstanding morals and another to raise money for the education of "heathen" children at home and abroad; there were two "Female Cent Societies" devoted to poor relief and a thriving "social library" with more than two hundred volumes. Boscawen's citizens took particular pride in their common schools, to say nothing of the uncommon number of more than eighty "young gentlemen" whom their longtime minister had prepared for college. What better investment, then, than a female academy to educate suitable wives for Boscawen's Latin-conjugating scions?

Perhaps leaving behind Fairhaven's bustle came at some cost for Martha. She had made at least one close friend there, Caroline Jenney, the daughter of a leading local merchant. But perhaps, too, Martha yearned to live nearer to her mother and younger siblings, and Boscawen lay only about twenty miles north of Dunbarton. What's certain is that she and Emily welcomed the opportunity to shape a rigorous curriculum for the new "school for young ladies." Besides English composition and arithmetic, course work would include "Geography with the Use of Maps and Globes—Drawing of Maps,—Ancient and Modern History—Rhetoric-Logic, Chymistry, and Philosophy." Conspicuous by their absence were the "ornamentals" so cherished by her former employer, Charlotte Gage Gould.

The contrast suggests that the Parker sisters aspired to number among those educators in New England and New York who were providing their female students with an academic curriculum as

demanding as that of men's colleges. Those trailblazing educators in the 1820s—Catharine Beecher, Zilpah Grant, and Emma
Willard—held that women possessed the same intellectual potential as men and that their minds deserved the same cultivation.
Emily's involvement in that enterprise ended with her marriage to
the Reverend James Kimball in January 1825. But Martha seemed
determined to make a go of the Boscawen school, and its promot-
ers, intent on recruiting students, advertised in a Concord newspaper several times in the spring of 1825. Their notice ran right
below that for Zilpah Grant's Londonderry academy and prominently featured in all capitals "MISS MARTHA PARKER." How
did she feel, seeing her name printed in the newspaper? Did it fill
her with excitement and pride, being announced as a teacher who
commanded many fields of knowledge? Or did suddenly becoming a public presence embarrass Martha as yet more unwelcome
"tribute"?

Both, most likely. As she entered her twenties, Martha Parker
embodied the contradictions of the evangelical culture that dominated rural New England. Unlike young women of middling or
better families today, she was very far from believing that the
world was her oyster. What tempered all of her strivings were
religious teachings that urged members of both sexes to annihi-
late the self and submit to God and instructed women to submit
to earthly male authority. Yet at the same time, evangelical culture inculcated in young women like Martha the importance of
formal education and accomplishment; its academies and seminaries created the new settings for that to happen and trained
many students to become the teachers who would multiply such
institutions. Similarly, religious periodicals publicized the lives of
women who exemplified spiritual virtuosity and social commitment, some of them, such as missionary wives, acting on a world
stage. The churches themselves offered women opportunities to
make their influence felt beyond the household by joining volun-

tary associations devoted to religious, benevolent, charitable, and moral reform endeavors.

All those new opportunities reflected a seismic shift in views of women rocking both sides of the Atlantic. As the Enlightenment lent impetus to the conviction that women were the intellectual equals of men, evangelical Protestantism emerged as an important carrier of the notion that the female sex was superior to the male in some ways. After centuries of being censured as Eve's easily tempted daughters, women found their spiritual stock rising rapidly in the decades after 1800. Those in the Parker sisters' generation had become accustomed to hearing ministers and moralists praise them as purer and more pious than men, qualities that prepared them not only to provide spiritual nurture to husbands and children but also to extend their moral and religious influence beyond the home in ways that reformed civic life. Indeed, by involving themselves in an array of voluntary associations—whether to support missions, to alleviate the sufferings of the poor, or to curb intemperance—women could validate their claims to spiritual superiority and "true womanhood."

For all those reasons, the world appeared to young women like Martha a place of more possibility than it had been for their mothers and grandmothers. And those prospects opened up wider than ever before her bedazzled eyes in the fall of 1825 when, her name newly emblazoned in print, she first crossed paths with Elnathan Gridley.

Their meeting was no twist of fate. It came about because James Kimball, the new young minister of a church in Townshend, Vermont, shared Isaac Bird's high opinion of Martha Parker. Fast friends at Andover Theological Seminary, they became brothers-in-law by marriage in 1825 when James wed Emily Parker, the

sister of Isaac's wife, Ann. Both men took an interest in their
new sister-in-law Martha's marital prospects, concluding that she
could do far better than what New Hampshire had to offer. And
what could be nobler or holier than enlisting in the missionary
cause? James deeply admired the zeal that had brought Isaac and
Ann Bird to Ottoman Syria, and he lamented being kept from
"missionary ground" himself because "my poor weak eyes, which
fail even now while looking at my own language, would not probably long endure to search the niceties of the eastern dialects."
Accordingly, James did a favor for another mission-bound friend
from Andover who had decided it was time to marry: he introduced Elnathan Gridley to Martha Parker, most likely sometime
in the fall of 1825.

Elnathan was a little older and she, at twenty-one, a little
younger than most New Englanders contemplating marriage. But
then, Martha was more than commonly attractive, and Elnathan,
now nearly twenty-nine, had been in no hurry to find a bride as
he made the most of many advantages. The son of a well-heeled
landowner in Farmington, Connecticut, he attended Westfield,
an academy much like Bradford, before taking a degree at Yale
College and then training for the ministry at Andover. There he
had found favor with both his professors and his peers: as James
Kimball recalled, he was popular, even "beloved." A secret society
known as the Brethren, who recruited the most able seminarians
to serve in foreign missions, tapped him for membership, and he
enjoyed cozy evenings in the study of his Andover mentor, Leonard Woods, who confided to the young man that he loved him "as
my own son." Thereafter he pursued the path followed by many
missionaries in training: he preached in poor neighborhoods and
served as a traveling agent for his sponsoring organization, the
American Board. In that capacity, he raised money, made useful
connections, and gathered local missionary societies and women's
auxiliaries in dozens of New England hamlets. By all accounts,

he excelled, fixing himself in the public's eye as a lively, charming fellow.

Even at the beginning of 1825, when the American Board decided to place him with the Palestine mission, Elnathan, now in his late twenties, still had no inclination to wed. On the contrary, he had resisted many "lectures and exhortations on that point"—the sort eloquently delivered by those who yearn for grandchildren—because he had "long been determined to throw no obstacle in the way of my going to the heathen." So if the board wished him to remain a bachelor, he assured them, "I will submit to it, and—cheerfully." In fact, he expected to find himself paired with another single man, "some fellow laborer, who should be to me what Fisk was to Parsons."

He was referring to a pair of pioneer missionaries now famed in evangelical circles: Pliny Fisk, a veteran of five years in the Levant, and his first partner, Levi Parsons. When Parsons died after only two years in the field, the board paired Fisk with Jonas King, who proceeded to make himself at least as well known to pious Americans through reports that hyped his experiences into swashbuckling adventures. Now, with King planning a triumphal return to the United States, the board had slated Elnathan Gridley to serve as his replacement and Fisk's new partner. "Read Mr. Fisk's and Mr. King's journals, and you may read your own in anticipation, and may draw your inferences," Jeremiah Evarts advised the board's new recruit.

What Elnathan read left him rattled. There were the shakedowns and arrests of missionaries by a venal Ottoman government. There were the weeks of travel across sweltering deserts and mountainous terrain beset by robbers and local warlords. There were the constant challenges from Muslims, Eastern Christian prelates, and Roman Catholic missionaries. Small wonder, in view of the risks they were planning for him to take, that the board "strongly advised" that Elnathan "go out single" to his mission field. Within a few short months, the dangers awaiting him had sunk in, and he bemoaned a future of "wander[ing] about in Western Asia; without a family, and without a home;—having no certain abiding place." Though hardly immune from peril in their headquarters at Beirut, the American Board's two married male missionaries in the Levant, William Goodell and Isaac Bird, did not go off in search of it like the bachelors Parsons, Fisk, and King.

All in all, it was enough to turn a man's mind to matrimony. If more incentive was needed, there was also the will drawn up by Elnathan's father, Elijah, who had died in 1822 during his son's ministerial training at Andover. His real estate encompassed hundreds of acres on both sides of the Connecticut River, and he apportioned a third of that land to each of his principal heirs: his widow, Hannah, and his sons, Elnathan and Omri. The will also stipulated that if one of his sons died childless, the dead brother's portion of the landed inheritance would go to the survivor, provided that he had fathered children. The old man's object was to keep his property within the Gridley family line and to ensure the continuity of the Gridley family name. A deeply pious man, Elijah thought it well and good for his eldest son to commit to the cause of converting the heathen. But as a man who took pride in the long line of Gridley patriarchs—great begetters—he could not countenance Elnathan's abandoning all obligations to his family, chief among them producing progeny. And the sooner his son produced, the better, given the incidence of mortality among missionaries in general and the particular risks faced by those in the combustible Middle East.

Such were the considerations that at last launched Elnathan on his quest for a wife. He had steeled himself to share the new plan with the American Board by the end of 1825, even though he had not, as yet, won Martha Parker's heart. At the time, he was attending medical lectures in Boston, a rudimentary training that some future missionaries received, and lodging at the home of Jeremiah Evarts. No sooner had Elnathan raised the possibility of his marrying than the two locked horns, arguing away a long, cold December evening. Other members of the American Board's Prudential Committee, which made the final decision in such matters, subsequently pressed Elnathan to "go unmarried." But he had made up his mind, and Evarts and the Prudential Committee at last relented. By remaining single, Elnathan insisted, "I shall go contrary to the wishes and feelings of one, to whom I am under greater obligations than to all the world beside, one who submits cheerfully to very great sacrifices to promote the objects of the American Board, and one too, whose feelings, on any point, it would be ingratitude in me, to disregard." That would be his widowed mother, Hannah—the person pestering him for those grandchildren.

It was months earlier, sometime in the fall of 1825, that Elnathan had first made his intentions—and his mother's fondest hopes—known to Martha Parker. James Kimball promoted the courtship, assuring Martha that she, like her sister Ann, could advance the great cause of converting the world. At his first ask, she demurred, but Elnathan was a hard man to resist—a chip off the old block once set on begetting. By all accounts, he possessed "an uncommon share" of "ardor and energy," which is to say, as did one contemporary, that he was "awake to all around him, and not at all disinclined to the labor of describing what [he] saw," often with "many intensives." According to James Kimball, Elnathan made "informal overtures" to Martha first in November 1825 and again a month later. She, yielding at last to his "intensives," agreed to their engagement in April, just as the spring of 1826 came on.

It was quick work, this six-month courtship, if not quite the whirlwind wooing of many missionary wives. Lucy Goodale became engaged to Asa Thurston after a single day's acquaintance, and less than a month later they married and embarked for the Sandwich Islands. Joining them at that mission were Sybil Moseley and Hiram Bingham, who wed a week after making their first acquaintance. Samuel Newell, widower of the celebrated Harriet, had never laid eyes on his second wife, Philomela Thurston, a woman recruited for him by the American Board, until she stepped off the boat at Bombay (Mumbai). So many impulsive couplings among these pious, prudent Yankees. No sooner had they wed than these near strangers set off together for the other side of the globe, expecting never again—at least in this world—to see the families left behind.

Their haste occasioned some embarrassment in evangelical circles, not least because the ideal of marriage based on love had come to govern the mores and expectations of many Americans of this era. People of middling means or better regarded their choice of a spouse as serving ends that went well beyond ensuring their economic security or consolidating family wealth. Weighing the worldly advantages of prospective partners had not dropped out of their calculus, but increasingly couples entered into engagements with the understanding that marriage would provide both partners with happiness and emotional satisfaction. In popularizing such companionate marriages as the goal of successful courtships, evangelical Protestants themselves played no small role: spousal love became a moral imperative among them. It prompted James Kimball to assure his future sister- and brother-in-law, Ann and Isaac Bird: "I once said to you when speaking on the subject of affection, I did not see how mine could be any stronger—But I never visit Emily [his fiancée] without finding it increase." Emily, in turn, believed that it would be "sinful in the extreme" to marry without love.

The many missionary couples who married on the fly was, then, a matter to be explained—or explained away. Pious memoirs sometimes took on the task by emphasizing that missionaries' wedded lives conformed to the ideal of companionate marriage. Harriet Newell alluded often to her love for her husband, declaring, "He is all I could wish; affectionate, obliging, attentive . . . every way deserving of my strongest attachment." Even Sarah Lanman Smith, who might have been too "fastidious," as she put the matter, to consummate her marriage to her husband, Eli, bragged that he brought her flowers every morning from their garden in Beirut. Within the ranks of missionaries themselves, it was understood that the urgent need to convert the world justified some speedy pairings off. Not a moment to waste, as they saw it, when it came to effecting the spiritual transformation of the earth's inhabitants that would usher in the millennium. As conservative evangelicals, too, they believed that all marriages should serve a higher end than satisfying the needs of the individuals involved. And as selfless missionaries, they accepted that serving this nobler purpose could be the sole object of their marriages. What mattered, then, was the strength of a prospective partner's devotion to saving the world: that spiritual conviction became his or her irresistible attraction, the basis for lifelong commitment, if not romance. These warp-speed weddings and the sacrifices they entailed might alert us to emotional lives in the past much different from our own. Then again, understanding marriage as a union that draws strength solely from serving shared ideals is not altogether unknown in the present.

The ability to value spiritual activism above other attributes when deciding to marry might have come more easily to missionaries for reasons unrelated to their religious convictions. First was their gimlet-eyed realism about the likelihood of early death dissolving their unions. Harriet Newell, for one, entertained consoling thoughts of returning to her family in New England in the event of her husband's untimely demise. Then, too, many missionaries abroad lived in compounds housing multiple people, both families and singles. In settings more like an apartment with multiple roommates than a single-family dwelling, those saddled with less than satisfying partners might find the missing intimacy among other members of a mission household. Hence Harriet's friend Ann Judson reflected on the "happy days" when the two couples, "Newell and Judson, Harriet and Ann, united in the strictest friendship—then anticipated spending their lives together."

But whether they accepted proposals after a courtship of mere days—or, in the case of Martha Parker, several months—all those brides-to-be seized a chance that would not come again. As missionary wives, they would gain an opportunity to see the world and to carve out a career beyond their households. Here was the opportunity of a lifetime, and one beyond even the imagining of most of their female contemporaries.

Elnathan Gridley never doubted that piety could substitute for ardor when it came to choosing a partner. Then he fell in love, and what had started as a calculated campaign to find a wife who shared his devotion to missions blossomed into a bona fide passion—quite possibly his first, judging by how hard he fell. "I love you and shall love you till I die," he wrote to Martha, and he meant it. One of those who knew him best, Leonard Woods, perceived that the young man's affection for his betrothed was "ardent and tender." What was not to love? She was perfection, not only in body and mind, but also in soul. Like Elnathan, she numbered herself among the "Redeemer's children," those hopeful of finding a place in heaven. Only a year before their first meeting, she had joined the church in Dunbarton "by profession" of her faith. As for her family, they seemed eminently respectable—one sister wed to a clergyman, another to a missionary, and the mother now connected with Dunbarton's leading clan.

Another stroke of luck for Elnathan was that Martha's mother and sisters adored him and eagerly joined with James Kimball in promoting the courtship. Many parents, even among the devout, forbade their daughters to marry missionaries, but not Martha Tenney Parker Mills. She was more than pleased, even eager, to commit not one but two daughters to the missionary cause. It pleased her even more that the Gridleys of Connecticut could hold up their heads even higher than the Millses of New Hampshire, her second husband's clan. Her prospective son-in-law had grown up in a household with expensive carpets on the floors, curtains on the windows, books and a clock on the shelves, and walls bedecked with a looking glass, pictures, and maps. At night he and other Gridley family members had slept soundly in fine feather beds, one of many comforts provided by the estate being amassed by Elijah, about half a million dollars in today's money. And no sooner than Hannah Gridley became a grandmother, Elnathan stood to inherit a considerable portion of it. What more could Madam Mills want for her daughter?

That leaves only the bride-to-be. There can be no doubt about Martha Parker's regard for her intended: she praised Elnathan's "affectionate disposition—his energy of character—his sincerity—his benevolence—his nobleness of soul, and his piety." Yes: that does sound more like an obituary, especially set against his own fervent declarations to her. Perhaps maiden modesty imposed a certain restraint, yet in all the surviving words she wrote and said concerning him, that telling four-letter word— "love"—turns up only once. The omission invites speculation about the reckonings of this young woman poised on the cusp of possibility in the spring of 1826.

She would not have felt that all the world lay before her. Yet Martha Parker knew that she was not without resources, options, and exemplars—more than those available to most women of her generation anywhere in the United States. She had the assets of some formal education and two models for how to make use of it: the redoubtable Abigail Hasseltine back in Bradford and the pioneering Zilpah Grant down the road in Londonderry. Her schooling had driven home the lesson that a woman should make her life count for something. Given hard work, good luck, and time, she, too, might become queen, reigning as preceptress over her own female academy. Or there might be other, more lovable matrimonial prospects awaiting someone such as herself, still just twenty-one, so attractive and accomplished and advantaged through the Mills family connection.

But no. To a woman in Martha Parker's world, Elnathan Gridley, as she had come to realize, presented a matchless opportunity—the chance, as we say, to have it all. For her, "all" meant that curious amalgam of selfless devotion, spiritual virtuosity, exotic adventure, and wide renown incarnated in the idealized images of missionary wives projected by the religious press. No matter if he did not arouse—or had not yet awakened—her passion: his piety—and hers—were enough. Together they would fulfill the fondest ambitions for her future harbored by the sister she idolized, even reunite her with Ann Parker Bird at the Palestine mission in Beirut. What were the satisfactions of running a school or falling in love compared with having a life that held such promise for this world and the next? Fortified by the encouragement of Ann and Emily and James—as well as Elnathan himself—Martha had come into a greater confidence in her possibilities. Daunting as it was to imagine herself following in the footsteps of Ann Judson and Harriet Newell, she took heart from those who believed that she might match their spiritual heroism.

But before that brilliant future could find her, the past—her past—caught up with Martha Parker. And only months after his sister-in-law's engagement, as the summer of 1826 turned to fall,

James Kimball came to know the remorse felt by matchmakers the world over when fate stepped in to defy his good intentions. "I sometimes think," he wrote to Elnathan Gridley, "if I had dreamed of such a thing as this taking place, I never would have introduced you to her."

CHAPTER TWO

The Redeemer's Children

It was a long ride, even in midsummer's fair weather, and the dread of what awaited her drew out those seventy miles. Knowing the worst could not come fast enough for Martha Parker. Worry over what he could and might do had haunted her for months. Back in March, she had tried to dispel it by writing to his sister Sarah, her old Bradford schoolmate, saying that she wished to "keep alive the spark of friendship enkindled some years since" and inquiring after her health and happiness and that "of those most dear to her." In May, she confessed to Sarah that she had "done wrong" by ending the engagement with her brother but not "designedly so," and told her that if he remained unhappy, she could never be happy. Several weeks later she wrote to Sarah again, calling her brother "the best friend I have on earth, (Mr. G[ridley] excepted)," and imploring her to plead with him "till he has forgiven me. Could I see him, on my knees would I beg his forgiveness." Now she would meet him, face-to-face, the man she had not married. No sooner had Martha received his letter in late July, its message confirming her deepest fears, than she arranged their meeting. Yes, she would see him—not at Dunbarton, where the neighbors would know of his visit—but in distant Townshend, Vermont, home to the couple whom she knew would take her part, James Kimball and his wife, her sister Emily.

As she fretted, the young man riding from Hanover to Townshend felt more hopeful than he had for a long time. He had known that his letter would force her to see him, even though for the last four months—ever since her engagement to Elnathan Gridley—she had refused all of his overtures. Now he would seize the chance "to convince her of the wrong of which she has been guilty" by breaking her earlier promise to marry *him*. If that failed—as his letter intimated—well, he just might satisfy the curiosity about their past that suddenly stirred among members of the American Board's Prudential Committee, men who oversaw the appointment of its missionaries. In their behalf, Jeremiah Evarts had lately written to him, posing some pointed questions about Martha's past. Seeing his opportunity, he wrote straightaway, telling her about Evarts's inquiry. She knew all too well that his answers could prove her peril. He knew that she knew, which meant that one way or another Thomas Tenney would be heard.

What had prompted the Prudential Committee's inquiries to Thomas was another letter, this one anonymous. Addressed to Evarts, it had come into his hands on June 15, shortly after he returned from a long tour of the South to recover his health and to visit Indian missions. Its unidentified author warned that "disclosures will ere long be made of her [Martha Parker's] conduct, which will give the enemies of Missions great occasions to triumph." By now Evarts had become accustomed to crank complaints about the board's missionaries. Before she sailed to India, the now-sainted Harriet Newell had come in for accusations of "wanting a great name"; a few years later, a cantankerous Vermonter charged a missionary headed to the Levant, Levi Parsons,

Jeremiah Evarts headed the largest foreign missionary organization in the nineteenth-century United States, the American Board of Commissioners for Foreign Missions. He also led the investigation into Martha Parker.

with pocketing money from collections meant for the Palestine mission. So this swipe at Martha Parker—anonymous at that— did not concern Evarts unduly.

Yet he was nothing if not a prudent man, so he reached out to the only other person named in the anonymous letter. That was the Reverend William Gould, Martha's onetime employer at the female seminary in Fairhaven, who replied that within the last year he had heard "unfavorable reports" concerning her from a friend of Thomas Tenney's. Only one member of the Prudential Committee had any acquaintance—and that in passing— with Gould. As for this fellow Tenney with the rumormongering friend, no one on the committee had ever heard of him, whereas two respectable gentlemen known to many—Benjamin Greenleaf, the head of Bradford Academy, and Walter Harris, Dunbarton's pastor—had weighed in with glowing testimonials to

Martha's good character. At the end of June, Evarts met the lady herself, a brief encounter that made him wish all the more to believe the best about her.

As for Elnathan Gridley's decision to marry, Evarts had long since reconciled himself to it. Indeed, far from being merely resigned to the match, this shrewd promoter of foreign missions now glimpsed the publicity bonanza that awaited the board from their stationing two sisters in the Holy Land. This second Miss Parker would make, he expected, "a very valuable accession" to the Palestine mission at Beirut. Accomplished as they were, either one of the Parker women bade fair to become another heroic Ann Judson if she managed to survive, a martyred Harriet Newell if she did not. How the legion, loyal—and largely female—readership of the religious press would glom on to that pair in that place! With so much to be gained, Evarts, ever the careful lawyer, wished to dispel even a shadow of doubt about the young lady, which meant tracking down Thomas Tenney. How reassuring that the fellow was a nonentity, a mere schoolmaster teaching in Hanover and studying for the ministry. Tittle-tattle from so obscure a person would come to nothing.

Most folks in New Hampshire would have responded immediately to any request from the gentleman known to all in those rustic parts as "Esquire Evarts." But not Thomas, who agreed, as Martha had asked, to see her before sending any response back to Boston. At the end of July, he rode to the Townshend parsonage and spent the weekend, joining Martha and the Kimballs. The foursome shared a long history, one charged with strong attachments, fond hopes, bitter disappointments, and deep resentments, emotions intensified by their nearly tribal connections. A fifth person, Ann Parker Bird, would make her presence felt in memory even from the distance of Beirut. Emily Parker Kimball had named her first baby, born about eight months earlier, Martha Ann, a sign of the love and loyalty bonding the three eldest daughters in the family. As for Thomas Tenney, the Parker sisters' intimacy with him dated from their earliest childhood. Second cousins to him through their mother, whose maiden name was Tenney, they had "always called him cousin Thomas," Ann later recalled, "and treated him as such." In their teens, all three sisters along with James and Thomas had attended Bradford Academy and converted in revivals while at school or thereafter to the same evangelical faith.

Thomas, it seems, outshone them all on the score of religious precocity. Ann judged his adolescent self, this future Dartmouth valedictorian, only "respectable" as a scholar but more striking as "a prodigy of piety." "I was the means of turning his attention to the subject of religion," she claimed—never reticent about the power of her influence—which put her "in the habit of conversing very freely with him of the state of his mind." It impressed her, "so completely did he appear to be devoted to the best of causes, and so great, apparently was his enjoyment of religion." Impressive, too, that Thomas could claim among his first cousins the missionary whose memory she venerated, Harriet Newell. On the downside, comparing herself with this "prodigy" left Ann "sometimes ready to question" her own salvation, because she "had been four or five years entertaining a hope in Christ" before feeling assured of her conversion. It must have struck her as odd: Weren't women supposed to be the spiritually superior sex?

Whether despite or because of his odor of sanctity, the Parker sisters kept some distance between themselves and "cousin Thomas." According to Ann, "tho' we respected him as a friend we never thought of him as a brother." The younger Martha might have regarded him as even less: Ann remembered her having such a "settled dislike to Tenney" that she "would spend most of her time in her chamber" whenever he paid a visit. A scrap that survives of his correspondence with a fellow Dartmouth alumnus, Bezaliel Smith, suggests another trait that would have irked the brainy Parker women. After joining a "weekly reading society"—a book club of four men and five women—he informed Bezaliel that at least in Hanover "the young ladies have much more of a taste for what is solid and sensible than is generally supported." He felt obliged to offer this appraisal, he admitted, "because I have sometimes done them an injustice." It's unclear whether Thomas had sneered at the literary judgments of all "young ladies" or only those in Hanover, but doing either within earshot of the Parker sisters would only have confirmed their low opinion of him. Oblivious of their disdain (yet another fault), he proposed marriage to Emily sometime in the winter of 1821–1822, leaving them, as Ann remembered, "astonished at his presumption." Emily promptly turned him down, as she had earlier rejected his elder brother. Evidently, the Parker sisters did not rate any of the Tenneys as being in their league. But what really cratered their opinion of cousin Thomas was his proposing to Martha little more than a year after he had offered marriage to Emily.

Getting entangled with more than one sister is rarely a good idea. Thomas made matters even worse by telling Martha, not even twenty at the time, that he had loved her passionately for the last three years—which would have included the period when he was paying court to Emily. It might have been to Emily he referred when writing to Martha, "If I should be engaged to another, and you will then let me know [that you can marry me] you will make me the happiest of men." It seems not to have crossed his mind that Martha would share this news with her older sisters.

Amazed that this wooing strategy would recommend itself to anyone—let alone a fellow who preened himself on godliness—Martha turned down what would be the first of Thomas's proposals. Confiding the news to Ann, she declared, "I really thought him destitute of his reasoning powers or surprisingly altered in his opinions, for you know how much he has ever been opposed to professors of religion marrying those who are apparently destitute of real piety." Among those "apparently destitute" of piety was Martha herself, a devout teenager, but one still struggling for assurance of her salvation. Ann confirmed her sister's opinion of Thomas's offenses: "You will observe that he is guilty of a lie, or of offering his <u>hand</u> to <u>one</u>, while his <u>heart</u> was in the possession of another." A liar for proposing to Emily, whom he did not love, and a hypocrite for proposing to the as-yet-unsaved Martha, Thomas had "greatly sunk in my estimation." Once he entered the Parker sisters' orbit as Emily's spouse, James Kimball concurred with that judgment. He sized up Thomas Tenney as a Christian, surely, from a respectable family, of course, but a fellow altogether "unprepossessing." Even unconverted, Martha deserved better.

Thomas's checkered history with the Parker sisters helps us to make sense of what at first seems the strangest feature of this meeting at Townshend. Despite the many years of intimacy among those he was to meet at the parsonage, he prepared for their encounter by composing a long account of his courtship of Martha. He wrote it in advance and then read this statement aloud to her and the Kimballs. Its delivery would have stretched to more than an hour, and much of what he recounted would have been familiar to all concerned. Yet he insisted on presenting his narrative so as to give Emily and James "a correct statement of the manner in which I had treated Martha" in order to convince them "that my conduct had been generous." Sounds like the self-serving sentiments of a man with lots of explaining to do. But we should hang on his every word, because Thomas's chronicle of love's labor lost—crowded with minute and unsparing detail and packed with long extracts of letters from the Parker sisters—brings us closer to young Americans whose inner lives seem, in some ways, much like our own, but in others, utterly foreign. Did they feel then as we do now? Can we ever know?

⌒∞⌒

Thomas omitted from his narrative any reference to his pursuit of Emily. Instead, he began by describing his long exchange of letters with Martha, a correspondence that continued throughout his time at Dartmouth College and during her years in Bradford and Fairhaven. When he first proposed to her in February 1823, he had received "a decided refusal" but hoped that she turned him down only "to test the strength of my affection." None of the three Parker sisters, it seems, had as yet shown their displeasure at his "presumption." Or perhaps they had, and he'd failed to pick up on it. Thereafter he and Martha spent time together, being cousins after all. They visited and wrote; they even took a trip down to Londonderry near the Massachusetts border to visit some of his friends and to attend the annual meeting of the General Association. A religious gathering that generated the excitement of a rock concert today, it featured sermons delivered by famous preachers. He thought that trip went well enough. So well that he'd no sooner returned to Hanover than he proposed again. The answer this time came not from Martha but from Emily, not yet married, who told Thomas that "she did not think my attachment would ever be reciprocated" because "Martha had informed her, that she never had seen a person she could love."

Interesting. Had Ann's concerns prompted Emily's intervention? Did the two elder sisters wish to help the inexperienced Martha discourage an admirer's unwanted attentions? Was there something high-handed about this interference? Did Emily take a certain satisfaction in disappointing the man who had asked for her hand even as he pined for Martha? But why, then, did she mention Martha's claim that she'd never laid eyes on a man worth loving? Could Emily have been trying to draw the sting of rejection by assuring Thomas that no man could pass muster with her picky sister? Some combination of all of the above? Whatever lay behind her letter, Thomas took Emily at her word, and he spent the next year trying to forget Martha. The sisterhood was powerful—that much he understood.

Gaining command over his feelings did not come easily, as he told the group gathered at the parsonage. But by the late summer of 1825, he felt certain that he "could regard Martha as only a friend." That confidence lasted until the moment when, as he bade farewell after a brief visit to the Parker home farm, she slipped him a note asking, "Is it <u>still</u> in the power of Martha to confer on you the <u>highest earthly happiness</u>? If so, her heart is all your own." Her contemporaries called that "encouragement"— making known a woman's interest and availability. It marked quite a change from the sentiments Martha had expressed only a year and a half earlier in response to Thomas's first proposal. "Perhaps it is unnecessary for me to say <u>to you</u>," she had then written to Ann, "that to accept . . . would make me completely miserable."

Taken aback—as are we—by this sudden "encouragement," Thomas resolved to remain "calm and cautious" until he knew why Martha had rejected his earlier offers of marriage. All the trouble, she explained, came about because of gossip that had impugned Thomas's character; after discovering "that the author was an enemy" to him, she concluded that "the report was false." But within weeks, Martha changed her mind and took back her heart, telling him that her doubts arising from some unspecified "obstacle" had returned. She wanted to be friends again, nothing more.

By now Thomas had lost the hard-won composure he had gained over the last year, as he readily confessed at Townshend. "I loved her more than ever," and "I had no doubt <u>she loved me</u>

<u>ardently</u>." He supposed "she was making sacrifice of her own happiness to principle," though he could not have said to what principle, because Martha refused to identify both the "obstacle" standing in the way of their marriage and the person who had warned her about it. Despite his letters pleading to know "what would thus wound the feelings and pain the heart of a delicate female," she would not tell. "Her feelings were such," Martha assured him, that "it was <u>impossible</u>" for her to say more and "that she now would rather have me to hate than love her." Thomas felt sure that "her happiness was at an end; I could only look on as a silent spectator and see <u>her</u> sink into the grave for an <u>imaginary</u> cause."

No shortage of "obstacles" might have given Martha Parker second thoughts about giving her heart to Thomas Tenney. As she and her cousin carried on their exchange in the fall of 1825, two other men were pursuing her. The first suitor, then unknown to Thomas, was Elnathan Gridley, who, thanks to his friend James Kimball, had entered Martha's life. The two would have met only occasionally as the aspiring missionary traveled the countryside raising money for the American Board and organizing local auxiliary societies. But sometime in November, Elnathan "took pains" to see her and raised the possibility of their marrying. Whatever he said stopped short of a formal proposal, or she stopped him short by declaring herself "not inclined to favor his addresses."

More fixed as a presence in Martha's life that fall was her second suitor, Elisha Jenney, a young man of Thomas's acquaintance, then a junior at Dartmouth College, the son of an affluent merchant family in Fairhaven. During her time teaching at the academy there, Martha had met Elisha through his sister, her new friend, Caroline. He became smitten, the two corresponded, and by the end of 1825 he was laying siege at Dunbarton. Since remarrying, Martha's mother had taken up residence at her second husband's home but continued to use what had been the Parker home farm as a boardinghouse. Elisha and Caroline Jenney lodged there without charge for some weeks that winter, keeping company with Martha and perhaps some of her younger siblings. Elisha might have taken an early leave from college to teach a winter school in Dunbarton, a common practice for Dartmouth students, but his main occupation seems to have been skewering Thomas Tenney. He warned Martha that Thomas fancied a woman in Hanover and also that he was "once engaged to a young lady, and after she became <u>tenderly attached to him</u>, he deserted her without assigning any reasons for his conduct." When Thomas returned to the Parker home farm at the end of December, hoping to propose again, there was Elisha, still firmly lodged, gloating to his rival that Martha's "feelings were <u>changed</u>" and that she loved her cousin no longer.

The news devastated Thomas, and his audience at Townshend got an earful about how much. "I was confounded, I was distressed, I was miserable! Never did such mental agitation distract my bosom! I felt that I lived only to be tormented." Unable to sleep that night, he "wrote a <u>crazy billet</u> [letter]" to Martha, demanding to know why she had encouraged his suit in the late summer only to spurn him now. The next morning, she told him that one of her sisters—most likely Emily—had threatened to disown her if she wed Thomas. When he pressed Martha, urging that her family would become reconciled to their marriage, she cut him off. Elisha had told him the truth, she admitted: her feelings had changed, and she "did not think she could be happy connected with me." Thomas crawled back to Hanover, hopes dashed.

Then—only a week later—what he called "business" brought him back to Dunbarton, and his hopes renewed. He stopped for tea at the Parker home farm and found Martha there, "much agitated." She urged him to pass the night and then "at length told me, I was the only person she had ever loved—said she could never love another—she could not be happy, if she saw me connected with another!" A long conversation ensued, during which she blamed Elisha Jenney for driving a wedge between them. She realized now that he had spread lies about Thomas, scheming to win her for himself, but "did not possess those qualities necessary to render her happy." Before dawn, Martha and Thomas had become engaged, and he "left Dunbarton more happy than I ever had been before."

That ecstasy lasted until the love letters he so eagerly expected failed to arrive. Days and then weeks dragged by as Thomas's "forebodings of the future" mounted. At last, sometime in February 1826, the ax fell: Martha wrote from the Kimballs' parsonage in Townshend that she could not gain Emily's consent to their marriage and broke off the engagement. "This is probably the last letter you will ever receive from the hand of Martha," she wrote in farewell. "And I now feel, that I wish not to meet you again, till we meet in Eternity." Martha was counting on that postponement until the next life, because by now, in her mind's eye, she was sailing to Beirut as Elnathan Gridley's wife. The missionary had renewed his "informal overtures" to her about that prospect soon after she had agreed to marry Thomas in December, and by April 1826 she and Elnathan were engaged.

Thomas still had no idea that Elnathan Gridley even existed, let alone that he had won the woman of their dreams. Convinced that Martha loved him still and that "some false report" had "prejudiced" Emily against him, he sent the latter a letter demanding to know why "she had determined to place herself between two, whose hearts were united and thus destroy all their earthly happiness." He had felt sure that he "possessed her confidence," because at their last meeting Emily had told him "how much pleasure it would give us all to see Martha connected with you." If, in fact, Emily had said that, she spoke like someone from whom assurance was being wheedled by her sister's importunate suitor. Thomas, desperate with desire, had mistaken civility for enthusiasm. Now, faced with his letter, Emily replied that she had withheld her approval of the engagement not out of any reservations about his character but because Martha didn't love him, and "for her to marry you, or any other person, without love, I should consider sinful in the extreme. . . . I should advise you to think no more of her." She weighed in again with the observation that Martha "has repeatedly told me, she never had found a person she could love; and she has probably told you the same."

That was Emily's story, and she was sticking to it. It must have struck her as more polite, to say nothing of more Christian, than disclosing to cousin Thomas the litany of faults that she and Ann had long held against him. Most likely, too, neither of her elder sisters wished to believe that Martha could be fond of him. In light of her views about marriage, Emily's insistence that Martha loved no one does raise an intriguing question: What did she make of Elnathan's courtship of her sister, a wooing—often right under the roof of the Townshend parsonage—that moved quickly toward engagement during the early months of 1826? Had Martha still "never found a person she could love" even a few short weeks before agreeing to marry Elnathan? Was it her love of the missionary cause rather than of the missionary himself that drew Martha toward marrying him? Had she confessed as much to Emily? Or was Emily gilding the truth about her sister's feelings in order to soften the blow for cousin Thomas—or to placate him?

Still more questions arise from the fact that the Kimballs had actively encouraged the match with Elnathan, even after they knew that Martha had accepted Thomas's proposal. The couple evidently felt free to persist because Martha had told them that her engagement to their cousin was "conditional"—pending

Emily's consent—which left room for both women to maneu-
ver. Martha felt free to back out of her "conditional" promise to
Thomas, and Emily, by holding back her consent, pushed her
sister into Elnathan's waiting arms. No doubt Emily believed that
her matchmaking—and unmaking—served the cause of missions. Possibly, too, she was evening the score with Thomas for his
earlier humiliation of her. She had refused his proposal a couple
years earlier, yet it must have stung, discovering that he much
preferred her younger sister. Even a minister's wife would have
felt the temptation, if offered a chance, to stick in the knife and
twist it.

Meanwhile, Elisha Jenney saw an opportunity in his former
rival's heartbreak. Questioned by Thomas, he denied "with much
promptitude and openness" that he had ever tried to turn Martha against his rival. To the contrary, Elisha insisted, it was she
who "had said and done" things "inconsistent with true affection" for her former fiancé. Thomas believed him. Indeed, the
two became friends, growing so close in their commiseration that
Thomas even gave him extracts of his many letters from Martha.
What Thomas might not have known is that at some point in that
eventful winter of 1825–1826, his new friend had also proposed to
Martha. For a time, Elisha might have been in the running for her
favor, but when he failed to "improve upon acquaintance," as she
put the matter, she dismissed him as "a mere boy." She rejected
his offer of marriage and, after he left Dunbarton, refused to cor-
respond with him and sent him a message, through Thomas, to
destroy all her letters. "I do not now approve of females corre-
sponding with gentlemen," she added primly, "and I regret that
I ever have." She would regret it even more once Elisha Jenney
served up his revenge.

∞

Jilted by Martha and convinced that she had never felt any "real attachment" to him, Thomas opened his final volley of recriminations. He accused her of being "irrational" and "deceitful," and he requested—superfluously, it would seem—a release from their engagement. She fired back: "You say you wish me to be a rational girl. I certainly must be so if I hope to be in any degree useful in the world. I profess to be a follower of the Jesus whom you love." (And she was by then, having been accepted for church membership.) Even so, she asked for his forgiveness, and "I did forgive," Thomas told the company at Townshend. He "cherished not one hard feeling"—not even a few weeks later, when at last he learned about her engagement to Elnathan Gridley. The capacity to forgive was important to evangelicals, and Thomas expressed something even more essential to their ideal of holiness by the admission that he had erred by his "unwillingness that my Heavenly Father should lead me in his own way." Yet once he divined "the design of God" in his romantic disappointment, he "felt I had reason to regard this as one of the most profitable occurrences of my life." Reconciled to the will of his sovereign God, Thomas felt happier than he'd been for many years—until, a few short weeks later in the late spring of 1826, he heard from Elisha, now back home in Fairhaven.

Submitting to God's will sat even less easily with Elisha. Or perhaps he believed that providence was offering him a prime opportunity to even the score when Martha and her new fiancé turned up in town. As the rest of Fairhaven flocked to Elnathan's sermon and fawned over the bride-to-be, the prominent Jenney family held back. Then Elisha took to following the couple about, looking "downcast," and when asked why, he identified himself as "one of Martha's rejected lovers." *One* of them? Ah, yes: this so-called spiritual paragon, this soon-to-be missionary's wife, had a habit of leading men on before cutting them dead, and to prove it, Elisha spread around town those extracts from

old letters to her other castoff, Thomas Tenney. Exhilarated by
the stir he caused, Elisha sent his news of taking their revenge to
Thomas, adding that Martha, when confronted, had even denied
giving the schoolmaster any "encouragement." For Thomas, this
news was too much—not Elisha's conduct, but Martha's unwillingness to admit and repent her flirtatious ways and their broken
engagement before all of Fairhaven. It "awaken[ed] in me the live-
liest sense of wrong," he told his hearers at Townshend, as well as
the conviction that she was "wholly unfit for the holy and sacred
employment" of a foreign missionary. He wrote to Emily and
to Martha, demanding a meeting. Then, out of the blue, he had
received that inquiring letter from Esquire Evarts.

So much sounds so familiar in Thomas Tenney's lament. It's the
story we've all heard, overheard, or at worst related ourselves
over a kitchen table, at a coffee shop, in a bar. It's the plot of
countless novels and plays, television shows and movies. Here's
the lover who cannot give up hope, the poor fool jerked around
by the object of his or her obsession. But listening closely to
Thomas's tale of woe also turns up some surprises.

What's most unexpected is that many young New
Englanders—conservative Calvinists who, to outward appearances, seem models of decorum and reserve—reveled in taking
a deep dive into and then a long wallow through their feelings.
Altruists all, they were committed to careers demanding personal
sacrifice—the ministry, foreign missions, and teaching. That did
not keep them from dwelling—and with no apparent awareness
of any contradiction—on their inner states of thought and emotion. The word they reached for most often was "feeling." That
term had first taken on a buzz back in the eighteenth century as
philosophers, writers, and artists in the West popularized a culture

of sensibility. Their message was that the capacity for experiencing profound emotion, particularly the power to sympathize with the suffering of others, ranked as humankind's worthiest trait, one to be prized and cultivated. Sensibility's elevation of feeling, in turn, prepared the way for the romantic movement, with its emphasis on freely expressing emotion and asserting selfhood. The immersion of New Englanders in the cult of sensibility—invoked to inspire their involvement in every good and pious endeavor—helps us to understand how romanticism struck root in the inhospitable soil of Calvinism, a creed that inculcated thoroughgoing self-denial.

Both Thomas's narrative and Martha's letters attest to how deeply this veneration of feeling took hold and how luxuriantly it flourished. Their intense self-involvement signals, too, that evangelicals shared in the wider culture's burgeoning individualism. Within this context, then, it seems less odd that Thomas would recount his courtship to an audience of three who were intimately acquainted with him and many of the events he described. His florid outpourings of anxiety and agony, the dissection of his hopes, suspicions, and fears packed into several closely written pages, showed him—or so he hoped—to be a man of feeling, not some insensitive lout deserving summary dismissal. Indeed, the long extracts of letters from Martha and Emily Parker he interspersed through his narrative lend it some resemblance to the period's popular epistolary novels, which proved so influential in spreading the cult of sensibility.

Martha shared his capacity for relentless self-dramatization. Like some other academy girls, she had picked up the habit of referring to herself in the third person, as if she were the entranced spectator of as well as the featured player in her own life. ("Think of Martha no more," she wrote to Thomas. "I trust you will find one, who will be better qualified to render you happy than Martha.") Even *he* sometimes used the third person when speaking or writing to her about her. Each, too, favored the other with melodramatic pronouncements about sinking into the grave and meeting in eternity, echoing the purple prose of those novels evangelicals were not supposed to be reading.

It was not a matter of two lone drama queens finding each other in a youth culture otherwise given to sober restraint. To the contrary, romanticism put so deep an impress on many young evangelicals of this era because of—not despite—their religious beliefs and experiences. What attended their coming of age were recurrent revivals premised on the conviction that the way to salvation lay through the heart, not the head. Those seasons of intense preaching targeted young men and women and gathered them into the churches. Martha and Thomas, Emily and James, and Elnathan and Elisha all experienced such "awakenings," which made them—as they liked to call themselves—"the Redeemer's children." In fact, what helped reconcile Thomas to his broken engagement during the spring of 1826—at least temporarily—was a revival that stirred the villagers of Hanover, the men at Dartmouth College, and his own students at Moor's Charity School. "The Lord was pouring out his Spirit in this place," he recalled, and "my school was <u>richly visited</u>."

The explicit message of such religious gatherings was that the self must be abjured. Indeed, conservative Calvinists believed that saving grace manifested itself by the ability to abandon self-interest entirely in pursuit of others' welfare and God's glory. It was never too early for evangelicals to learn this habit of the heart, and it was one of the lessons that the foreign missions movement aimed to impress upon even the very young. Typically, Emily Kimball planned to tell her daughter, Martha Ann, still a toddler speaking a language all her own, about "the poor heathen" that the little girl might learn to "sympathize with their sufferings." What better way to instill feeling for everyone in the family of

man, a "disinterested benevolence" that would banish every trace
of self-involvement?

But experiencing the conviction of sin and the joy of conversion also pulled revival participants in the opposite direction,
to places deep within themselves. Many, addicted to the satisfactions of that inward gaze, kept coming back. Observers routinely
described New England revival participants as experiencing "overwhelming emotion" or being "overcome with emotion." In those
settings and in smaller gatherings, evangelical culture broke down
the habit of self-withholding among ordinary people and over-
came the resistance to reckoning with their inner lives. It encouraged exploring and sharing thoughts and feelings, no matter how
threatening or overwhelming. It fostered frequent exchanges in
which friends and lovers monitored each other's elation at spiritual progress or disappointment, even deep depression, over set-
backs. It made knowing another's religious condition and taking
measure of his or her feelings—and being known in turn—the
mark of true closeness. In all those ways, evangelicalism both cultivated individual inwardness and made intimacy—mutual disclosures of the innermost self—the gold standard for every near
relationship, including marriage.

Positioning Martha Parker at this intersection between romanticism and revivalism, a cultural crossroads for many private
lives in the early republic, brings into sharper focus what shaped
her choice of mates. What we'd like to know, first, is why she
offered her heart to Thomas Tenney in the late summer of 1825
and then, after much hesitation, agreed to wed him at the end of
that year. She knew that her elder sisters held him in contempt,
and Martha professed to share their aversion—until suddenly

she did not. Of course, for centuries before and after William Shakespeare outshone all competitors, comedy has thrived on the mysterious way that indifference, even downright dislike, might transmogrify in a twinkling into love. Maybe that's what happened to Martha.

It wouldn't come as a complete surprise, because to read their letters is to recognize that she and Thomas were, in some sense, a pair—though hardly one singular among young folks in their circle. Supremely self-absorbed, steeped in hothouse emotions, and skilled at working up themselves and each other, they had, over many years, become addicted to the drama of their relationship, the thrill of playing out their lives like characters in a novel. Ann Parker Bird offered the diagnosis that Thomas Tenney was "a little crazy after a love disorder of six years standing." But it took two: Martha had acted her part in that derangement. Everyone knows couples like this, their involvements giving off a whiff—or a blast—of folie à deux.

Less common now is what seems to have generated intensity between Martha and Thomas, as well as many other pairs, back then: religion. No one of his acquaintance called him charismatic or even close, but Ann spotted in her cousin, even from boyhood, a sanguine confidence in his righteousness that aroused her envy—even prompted her own spiritual self-doubts. Martha was his opposite: far from being precociously pious or serene about her eternal future, she struggled through adolescence for a deeply felt assurance of salvation. Unlike her sisters, who joined the Dunbarton church in their mid-teens, Martha held back from professing faith and presenting herself for church membership. Beset by scruples and uncertainty, she would have felt both comforted and burdened when others in the family—including James Kimball—openly expressed concern about her spiritual impasse and prayed for a breakthrough. Even her adoring sister Ann deemed Martha "a rich prize [as a spouse] for anyone, <u>but</u> a Christian," believing that professors of religion should not, as evangelicals liked to say, become "unevenly yoked" to unsaved mates. Telling, too, is that Martha's mother, far from sharing the rest of the family's distaste for Thomas, urged her daughter to accept his first proposal. "Mother is exceedingly fond of him," Martha wrote to Ann, "and called me a foolish girl for refusing a man of such ardent piety." Here was the perfect partner, her mother hoped, to smooth her daughter's path to heaven.

Taken together, the evidence points toward Martha's convincing herself that to marry cousin Thomas would ease, perhaps even banish, her spiritual insecurity. There he was, a struggling young teacher, an aspiring minister, pining away from unrequited love. His misery inspired her sympathy, even her solicitude—sentiments falling so far short of pulse-racing rapture that to marry him would amount to an act of genuine self-sacrifice. To wed him would attest to her capacity for disinterested benevolence, the mark of the truly godly. Thomas himself knew it: in the letter breaking their engagement, he recalled Martha once admitting that "she had been attempting to force herself to love me from pity of my deplorable condition."

As appealing to Martha might have been her cousin's cast-iron certainty about numbering among the elect destined for heaven—the same quality that unnerved Ann. How comforting to Martha that a man of such conspicuous sanctity would choose her, confident, as he assured her, that she, too, "would soon become a follower of Christ." Her decision to accept his offer would give proof of her piety. She would save him from heartbreak; then he would save her from hellfire. And sure enough, about a year after his second proposal, Martha, as if emboldened by the imprimatur of his steady affection, finally presented herself for membership at the Dunbarton church and received admission.

What surfaces in Martha's calculations about marriage is an important difference between the emotional world inhabited by her, to say nothing of generations in Western Christendom who lived long before her, and the one inhabited by many—maybe most—Americans today. For those past actors, concerns about the afterlife made up much of the interior drama in their waking lives. Pondering their eternal outcomes held the foreground, not the background, of their thoughts and feelings. Whether it took the form of devoted daily reflection, occasional bouts of niggling doubt, or nights of searing, sweating dread, concerns about their soul's estate and its ultimate fate loomed large in what and how people were feeling. Religious preoccupations in turn influenced other emotions—like Martha's sudden willingness to give herself to cousin Thomas.

Then, too, he possessed the charm of the familiar. For many Americans of that era and later, pairing off with a relative, often a playmate since youth, would have held little risk while offering considerable emotional security and the comfort of weaving ever more tightly the web of kinship. And this particular cousin was so steadfast in his devotion and—as he seemed at first to Martha—so easily managed. What did it matter if he was Emily's castoff? Perhaps Martha had guessed, as Thomas later admitted, that he had courted Emily while loving only her. That dogged attachment, enduring despite years of Martha's indifference, might have drawn a woman who, as a little girl, had suffered the traumatic losses of her father and older brother. Whatever else anyone might say about Thomas Tenney, he wasn't going away. He was also launched on a career that dovetailed nicely with Martha's own hopes for the future. Marrying a schoolmaster and clergyman had enabled Charlotte Gage Gould to become the preceptress of her own female seminary in Fairhaven, suggesting to Martha that partnering with her cousin could allow them to do the same. Plenty to like about those prospects—more than enough to incline her toward the man who promised to deliver them. Veterans of today's digital dating scene, scarred by encounters ranging from the unsatisfying to the humiliating, might sigh with envy.

All those advantages gave Thomas the edge over his archrival, Elisha Jenney, as the two battled for Martha's favor during the fall and early winter of 1825. Flattered as she was by Jenney's pursuit in those months and perhaps gullible enough at first to swallow his gossip about her cousin, Martha quickly grew disenchanted with this "mere boy." The further she retreated, it seems, the more he pressed his attentions on her. That might account for Martha's being "much agitated," as Thomas described her, on the late December evening when she professed her love and consented to their engagement. It sounds like the behavior of someone who believes that she's dodged a bullet—or escaped a bully.

Why, then, did Martha change her mind so quickly when Elnathan Gridley resurfaced at the end of December and renewed his "overtures"? Why hadn't she "encouraged" him at the time of his first approach a few months earlier? Most likely, Martha had then regarded Elnathan as a risky and even daunting choice. He was far more accomplished than the young men to whom she'd been accustomed, and his family was even wealthier than that of Elisha Jenney. (He who had whined to her in Fairhaven, "You may obtain for a companion, a man of greater wealth than myself, but never one that loves you more.") Still more overwhelming would have been Elnathan's career plans. Not only was there a good chance of one or both of them meeting with early death a world away, but Martha also faced the challenge of living up to the high standard set by women whom she idolized as religious virtuosos: Harriet Newell, Ann Judson, and her own sister Ann. Could she, Martha, the recent convert, still shaky in her faith, ever hope to match them? How much safer to marry cousin Thomas or to bide her time and keep school while awaiting some other marital prospect.

But Elnathan had persisted, and James and Emily Kimball

did too, all of them assuring Martha that she could rise to the challenge being offered. (Probably it was no coincidence that she wrote the letter ending her engagement to Thomas from the Kimballs' parsonage.) Heady words to hear, especially for a young woman accustomed to thinking of herself as the spiritual runt of the Parker litter. Within a few short weeks, their urging took effect: a missionary career became Martha's dream and Elnathan, her dreamboat, the man who would sail her to a future promising a superabundance of assurance. If she was looking for a partner to banish those besetting doubts about her own salvation, Elnathan Gridley, committed as he was to the self-immolating career of a missionary, outclassed even Thomas Tenney.

If the present's emotional estrangement from the past owes in part to religion, time's gulf yawns wide again when it comes to talking—or not—about sex. That subject stars in our own breakup stories, because many people construe physical intimacy—its duration, exoticism, satisfaction—as a measure of (well, at least a clue about) emotional commitment. So one big surprise awaiting any time traveler to the early nineteenth century is the deafening silence that surrounded sex among courting couples. Nowhere did Thomas or Elisha mention engaging in any intimate acts with Martha, nor she with them—not even a kiss. As for Elnathan, he acknowledged only running his fingers along "the lineaments of her face." A lover who wished to take liberties would have had no shortage of opportunity, because Martha, without the regular presence of her mother or stepfather, looked after the boarders and visitors at the Parker home farm during the winter of 1825–1826. Elisha lodged there for months, and on at least two occasions Thomas spent the night, keeping company with her until late in the evening. The custom of bundling had vanished decades earlier, but a New Hampshire December might well have inspired options besides sitting closer to the fire. Bear in mind, too, that more than one out of five New England brides in this decade produced babies less than eight and a half months after marrying, which means that even more were tempting fate.

On the other hand, all concerned belonged to an evangelical culture that was incubating Victorian sexual mores, including the notion that women were naturally inclined and morally obligated to maintain chastity. Monitoring a couple's purity during court-ship came more easily to "the delicate female," as Thomas once described Martha, because no decent girl had a sex drive. As for the Christian gentleman, this paragon of purity had mastered all of his desires: Jeremiah Evarts expressed full confidence that edu-cated men, "born in a Protestant country, bred in the practice of pure morals," were "accustomed to restrain all their passions to the age of 28 or 30." Whether or not the force of those ideals actu-ally kept Martha and her beaux from kissing, embracing, or more, it certainly kept them from talking about it. But the possibility that Thomas, in particular, had the recourse of revealing more—true or false—about the liberties Martha had once permitted him surely crossed the minds of all at Townshend.

About a decade earlier, retaliation of this sort—a pioneer of today's "revenge porn"—had even found its way into print. Com-posed and published by another spurned fiancé, one Aaron Big-elow, *A Sketch of Courtship* shouts out for our attention because of the near silence that prevails even in most diaries and letters. Its fifteen pages set forth Bigelow's thwarted passion for his fiancée, Susan Griggs, whose grasping mother derailed their engagement after he lost his property. Bigelow retaliated with fond recollec-tions of amorous couplings in which he "received all the satisfac-tion I could enjoy from my intended wife." His aim—at least the one he professed to his readers—was not to ruin Susan's reputa-tion but rather to stake his claim to her and to ward off all rivals.

"I now feel it a duty to myself and my God, to caution any gentleman against paying any attention to the said Susan, under the
pretense of marrying her in my absence," his *Sketch* concluded.
Should anyone try, Bigelow, who had enlisted as a soldier in the
War of 1812, swore to meet that "paltroon" (poltroon) in a duel,
"should I live to return from the United States service in which I
am now engaged."

Thomas Tenney was no Aaron Bigelow, but he, too, was pursuing a bold course to reclaim the woman he loved. None
of the other three people at Townshend disputed his version of
what had happened between him and Martha, only the intent or
significance of specific actions. And they all realized that a none-
too-veiled threat lurked in his recollections. He was sending the
unmistakable message that his revelations could do real damage
to Martha's reputation, far worse than the gossip of a callow college boy like Elisha Jenney. Thomas's narrative told Martha and
the Kimballs in no uncertain terms that she had, in his righteous
judgment, too much of a past to deserve any future as a foreign
missionary. He had a religious duty to keep a woman so spiritually unfit from serving, of all places, in the Holy Land.

Thomas's ultimate aim was not to avenge himself by dragging
Martha's name through the mud. To the contrary, he wished to
keep her past—their past—from the prying gaze of the American
Board and from any more public notice. He would take on that
damage control, even dealing with Esquire Evarts himself, as he
pledged to the others at Townshend, once Martha had given him
"Christian satisfaction." As James and Emily looked on, he told
Martha "that her conduct left him no reason to hope that she
was a Christian"; then he demanded a show of repentance for her
conduct at Fairhaven. Satisfaction he got—a little, anyway. Yet

again, Martha asked Thomas for his forgiveness. She also assured him that she had been sincerely attached to him and had broken off their engagement "in a hasty moment under the influence of wrong impressions." She had engaged herself to Elnathan at her brother-in-law's "solicitation," she explained, believing that her behavior had estranged Thomas.

Events themselves—even in Thomas's recollection—did not remotely support those excuses. But taking the full measure of her danger had shaken Martha to the core. Once spread beyond Townshend, Thomas's version would not only ruin her chances of marrying Elnathan and becoming a missionary but also compromise her ability to support herself in spinsterhood by keeping a school or to find another husband. Disaster loomed, unless somehow her former fiancé could be placated. She would say anything to satisfy his pride. She promised to withdraw from the Palestine mission.

That was enough to hold him at bay, at least for the moment. Lame as her explanations were, Thomas felt vindicated, having shown them all how well he had behaved in his past dealings with Martha—and how dangerous he could become in the future. He rode back to Hanover, certain that Elnathan Gridley would sail off to the Holy Land as a single man. And then, he promised himself, Martha Parker would become the wife of Thomas Tenney after all. He would have felt even more confident had he known that others stood at the ready to help him gain his heart's desire, men far more prominent than he who were facing even bigger problems with women.

CHAPTER THREE

Patriarchs Under Pressure

Nothing could have suited Bennet Tyler better. It was altogether fitting that Esquire Evarts reached out to him about the Parker girl, only proper that the president of Dartmouth should weigh in on this matter. Others might have been less impressed with his position, especially those who recalled that no one else had wished to assume leadership of this cow college struggling for solvency. But Tyler had plans for the place and for his boys, the poor fellows. Many were older and rougher than his Yale classmates, some still stinking of the barnyard. A quarter century earlier, he had been a hayseed himself, blown from his family's hardscrabble Vermont farm to New Haven, where he trained for the ministry. For many years thereafter, he pastored a country church in a Connecticut backwater where he "had paid little attention to science and literature." How Tyler even came to be considered for the Dartmouth presidency back in 1822 no one seemed to know—or was inclined to tell. It helped that he at least looked leader-ish with a strapping physique and a luxuriant thatch of dark hair framing his fleshy face. It helped even more that he knew the right men, the most influential ministers in the Congregational and Presbyterian churches.

Among them, none was more righteous than the Reverend Lyman Beecher. If Protestants had elected popes, Beecher's Holy See would have encompassed most evangelicals in the North during the opening decades of the nineteenth century. He spearheaded campaigns to conform all Americans to his faith by blanketing the country in Bibles and religious tracts, stopping business on the Sabbath, banishing duels, sobering up drunks, reclaiming prostitutes, and, of course, converting the rest of the world to his kind of Christianity. Visitors to Boston searching for the headquarters of the American Board would not have been surprised to find themselves directed to the basement of the Hanover Street Church, a great Gothic pile over which Beecher presided as pastor. But before moving to this prestigious Boston pulpit—by which time a shock of white hair lent more dignity to his homely face and squat figure—he had ministered to a Connecticut church neighboring that of Bennet Tyler. Over their long acquaintance, Beecher found his colleague never once "mistaken in his judgment," implying that Tyler had plenty of practice arraigning sinners before his bar.

An even deeper intimacy had developed over the decades between Tyler and his Yale classmate Asahel Nettleton. If Beecher reigned as an evangelical pontiff, Nettleton enjoyed the stature of an apostle thanks to preaching that packed a wallop. Celebrated as the most eloquent pulpit speaker of his day in New England, this wisp of a fellow—pale, thin, and, in his later years, consumptive—summoned revivals that elicited an impassioned response. He must have looked even scrawnier standing next to the ruddy, rawboned Tyler, who, whatever his deficiencies, knew how to surround himself with powerful allies who could endow him with every advantage. Among those perks was his appoint-

Bennet Tyler, president of
Dartmouth College and
mentor to Thomas Tenney

ment to the American Board's Prudential Committee, which
oversaw all dealings related to missionaries.

That was why, when Jeremiah Evarts went in search of Thomas
Tenney, he had no choice but to approach Bennet Tyler. Ah, yes,
Thomas had been one of his collegians, the president wrote in
reply, and since his graduation in 1825 the young man and his sister Sarah had presided over Moor's Charity School in Hanover. A
great favorite with Dartmouth's faculty of several professors, still
chummy with some of its hundred-odd students, Thomas was a
young man of "a most excellent character," being both "ardently
pious" and "very judicious and discreet." So much so that "nothing but an imperious sense of duty would induce him to open
his lips" concerning his sorry dealings with Martha Parker. But
now, thanks to the president's counsel, Thomas was "willing to
make a disclosure of the whole, if the cause of Christ demands
it." The young man had confided in him fully concerning his
disappointments in love. He had also told Tyler about his plans to
visit Townshend and his hopes that once she realized that he had

Lyman Beecher, the most
prominent evangelical leader
in the early republic, 1842

"her character in his hands," Martha would withdraw from the
Palestine mission. He had already followed the president's advice
by drafting that long statement he would deliver to her and the
Kimballs.

The girl's comeuppance could come not a moment too soon,
Tyler believed, because one so wanting "as to truth and verac-
ity" was unsuited for "the high commission of a Christian missionary." Given the gossip about her circulating in Fairhaven and
beyond, "some of the facts have already become so public," and
if she somehow passed muster with the Prudential Committee,
"reproach would be brought upon the cause of missions." As for
Elnathan Gridley, Tyler advised against his marrying her until "he
had made himself acquainted with the manner, in which she has
treated at least two other young men of excellent character." That
second suitor would be Elisha Jenney, whom Tyler praised as having "irreproachable moral and christian character."

Elsewhere in New England and throughout the North, a formidable phalanx of historical forces was challenging the rule of

patriarchs, both literal and figurative, in families and communities, churches and colleges. The changes ushered in by more market-oriented economies, the masses of Americans on the move westward or into cities, and an expanding electorate sapped the power of fathers to command their children, gentlemen politicians to overawe voters, and clergymen to lord it over their congregations. There were even some who challenged husbands' claims to dominion over their wives and the prerogative of men generally to prevail over women. But if the rule of fathers was coming under siege, the 1820s would not write its epitaph. Patriarchs still held their own and more, and Bennet Tyler was one of them, exuding an unwavering confidence in his ability to manage those lesser mortals committed to his oversight.

"Commanding" was how the Dartmouth men recalled him, but Tyler seems to have been lenient, even indulgent, when it came to reining in their rambunctious ways. He succeeded better at a campaign to provide scholarships, thanks to an appearance that made him a natural fund-raiser. And although he was no Nettleton, he led a religious revival that rocked all of Hanover in the spring of 1826. As students filed into the chapel each morning, Tyler's was the first figure they saw, a "large manly form" wrapped in a cloak, as one remembered him, and with the Bible open before him at the pulpit. His "heavy smooth bass voice" intoned an unadulterated Calvinism in sermons flowing out of him like sap from the trunk of a stout maple. And as his words sank in, one student recalled, the president "went from room to room instructing and exhorting his beloved pupils, and praying with them" like "a loving, anxious father."

A few months later, in the midsummer of 1826, Tyler brought the same zeal to redress the wrongs done to one of his own. He took Thomas Tenney at his word, never doubting that young man's description of Martha Parker. Why bother to hear her side of the story? Women, of course, had their uses—Tyler himself sired twelve children—except when they did not, as his friend Nettleton, who took a vow of celibacy while still in college, had decided. But there were others in evangelical ranks—indeed, others among its leading men who also hewed to an arch-Calvinist theology—who harbored a higher estimate of women and a different view of their relationships with them.

Such men followed their convictions about women's intellectual equality and spiritual superiority to a logical conclusion. They believed that women deserved access not only to formal education but also to opportunities for activism, even leadership, in benevolent and reform organizations. If those who undertook such roles in the churches and civil society met with opposition, be it from bullying or slander, they deserved protection. If charged with misdeeds of any sort, they were entitled to a fair hearing and a full investigation of the facts. Evangelical men of this stripe were far from advocating anything so radical as full political citizenship for women. And they shared with Bennet Tyler a firm conviction about the propriety of men's holding women's "character" in their hands. But they also believed that women had certain privileges and rights that men were bound to respect and uphold, not out of chivalry, but out of simple justice. And Jeremiah Evarts meant to do exactly that in the matter of Martha Parker.

The case you must perceive to be a delicate one," Evarts wrote to Tyler, already suspecting that he did not. All the more reason for Evarts to make this letter a long one, spelling out the reasons for the president to reconsider his summary judgment of Martha Parker. Even if she had treated two young men improperly, did "the cause of Christ" demand "an exposure of her frailty"? Of course not: she might have "thoroughly repented," and if she had, did she deserve to have her reputation besmirched by scandal? Evarts invoked the example of Jesus, who told the woman taken in adultery, "Go and sin no more." Couldn't Thomas forgive Martha for a much lesser offense? Evarts concluded by citing "the habits and feelings" of most Americans, who regarded women as "the weaker sex," which won them "the sympathies of both sexes." Women "cannot select husbands," he observed, so "their only privilege is that of rejecting; and unless the circumstances are very aggravated, they will be supported in rejecting." Mystifying as it might be that a young lady would turn down any Dartmouth man, public opinion would uphold her right to make that mistake.

Deaf to all these arguments, Tyler stood fast. He could agree that the "matter should be hushed," but only to protect the reputations of those "two excellent young men," Thomas and Elisha. As for Martha, if she did not choose to withdraw from the Palestine mission, the Prudential Committee might "'put her away privately,'" just as the biblical Joseph "was minded to do" when his betrothed wife, Mary, told him of being impregnated by the Holy Spirit. Indeed, Tyler continued, because "the character of our missionaries should be not only above reproach, but above suspicion," it was not necessary for the Prudential Committee to prove Martha guilty of immoral conduct. Becoming the subject of gossip alone convicted her, and their concern that she might not be "a suitable person" was sufficient grounds for dismissing her. Between Joseph and Julius Caesar, those patriarchs of Nazareth and Rome, Dartmouth's president had learned all he needed to know about how to handle females.

But what appeared a simple matter to Bennet Tyler—showing the door to a wayward girl who really had to go—Jeremiah Evarts knew to be far more complicated. In fact, it was so fraught with the potential for disaster that even a punctilious lawyer might put a foot wrong and live to regret the consequences. What a trial, his having to deal with Tyler in this matter—a good man, to be sure, but a dullard fit only for the wilds of New Hampshire or somewhere even farther north. Perhaps he had spent too long in Dartmouth's monastic precincts, but somehow it had escaped the president's notice that the foreign missions movement—to say nothing of all evangelical churches—owed their numbers and vitality mainly to the support of women. They were legion, all eminently useful to the evangelical movement and insatiably curious about the lives of missionary wives. Many would be watching and listening for any news about Elnathan Gridley's bride-to-be. That meant whatever the Prudential Committee decided in the matter of Martha Parker, it would need to proceed very, very carefully.

Then, too, the more that Jeremiah Evarts learned about Thomas Tenney, the less he liked him. For starters, he quickly came to suspect that Thomas himself was the author of the anonymous letter prompting the Prudential Committee's investigation. What pointed to the schoolmaster was another letter, one that he had dispatched to Evarts shortly after the Townshend gathering. True, a close examination showed that Thomas's handwriting did not match the script of the anonymous letter. But, as Evarts reflected, Thomas might have dictated it with another person transcribing "at his request, or by his direction." And even if he had played no part in crafting the anonymous letter, the one he'd lately sent to Evarts made it clear that Thomas Tenney was far from being a disinterested party. No, he was a man with a plan.

His letter to Evarts began by describing Martha as "this poor, bewildered girl" who had been carried away by her "imprudence." Here already was someone unrecognizable as the self-possessed young woman whom Evarts had met in Boston a month earlier. Should it be necessary, Thomas continued, he would risk disclosing every detail of their romantic past, because "if the Lord required me to sacrifice my own reputation to the general interests of the church, I ought to be willing to make even this sacrifice." Finally, he lectured Evarts, of all people, about the importance of cultivating public support for missions, warning that even now, although Martha might be "penitent for her conduct," the cloud of rumors ensured that "her departure from this country would probably be the signal for the enemies of missions to raise their voices." That being the case, he announced, Martha had decided during their meeting at Townshend to withdraw from the Palestine mission. He added that President Tyler himself wished him to say that he thought this outcome "the <u>very best result which could have been hoped</u>."

This letter's tone—which rose from the condescending to the self-righteous before settling into the presumptuous—set Evarts's teeth on edge. By now, too, he was receiving plenty of encouragement from another young man, one in whom he had a great deal more invested, to dismiss Thomas Tenney as a disappointed lover who would stoop to the lowest tactics to win back a woman far too good for him. Evarts might still have felt some disappointment at Elnathan's sudden insistence on finding a wife before taking up his mission, but it had not lessened his esteem for this young man who, by the beginning of August, had much to convey on his fiancée's behalf—and to the discredit of his rival.

At the end of July, the unsuspecting Elnathan Gridley had made the long trip from Boston to Dunbarton, eager to reunite with Martha. The two would marry within the week, he believed, and then set sail for the Mediterranean. But instead of a radiant bride-to-be, he found a woman on the edge who had just returned from that fateful meeting at Townshend. Elnathan thought "her whole nervous system deranged," even showing "signs of delirium." Still more alarming, she was experiencing a spiritual crisis, doubting the authenticity of her conversion and losing the assurance of her salvation. It would be a mistake to discount Martha's flair for the dramatic, but she had every reason for real distress. Her encounter with Thomas at Townshend only a day or two earlier had dashed her hopes for this world and the next.

Possibly Martha could not even bring herself to confess to Elnathan that she had once consented to marry another man, because no sooner had the two reunited than she sent him to Townshend. There Emily and James Kimball told him about the confrontation with Thomas and, no doubt, a good deal more. None of their revelations cooled his ardor. James's lukewarm assurance that "after all . . . Martha is not so bad a girl" Elnathan met with more heat, vowing that if the American Board found her unfit, he would give up his missionary career and "turn his attention to some other field of labour." To leave Martha under these circumstances, he declared, would be "base and wicked." Then he went back to Dunbarton and, despite whatever else about her past she then disclosed, pressed her to proceed with their nuptials that very week.

After six days together, Elnathan, still unwed, "left her in despair." But he had managed to persuade Martha not to withdraw from the Palestine mission and to let the Prudential Committee's investigation go forward. By the beginning of August, he had brought her case—now their case—back to Boston and started lobbying the committee's members. In private conversations with Jeremiah Evarts—and doubtless with his mentor, Leonard Woods, as well—Elnathan described how no fewer than three other people were prepared to attest to Thomas Tenney's determination to "obtain" Martha by any means, no matter how foul. By the middle of August, he had composed a long statement to Evarts and the rest of the Prudential Committee recounting his fiancée's romantic history. Having been clueless on that subject until recently, Elnathan would have relied on the version told him by Martha and the Kimballs, perhaps adding a few of his own flourishes. How could he resist, being a young man, as Evarts once observed, whose "feelings were always warmly engaged, in any cause which he espoused," to say nothing of a besotted lover who believed that no man had ever risen higher in Martha's esteem than himself?

To read Elnathan's statement is to meet another Thomas Tenney. This Thomas stalks Martha like a man possessed, one who would not take no for an answer. After striking out with her sister Emily, this Thomas switched his attentions to Martha, bombarding her through the mail. ("I do not send you but a small part of the letters which I write.") When she failed to answer him promptly, he accused Dunbarton's postmaster of "detaining her letters," which so wounded that officer's federal pride that he sued the hapless swain. All that saved him from prosecution was "a humble confession," coupled with an "intreaty" from the village minister, Walter Harris. "No art was left untried, that could operate on her feelings," Elnathan declared, "and knowing her to be kindhearted in the extreme," this Thomas "long sought, by moving her to pity, to gain her affections." It worked: Martha came to regard him as "a man of talent sinking rapidly to the grave,—and from love to her." She accepted his proposal of marriage, but only because of an excess of sympathy on her part and of persistence on his. Then she thought better of the matter and withdrew her consent, "and there she supposed that the business was ended and regarded herself as absolutely free from all matrimonial engagements."

Elnathan's statement did more than echo Evarts's sympathy for women who had only the power of rejecting proposals. It depicted Martha as the reluctant object of "unsolicited attention," all but trapped into betrothing herself to Thomas and then beset by Elisha Jenney. Fingered by Elnathan as he "who does in fact, lie at the bottom of the whole difficulty," Elisha "deliberately plotted the ruin of one of the worthiest females merely because she would lay herself under no obligations to him—politely rejected his addresses." He pressed his suit after Thomas cavalierly told Elisha that because "I cannot get Martha, you may now try." When Elisha, too, failed, he retaliated with the smear campaign that had "rung [her] through Fair Haven as a liar." In Elnathan's telling, disappointed suitors subjected Martha to harassment and character assassination, and her many admirable qualities had made her all the more vulnerable.

In his view, too, Martha inspired envy even among people who were not competing for her favors, most notably her former employers, William Gould and his wife, the former Charlotte Gage, who had hosted the engaged couple during their visit to Fairhaven. "From the time I was introduced, till I bade them farewell," Elnathan recalled in his statement, both Goulds were "unceasingly lavish in their praises of Martha." But all the while, this two-faced pair were gloating over Elisha's gossip. William Gould remarked within earshot of others in Fairhaven that "Martha would outwit the Devil himself in deception," while his spouse "engaged to catechize [question] Martha in private, and to draw from her, if possible some cause for accusation" that she had wronged her former suitors. "Little did I dream," Elnathan added, "that the family to whose hospitality I felt myself very greatly indebted, were acting as spies, upon our conduct." But then, "Mrs. Gould, is the lady, let it be recollected, to whom the reports unfavorable to Mrs. Judson's character were traced." That would be the missionary Ann Hasseltine Judson, known to both Goulds from their connection with Bradford Academy and whose fame had evidently aroused Charlotte's spite. And now here was Martha Parker, whose academically rigorous curricu-

lum for her own school excluded such "ornamentals" as painting on velvet and who, still more mortifying, might well become
the next Ann Judson. How Elisha's tattling must have tickled
the ears of this couple, consigned to their humdrum lives in
Fairhaven.

A shrewd observer of the passing scene, Elnathan captured
the petty jealousies pervading evangelical New England even as
he exposed the predatory behavior of some of its men. But he did
not cast Martha as a helpless victim. To the contrary, his statement
portrayed her as "one of the worthiest females," a woman remarkable for her sympathy, strength, and virtue. She was too good
for her own good—too promising in every way for a woman in
this time and place. The same qualities that made Martha Parker
ideal as a missionary's spouse also made her a target for those who
envied her talent and resented her prospects.

Only a week after his return to Boston, Elnathan's efforts had
found a receptive audience with the one man there who
mattered most. "Your impression that Miss Parker desired to
withdraw herself from the Board, was no doubt authorized by her
feelings at the time you saw her," Jeremiah Evarts wrote to Thomas
Tenney, "but subsequent reflection, in cooler moments, has produced a change, and she still desires to go on a mission." Then he
lectured the schoolmaster on the "very intimate and sacred" rights
of "an accepted missionary," explaining that the board was bound
to shield them from "unjust accusations" and to ensure, likewise,
"that a missionary suffer not a retribution for <u>actual</u> transgression
beyond what the limits of equity would prescribe." Nor should the
board "follow public opinion blindly." After putting Thomas in
his place, Evarts assured him of having done no such thing—that
his remarks were not intended "in the way of censuring"—and

then, for good measure, ordered him to "set right" anyone whom he had told about Martha's withdrawing from the mission. She wished to do no such thing. Perhaps, Evarts speculated privately, Thomas might have "mistaken his commission, and transcended his powers," or Martha "might have decided hastily, from sudden fright, and without good reason." Whatever the case, Evarts recognized the need for conducting a closer investigation and finding "the best and fullest evidence."

Other members of the Prudential Committee joined in his support for Martha, sometimes echoing Evarts's views in even "stronger language." Based on Bennet Tyler's report, they conjectured that her conduct might not have been entirely blameless. It appeared that she had rejected the "addresses" of two young men "after giving them more or less encouragement" and even "entering into engagements more or less sacred." She might also have offered false reasons for her refusals or dwelled too much upon minor reasons and "too little upon the really operative ones." Yet "duplicity" of that order did not strike them as disqualifying Martha from the mission field. And besides, they thought it entirely possible that Tyler had "judged too severely" after hearing only Thomas's side of the case. They believed that if their investigation vindicated Martha, "it would be our duty to send her, even at the expense of some disaffection and complaint among the best friends of missions."

The member of the Prudential Committee most eloquent in her defense was Elnathan's mentor, Leonard Woods. He shrugged off the reports of Martha's supposed misconduct as "a mere girlish freak, just such as pretty girls, and sometimes good girls are capable of—without any deep wound to their moral or religious character." Himself the doting father of ten children, Woods had managed to hold in his own memory all of youth's passions, wayward and ennobling. As a professor who saw plenty of both, he had developed a deep admiration for prospective foreign missionaries and their

Leonard Woods, professor of Christian theology at Andover
Theological Seminary and mentor to Elnathan Gridley

wives. And as someone who regarded Elnathan as a son, he knew
that the young man had set his heart on Martha—as surely, he
believed, as she had set hers on him. Then, too, Woods regarded
it as "mean"—far beneath any gentleman, let alone Elnathan—to
"win the affections of a lady and then leave her."

Woods might also have felt personally invested in the future
success of this golden couple. He had already earned renown
as the memoirist of Harriet Newell, and the signature achievement of his later career would be a collective biography of other
missionaries who had died in the field. In other words, Woods's

intimate connections with the foreign missions movement's most promising prospects enhanced his own stature. When it came to his status as a theologian, none of his contemporaries took him for the second coming of Jonathan Edwards, but demonstrating the ability to discern extraordinary souls provided Woods with another way to burnish his reputation among evangelicals. "I rejoice that, after the most intimate acquaintance with that excellent woman," he boasted in his memoir of Harriet Newell, "I am able to say, that she happily exemplified the character which I have drawn." It's likely, then, that Leonard Woods saw in Martha Parker the second coming of Harriet Newell. Yet another reason that he judged it only right to stand up to her critics among those "sincere friends and grave clergymen"—meaning Thomas Tenney and Bennet Tyler. "They take only a superficial view of the subject," Woods declared, "and judge in haste."

The deeper view of that subject—the one held by Leonard Woods and Jeremiah Evarts—recognized the pivotal importance of women generally to the future of evangelical Protestantism in the United States and throughout the world. The two realized that women of all ages took a particular interest in the fate of Martha Parker, because so many had developed a personal and intensely emotional investment in foreign missions. Indeed, one of the most powerful influences promoting their attachment to the missionary cause was the work of Woods himself. His memoir of Harriet Newell made her a spiritual heroine and a patron saint of Protestant missions, and it sold steadily for decades. Her celebrity inspired thousands of parents—Woods and his wife among them—to name daughters after her.

Evarts, too, had pioneered the enlistment of women in the cause of missions. Beginning in the 1810s, he had encouraged the formation of hundreds of auxiliary missionary societies through-out the United States, and their membership often consisted pre-dominantly or exclusively of women. His own wife, Mehetabel Sherman Barnes Evarts, served as an officer in just such an orga-nization. Hearts set afire by Woods's account of Harriet, women of every age—widowed, wed, and single—swelled the ranks of groups such as the Female Beneficent Society and the Female Bombay Society, the Female Cent Society, and, inevitably, the Female Newell Society. These women's auxiliaries were often small organizations, meeting in members' homes and laying plans to raise money for missions locally; they channeled their collections directly to the male-run American Board. They seem conservative groups, especially when set next to the women's associations that began to appear in the 1840s to battle against slavery and prostitu-tion or in support of women's rights.

But upon closer inspection, these local missionary societies can surprise us. Not a few of their members had definite ideas about the conduct of missions. On a tour of Vermont to drum up donations, one of the board's agents ran into one woman who "undertook to show the impropriety of [mission schools] educat-ing male children to the neglect of Females." When he explained that such decisions were "left to the discretion of the Board and the Missionaries," she shot back, "No matter for that, if I subscribe, I wish to direct!" When female benefactors spoke, Jeremiah Evarts had no choice but to listen, because the board relied on women to "keep up the missionary zeal" by forming new societies, locating prospective donors, and raising money themselves. Many women found that their involvement in missionary societies—and in any number of other evangelical associations—enabled them to dis-cover an entirely new set of interests and talents. Most members worked in their home communities, talking up the cause to their neighbors, taking up collections by going door to door, and organizing fairs and other fund-raisers. But for a few of those eager to "direct," the cause became a career opportunity.

Consider Louisa Battelle. A single woman of independent means and spirit, she traveled a circuit that stretched from Saratoga Springs, New York, to Washington, D.C., drumming up donations and signing her reports to the board with a proud flourish, "Louisa Battelle, Agent." When Evarts intimated that she was shaking down her targets in Philadelphia too hard, prompting some to criticize her "misguided zeal," she fired back that "a Gentleman on the same business, would never have collected half as much in this City." Yet even as he harbored misgivings about Battelle, Evarts kept on the lookout for other women to serve as agents to raise money and "correspondents" to keep him informed about the progress of local missionary groups. During his tours of the South, he cultivated and praised likely prospects—all former northerners—including one Miss Thompson, transplanted from Albany to Savannah, "a woman of rare accomplishments and great activity of mind."

That formidable base of female support—what they owed women, what they hoped to gain in the future from women—never strayed far from the minds of Evarts, Woods, and some other members of the Prudential Committee as they weighed what to do about Martha Parker. True, as Bennet Tyler had insisted, the Prudential Committee should appoint no missionary "whose going abroad would create extensive dissatisfaction among friends of missions." But dissatisfaction could cut both ways and much to the disadvantage of missions should significant numbers of women come to believe that Martha Parker had not received just and equitable treatment as the investigation of her case went forward.

And who might arouse their suspicions? Who would be capable of broadcasting far and wide the message that the Prudential

Committee, far from protecting Martha, had abandoned her at the first hint of scandal? That would be her most ardent defender, the man "not at all disinclined to the labor of describing what [he] saw," often with "many intensives," Elnathan Gridley. Those who knew him best feared that he would prove a loose cannon, his scattershot shredding Martha's reputation along with that of the American Board. "All I have to say, Brother Gridley," James Kimball warned in mid-August, "is do nothing rashly." Evarts voiced the same concern, fretting that "Mr. Gridley might very probably be much carried away by his feelings. He might be impetuous and uncontrollable, and he might suddenly give the matter a publicity, which he would afterwards regret." Nor were those fears misplaced. Thanks to his years on the road as an agent and fundraiser for the American Board, Elnathan enjoyed a wide circle of contacts within the dense network of local missionary societies. Only a few letters to the right ladies would set tongues wagging at tea tables in every New England hamlet about the Prudential Committee's shocking mistreatment of Martha Parker.

Set against those concerns was the danger that Martha's foes rather than her friends would seize control of the narrative and persuade the public—women and men alike—that her character could not bear scrutiny. In that event, the casualties would be steeper than the future prospects of one young woman. No one knew better than Evarts the risk of butting heads with the likes of Bennet Tyler—or worse, his formidable allies Asahel Nettleton and Lyman Beecher. All three men had heretofore shown themselves fast friends of the missionary cause in general and the American Board in particular. So far, so good, but the foreign missions movement had been afoot in the United States for not even two decades. Its outsized ambition to convert the world probably drew as many critics as it did defenders in the forum of public opinion, and as the man charged with keeping his eye on the bottom line, Evarts was painfully aware of the board's fragile finances. All the more important to avoid doing anything that might alienate powerful allies within evangelical circles.

That meant, as Evarts concluded, "satisfaction" must be given, "if possible, to those who, like Dr. Tyler, conscientiously doubted whether Miss Parker were a fit person." The Prudential Committee must pursue its investigation, and if, as Evarts hoped and still expected, its members found nothing more than "a girlish indiscretion," then she would sail for the Mediterranean with Elnathan Gridley at the first opportunity. Above all, Evarts wished to keep events from getting out in front of him and spiraling beyond his control. If Martha Parker were to go abroad without the committee's having cleared her name, Evarts believed, "there was a moral certainty that the stories would be circulated with great avidity." Bad enough if she lost her reputation, but he foresaw disaster if those stories reflected badly on the foreign missions movement.

These diverse responses of the men in her world to Martha Parker provide us with a vivid sense of the complex, even contradictory ways that the evangelical movement shaped the lives of American women during the first half of the nineteenth century. As a source of unprecedented opportunities, it was unsurpassed. Evangelicals like Jeremiah Evarts and Leonard Woods celebrated their faith for founding educational institutions for young women and establishing an array of societies for those of all ages devoted to religious outreach, charitable relief, and reform. From the vantage point of the present, it's hard to grasp the impact of those schools and associations until we recognize that they offered women in the early republic a complete historical novelty. Here, for the first time, were sanctioned avenues of escape from the bounds of the household, a chance to develop skills and aspirations unrelated to their domestic roles, and forums to make their influence felt in civil society. Evangelicals not only created those new institutions but also popularized the notion of a purer, spiritually superior female sex that justified women assuming this new public presence. That meant their movement held the potential to effect even more profound changes in women's lives and relations between the sexes.

By the 1820s, this realization had begun to dawn on believers. The prospect delighted some but alarmed others, who feared that their faith was already giving women too many ideas. In the years that followed, the latter played a prominent role in writing and distributing the advice books, sermons, essays, poems, short stories, and even novels that sought to circumscribe the scope of women's ambitions and activities. They promoted the view that biological differences made women more emotional and less rational than men, ideally suited to nurturing their children, submitting to their husbands, and providing spiritual inspiration and moral influence to both. But, they insisted, nature had not equipped women to stray beyond their households: the female sex had no head for business, no stomach for politics, and none of what it took to play a prominent role in civic life. The power of this notion of "separate spheres" prompted even evangelical women involved in various voluntary associations to insist that far from challenging male prerogatives, their activism was merely another way of fulfilling their domestic responsibilities.

There was no question about where within this protean evangelical movement, one abounding in mixed messages about women's empowerment, Bennet Tyler's sympathies lay. He saw where the course being charted by men like Evarts and Woods might lead, and he feared the price to be paid for their readiness to celebrate women's religious charisma and to mobilize their energies in voluntary associations. In fact, he had already spotted its pernicious effects in the lives of his young men at Dartmouth like Thomas Tenney and Elisha Jenney. No penman, Tyler none-theless felt confident of finding other ways to ensure that believers of his stripe would prevail in the contest over Martha Parker and others like her.

CHAPTER FOUR

Satisfaction

The stories were spreading. Like a pebble tossed in a pool, the rumors that had started in Fairhaven moved outward in widening circles. By early August, all of Hanover—150 miles to the north—was abuzz, and who knew where else? "Miss P[arker] is so well known to many in this place [Hanover]," Thomas Tenney explained to Jeremiah Evarts, "and so many were acquainted with the fact, that she was going on a mission, that the least thing awakens curiosity." Inevitably, a rumor rippled through the village that Martha herself was about to appear there, which, Thomas tutted, "has given rise to many unpleasant stories" because of "the little vague knowledge, which several had of some things, which have in time past occurred in relation to Miss P[arker]." How could the American Board even consider sending her to the Palestine mission amid this swirl of scandal?

Self-serving as his remarks might have been, Thomas did not exaggerate the community's curiosity. A Hanover correspondent informed James Kimball that the "whole college has been in agitation in relation to this business" and that "a story has come from some quarter" intimating "something very 'tragical' has happened.

Every body is busy to find out what it is." A dismayed Evarts, fearing even worse to come, reflected that "very little was necessary to set people, in different parts of the country, to conversing on this subject." Of course, like pebbles landing in pools, rumors do not make their way abroad unassisted, and it was a long way from Fairhaven to Hanover. Some person or persons—those "several" with "the little vague knowledge" of "some things"—were creating what Evarts called the "public clamor" about Martha Parker.

Hanover itself provided a perfect spot for scandalmongering. Today's postcard-perfect town and the manicured campus bear little resemblance to the place in 1826, when the college, numbering several professors and about one hundred students, consisted of a single spartan structure (Dartmouth Hall) and a drafty chapel set within a village of about seventy homes. Past that tiny perimeter of settlement, the mountains rose and the forests closed in, socketing Hanover in any season, burying the town even deeper during long winters. Locals wagged their heads at "the tattle of a village like this," prompting one professor's wife to make it her rule "to believe all the good that she heard and none of the evil unless she was compelled to." Few followed her example.

William Parker's enrollment at Dartmouth might explain how his sister Martha, younger by two years, came to be "so well known" there even before the summer of 1826. Some sixty miles separate Hanover and Dunbarton, but she would have had occasion to visit her brother there as well as her friend and fellow alumna from Bradford Academy, Thomas's sister Sarah Tenney. A retiring youth, William passed through the college without winning any distinction. He spent the rest of his life as an itinerant schoolmaster, moving to a new town every few years, as if he wished to avoid becoming too well known. A good guess would make him James Kimball's Hanover correspondent, a young man mortified on his younger sister's behalf and unburdening himself to his brother-in-law.

Martha might also have numbered among those members of the general public who sometimes attended chemistry lectures at the college. Armed with a "battery," the professor of that subject gathered members of his audience into a ring and administered "shocks," a most amusing curiosity to all involved. Those in attendance included the chief of a neighboring indigenous nation as well as "lady listeners" who, as one student in William's Dartmouth class recalled, sometimes "grace[d] the front row" to take in this demonstration and other chemistry lectures. Had she been among them, Martha seems likely to have offered such a distraction to the men seated around her. Note, too, that the advertisement for her Boscawen school offered instruction in chemistry, which was not part of her curriculum at Bradford. Perhaps she availed herself of Dartmouth lectures in order to teach that subject.

However often Martha herself might have turned up in Hanover, many young men at Dartmouth knew her name. Steeped in evangelical culture as their college was, most of the students would have heard or read about her being engaged to Elnathan Gridley and thus accepted as a missionary. Then, too, there was Thomas Tenney's habit of taking others into his confidence. Perhaps all those years of being disappointed in love inclined him toward oversharing. To at least one of his friends, Elisha Jenney, he not only poured out his romantic woes but also entrusted the long extracts he had copied from Martha's letters before, at her request, returning the originals. Like Thomas, Elisha was still seething over her rejection, and according to Martha he had threatened to retaliate, vowing to "nettle [her] to the quick." Hanover offered the ideal place to begin. Making her the subject of common gossip in the college would have appealed to him all the more because Martha's brother William numbered among his classmates. Perfect: Elisha could entertain his classmates by humiliating both brother and sister.

In his youth at Dartmouth College,
Silas Aiken became a close friend of
Thomas Tenney.

That flair for casual malice makes Elisha a natural to have authored the anonymous letter that had reached Jeremiah Evarts back in June and set in motion the Prudential Committee's investigation. But in fact, that letter was the doing of someone else. Although Evarts had at first suspected Thomas of having written or dictated it, the schoolmaster claimed not to have known of the letter's existence. And in early August, when shown it by Evarts, Thomas readily identified the handwriting as that of his friend Silas Aiken, another trusted confidant. "He [Thomas] declared the handwriting to be that of a tutor in Dartmouth college, with whom he had, some months before, had conversations respecting Miss Parker," Evarts recalled, "but the writer had never informed him that he had written, or intended to write."

The beefy son of a prosperous New Hampshire farmer, Silas Aiken had graduated with Thomas in the Dartmouth class of 1825. Thereafter the two remained close: Silas served as a tutor on the faculty for three more years while Thomas taught younger boys at Moor's Charity School, and both men studied for the ministry under Bennet Tyler. Unlike Thomas and Elisha, Silas was no heartsore swain. Indeed, he might have known Martha only by reading her letters, but something—and perhaps someone— prompted Silas to write anonymously to Evarts, warning that certain "disclosures" were about to sully Martha's reputation and alluding to the rumors in play ever since Elisha had confronted her in Fairhaven a month earlier.

The timing suggests that Thomas's two confidants had worked in concert. Elisha ambushed Martha in Fairhaven and spread gossip about her past—a campaign of harassment he reported in full to Thomas—and then Silas followed up a month later with the anonymous letter. But whether the two acted together or separately, why did they do it? True, Martha's rejection stung Elisha, but he had flirted with her for a few months at most and, unlike Thomas, who had pursued her for years, stood no chance of catching her on the rebound from Elnathan. Silas might not ever have set eyes on her. Why, then, were Thomas's two friends so intent on ruining his former fiancée's reputation? And was he, in any way, the author of their actions?

Dropping into Dartmouth and getting to know some of its denizens—as Martha did two hundred years earlier—afford us an opportunity to answer those questions. For a moment, then, let's step back from the events that unspooled as the rumors spread and take a closer look at those men bent on her undoing. Making their acquaintance and exploring their possible motives will reveal an evangelical movement that encouraged women as activists both at home and abroad and promoted women as charismatic religious figures even as it strove to contain them.

It was only Thomas Tenney who stood to gain anything if the board judged Martha unfit for missionary work. He dearly wanted to get back at Martha and to get Martha back. He wished to possess her, preferably after she had been humiliated into submission. That means he must have encouraged his Dartmouth friends to spread the gossip in Fairhaven and Hanover and to write that anonymous letter, yes?

Well, no, and here's why: Recall that Thomas's announcement that Martha had withdrawn from the Palestine mission provoked a scolding from Jeremiah Evarts, a reproof that sent the schoolmaster into a defensive crouch. He had not used "any improper influence" when the two met at Townshend, he shot back. Then he leveled a threat: if Evarts would not credit his charges against Martha, Thomas would make public his correspondence with her. Those letters "should show myself weak and credulous perhaps," but he would take the risk, because "I should not fear censure; except for want of proper spirit. I mean [that] I should be thought too passive under injury." A foretaste of such ridicule he had already endured upon hearing from Elisha Jenney that "I have been censured at Fairhaven with unsparing severity because I have been so lenient."

Loosely translated, Thomas—and evidently many others— regarded his failed engagement as an embarrassment. It follows that the last thing he would have wanted was for his past with Martha Parker to become even more widely known, because it would have impeached his reputation for manliness, made him appear "weak and credulous," wanting "a proper spirit," and "passive under injury." Many within the precincts of Fairhaven had already made him out to be all that—at least in Elisha Jenney's telling. Even Elnathan Gridley implied that Thomas had been Martha's doormat, jibing that it took Elisha's taunts to arouse "Br. Tenney to his duty, else, probably he had, even now, been slumbering." Yes, Thomas told himself, he had been far too lenient in dealing with this girl, and by the middle of August he was determined not to make that mistake again. It answered to his aggrievement, the prospect of having "her character in his hands."

Understood in this way, the campaign to discredit Martha Parker parts the curtain on the ways in which men in the early-nineteenth-century North understood and performed masculin-

ity. The actions of his Dartmouth friends suggest that they were
at least as concerned to prod Thomas into a response that would
restore his manhood as they were to punish Martha for diminishing it. Elisha's confrontation with her at Fairhaven and Silas's
anonymous letter sent Thomas the message that it was important
for men to stick together and hold up the side. They had done
their part—what were friends for?—and now it fell to Thomas
to do his. He should demand and receive "satisfaction" for injuries suffered. Acting the part of a man, as they understood it,
meant putting and keeping women like Martha Parker in their
place. But the question remains, why were his friends so intent
on helping Thomas Tenney do just that? What made her so
threatening?

More was at work here than the predictable hypocrisies of
the conspicuously pious, Bennet Tyler's fine young men
of "irreproachable moral and Christian character." What bears
notice at the outset is their habit of making behavior toward
women an important measure of their masculine bona fides. It's
a calculus standing in stark contrast to that of their contemporaries among white men in the South, for whom gaining personal
honor and the validation of manhood came exclusively from their
interactions with their male social peers. The notion of demanding "satisfaction" from a woman—or anyone deemed inferior
because of class or race—would have struck them as laughable.
But farther north, some women had evidently acquired the power
to injure a Yankee man's reputation by impugning his masculinity. Hence the burr of anxiety buried in a joke that circulated
among the members of Dartmouth's debating society: their "common law" stipulated "any act of gallantry to a young lady was

among the most heinous of offences, constituting the crime of manslaughter."

Bad enough, as many Dartmouth men saw it, that head turners like Martha Parker possessed the allure that could make even a Samson "passive under injury." Still worse were the other ways in which this Dunbarton Delilah had reduced their friend Tenney to . . . well, acting like a girl, even as she assumed the role usually assigned to men in their culture's courtship script. No doubt they were as surprised as Ann Parker Bird had been that the righteous Thomas had pursued Martha well before she experienced conversion and applied for church membership. Typically, it was women who reluctantly accepted being "unequally yoked" to men of little or no evident piety. And even though Ann professed to know a number of young women who broke off engagements, men of that time were more notorious for doing the jilting. Not a few of those jilters even ended up facing civil suits for breach of promise, a subject that invited sarcasm from Ann's husband, Isaac Bird, who wondered how Thomas might respond if Martha persisted in wanting "nothing to do" with her former fiancé. Would the poor fellow "sue for damages? We have heard of young <u>ladies</u> prosecuting for breach of promise in such a case but that a young gentleman should do it, would be <u>a new thing under the sun</u>."

Unsettling as these reversed roles were to Thomas's Hanover friends, they were not the worst of Martha's offenses. What rankled them even more was that she numbered among the growing number of young women in the North who were now entering into direct competition with young men. They were vying for scholarly distinction in academies, teaching in and even heading such schools, and distinguishing themselves as missionaries abroad or community activists at home. Small gains if measured by twenty-first-century standards: women in Martha's world could not attend universities, enter the professions, get ordained as ministers, vote and run for political office, or rise to prominence as business leaders. But to those who lived two hundred years ago, it felt like a sea change. For the first time ever, opportunities to gain visibility and a voice in religious and civic matters were opening to some women. And their entry into some of the most important venues—academies, voluntary societies, and missions—came with the approval and even the assistance of some evangelical churches, ministers, and male lay leaders like Jeremiah Evarts. Here was tinder for the resentment of Martha Parker that smoldered within Bennet Tyler's upstanding young men.

There were many other devout northerners of both sexes who did not welcome the changes enabling women to excel outside their households. Even as evangelicals founded and taught in the first female academies, women of an intellectual bent made some believers uneasy. Among them were the "genteel" wives of some Dartmouth faculty members: Benjamin Hale, a chemistry professor newly arrived at Hanover in 1827, teased his wife, "The ladies here have an apprehension, that you are very literary, and I understand are a little afraid of you. How do you like the idea of inspiring terror in this manner?" Just as some were alarmed by the results of too many educational advantages for young women, not all admired missionary wives. Unlike Bradford's Abigail Hasseltine, Charlotte Gage Gould (she of the painting on velvet at Fairhaven's female academy) joined in the chorus of those within and without evangelical ranks who accused Ann Judson of deserting Burma to tour the eastern United States because she yearned "to excite attention and applause." The same resentment surfaces in the snarky advice that one Massachusetts minister offered to a young woman planning to teach poor children in a charity school. In that humble situation, he counseled, she would "borrow no aid from vanity. Neither Europe nor America will gaze on her fortitude. Nor will extracts of letters from China or Labrador trumpet her praises."

E ven those evangelical leaders who advocated for enlarging women's sphere of action were not without ambivalence about the results. As early as 1820, Jeremiah Evarts wondered aloud to a colleague who was preparing the annual report for the American Board "whether it is worth your while to look up the Christian names of the wives of our missionaries," and quickly decided that "where the name is not known to me, let it stand Mrs. Smith, Mrs. Cushman, etc." Those mixed feelings found even fuller expression in the writings of Evarts's ambitious subordinate at the American Board, Rufus Anderson. As a Bowdoin College student and aspiring missionary to India, he had seen the possibilities of connecting with the right woman and fantasized about marrying a sister of Harriet Newell's. With her by his side, who could equal them as a power couple? By 1825, Rufus had relinquished his dreams of saving the subcontinent in favor of succeeding Evarts at the board in Boston, but he had lost none of his appreciation for what a charismatic woman could do for his career. In that year, he produced a best-selling memoir of Catharine Brown, the mixed-race daughter of an elite Cherokee family and one of the few converts among Native people won by the board's missionaries.

Like Leonard Woods before him, Rufus recognized what he stood to gain by celebrating female sanctity: as Catharine's hagiographer, he basked in the reflected glory of his subject's charisma, heightening his visibility in evangelical circles. Yet what his memoir stressed about Catharine—whom he had never met— was less her spiritual gifts than her modesty, meaning the refusal to flaunt her fame. That emphasis echoed Leonard Woods's earlier description of Harriet Newell as "a modest, unambitious female." The same could not be said of that tireless traveling fund-raiser for the American Board, Louisa Battelle, whose take-no-prisoners

Rufus Anderson served as
Evarts's right-hand man on
the American Board and
succeeded him as its head.

approach to her targets drove Rufus to distraction. "Loud complaints are made respecting her—complaints from Philadelphia,
and other places," he fumed. "Last evening one of the most
promising young men in that city, gave me such an account, as
went towards confirming an impression I before had, that her
agency is, perhaps, no real service to the cause. . . . Reproof and
advice can not make her prudent. . . . I know not what should be
done."

Chances are that Rufus had a pretty good idea—or at least a
fantasy—of what to do about Louisa Battelle. But for the present, he and his "promising" young male friend in Philadelphia
could only fume and feel threatened. Here were women entering
and establishing an increasingly prominent presence as teachers
in schools of advanced learning, as organizers and administrators in religious and philanthropic institutions, and as missionaries abroad. All were arenas in which men alone had held sway,
but now a rising generation found themselves challenged by the
intrusion of young, well-educated women. Bad enough was this
sudden, unexpected competition. Downright unnerving was the
prospect that young women's gathering presence might feminize
those very professions—including the ministry—in which young
men hoped to succeed.

That possibility was not remote. During the same decade that witnessed the growing association of women with organizations promoting education, religion, and reform, many Americans were coming to identify another realm entirely with real masculinity. By the 1820s, electoral politics was becoming the exclusive and jealously guarded preserve of men. The hunt for votes, the quest for patronage, the lobbying for influence, and the debates about government policy took place in milieus such as taverns, clubs, barbershops, caucuses, and polling places, all rowdy venues that law or custom secured from female encroachment. In the estimate of this expanding brotherhood, engaging in partisan political activism affirmed manhood, but taking part in churches and voluntary associations called it into question. Real men didn't attend prayer meetings or join missionary societies. Instead, they reveled in clashes of interest and contests for power, reviling those who disdained the rough-and-tumble of politics as effeminate "Nancy men."

Among the many men who felt a slow burn over these developments was William Gould. Recall that he was the minister and schoolmaster who had told Evarts of hearing "unfavorable reports" about Martha in Fairhaven and even gossiped to friends there that she could "outwit the Devil himself in deception." It seems odd that he assisted in her undoing, because William had once deeply admired this young schoolteacher. Martha had boarded with him and his wife while a student at Bradford Academy, and when she was in their employ, she wrote to her sister Ann in Beirut, exulting in her success at Fairhaven's female seminary. Both of the Goulds entrusted her with "more than an ordinary degree" of the school's "direction and government." They made her "a confidant in some of their most intimate family secrets." The students and their parents respected her as a person "of judgment and stability." So impressed was William himself that he employed her to teach for three terms at his academy, and in an effort to persuade her to stay even longer, he offered "to pay her expenses and even to accompany her, on a journey to New York or elsewhere for her health." For two years after she left Fairhaven, he repeatedly asked her to return to the school, because "he never expected to procure another teacher so good as she had been."

Attention so solicitous comes off in any place and time as more predatory than professional. Consider, too, that when the lovely young Martha turned up in Fairhaven, Charlotte Gage Gould, five years her husband's senior, was the mother of three and closing fast on forty. Well within the realm of possibility, then, that William, a man nearly the same age as Elnathan and Thomas, had made—or had hoped to make—some "overtures" of his own to Martha. That would explain why, as she told her sister, it was "contrary to her own inclinations" to have spent as long as she did in Fairhaven. What's all but certain is that if her husband's eye had wandered, Charlotte knew nothing about it—at least not in 1825, when the couple named their fourth child Martha Parker Gould, an extraordinary tribute to someone with neither fame nor a family connection. Seen in this light, what might have suddenly soured William was that Martha had escaped his reach by taking a teaching position in Boscawen. Still more humiliating, she had managed to strike out on her own. He felt betrayed, even deceived: how content she had seemed for those three terms as his subordinate. Even more irksome, with the prospect of becoming Elnathan Gridley's wife and joining the Palestine mission, Martha gained the possibility of rising higher still in the world's estimate.

Like William Gould, Silas and Elisha and Thomas saw in Martha Parker more than an unobtainable object of desire: she was someone who stood to surpass them. To sound the depth of their disappointment, look in on these three college students as they forged their friendship—and their future hopes—in a Dartmouth club known as the Society of Inquiry. Such clubs were common on college campuses and seminaries, springing up among undergraduates and divinity students because, as the Dartmouth society's constitution explained, "it appears very necessary that a large number of young men should be inspired with a <u>missionary</u> spirit." Once elected on the basis of taking a "special interest" in missions, members presented "dissertations" on subjects of their particular interest. Silas, chosen in April 1822, delivered a "Sketch of the Jesuits," and the year when he and Thomas served as officers of the club, there, among its newly elected underclassmen, was Elisha Jenney. By then Thomas's interest in missions in the Middle East had become particularly keen. In August 1825, he joined with another member who read a dissertation on "prospects of the Palestine mission" to review the life of Henry Martyn, the first British evangelical to proselytize in Persia (today's Iran). In other words, what the three young men had in common besides their resentment of Martha Parker were their own long-standing desires to enter the mission field—a goal that she had attained so easily (and at Thomas's expense) by engaging herself to Elnathan Gridley.

No doubt, too, the possibility of being outshone by a woman when it came to winning a reputation for sanctity galled these devout young men. Keep in mind the pivotal role played by religion in Thomas's appeal to the once spiritually "destitute" Martha—what her mother praised as "his ardent piety." Then note that in response to her ending their engagement, he retaliated by attacking the sincerity of her Christian convictions, and she shot back, "I profess to be a follower of the Jesus whom you love." But reminding him that they were now spiritual equals—fellow professors of religion and church members—did not deter Thomas. At their Townshend meeting and thereafter, he repeatedly took aim at the authenticity of Martha's conversion. Condemning her as "a base girl, a deceiver, a liar," he "laid many and grievous sins to her charge" and "denied her claims to the Christian character until she should be brought to deep repentance for these sins."

Specifically, Thomas charged that Martha stood in need of God's forgiveness for failing to tell the truth—or the whole truth. That deceitfulness surfaced in the way that she had treated him and Elisha Jenney, spurning them but giving "no satisfactory explanation of her treatment of me, or Mr. J." How could she trust her recollection of what had passed between them over their own? To make matters right, Martha must embrace their version of events. "Tear from your bosom <u>every shred of insincerity</u> and review all that has passed between you and Mr. Jenney," Thomas urged her, "and see if you cannot recollect any thing like what he states." How could Elisha be wrong? After all, "he certainly thinks he is correct." Correct, that is, in all he'd disclosed to Thomas about the hurtful things Martha had said about and done to him, words and actions "inconsistent with true affection." Correct, too, in his insistence that Martha had treated both men shabbily, giving them "encouragement" and then, for no "satisfactory" reason, rejecting them. Her cavalier ways with young men, Thomas insisted, had made for Martha's misfortune. She should "examine anew the motives which had led her to think of so holy a work [as missions] and strive to make Christian satisfaction to Mr. J. and his friends, before she left the country." "O may this event be the means of your conviction," Thomas implored—as if she had not yet experienced a true conversion—"it may save your soul from <u>eternal death</u>." Here were tactics that revealed as much about his own anxieties—the prospect of her reputation for spirituality surpassing his—as they did about his keen awareness of Martha's vulnerabilities.

Bad enough, her ways with men. But the worst of Martha's "deceitfulness," according to Thomas, was concealing from him the real reasons for their breakup. Martha had practiced "intentional deception" by telling him that Emily's opposition had ended their engagement. As he saw the matter, Emily had objected to the marriage only because Martha had not admitted to her sister that she loved Thomas. It's possible that Martha had concealed her attraction to him from her sisters, knowing that neither would approve. Or possibly Martha had lied to Thomas or to herself or to them both about loving him at the moment of their engagement. What's certain is Martha badly needed not to love—and never to have loved—Thomas by the early winter of 1826. By then she was succumbing to another passion entirely, the desire to pursue her dreams of winning public acclaim and spiritual virtuosity by marrying a missionary. And in the end, she chose, as Thomas saw it, glory over love . . . well, his love anyway. Still more damning, she hid her ambition from him—her yearning for all that she might attain as a member of the Palestine mission—by lying to Emily about her feelings and then blaming her for the broken engagement. The best that could be said about a woman like Martha Parker—at least by Thomas Tenney and his friends—is that she felt ashamed about wanting so much to make something of herself.

But not all young men—or their elders—resented women who wanted more. Not all of them felt threatened by those who were emerging as charismatic presences in the churches, dynamos in voluntary associations, and players in the mission field. Consider not only Jeremiah Evarts, Leonard Woods, and Elnathan Gridley but also James Kimball, who was studying for the ministry at Andover and still longing for a missionary career in the spring of 1823. One day he and his sister Lydia dropped by the Boston headquarters of the American Board, "when who should come driving into the [Missionary] Room," but Ann Judson. When Kimball had seen her three months earlier, she was so ill that her returning to Burma seemed unlikely. But now she had rebounded and greeted Lydia as they did when "playmates" at

Bradford Academy. Just returned from meeting with Baptist leaders in Washington, D.C., "she says her book is out and that she has established [missionary] societies in most of the towns at the south thro[ugh] which she passed." Now she was looking to book a passage to Calcutta and "says she is ready to go back and is very anxious to go soon." In awe of Ann Judson he might have been, but her accomplishments don't seem to have bothered him.

It was not merely their implacable demand for "satisfaction"—the culture of entitlement among Dartmouth's young men—that brought on Martha Parker's troubles. The forces that conspired against her went right to the top. James Kimball, for one, suspected as much. "Though Tenney has been very imprudent in relation to this affair, he has done nothing compared with some others," he wrote to his friend Elnathan. No, Thomas was not chief among the culprits, but a man desperately besotted—which made him the dupe of others far worse. "If I could believe all, who were concerned in this business were good men, I should not feel so much troubled about it," James continued, "but I have too much reason to believe they are not, but will do all the mischief they can." Most likely, Martha's beleaguered brother William had been filling his brother-in-law's sympathetic ear with tales of his trials at Hanover, brought on by the "mischief" of Elisha Jenney and Silas Aiken. And both William and James would have known that such mischief could not run amok at Dartmouth College—at least for long—without the permission of its president, Bennet Tyler.

Tyler had long taken an interest in the fate of Martha Parker. When he received Jeremiah Evarts's inquiry concerning her in mid-July, he had met with Thomas Tenney, enlisted himself on the schoolmaster's side, gained his confidence, and advised him to come forward, as the Prudential Committee had requested, with a full disclosure of his dealings with Martha. He won the young man's trust so fully that Thomas had read to him the statement he would deliver at Townshend after writing it at his behest.

It's possible, too, that Tyler had some involvement even earlier with the anonymous letter that first raised concerns. When that letter came into his hands, Evarts engaged in some amateur sleuthing. He tagged its author as a gentleman because the penmanship was good, suggesting a person of some education, most likely connected with Dartmouth because it bore a Hanover postmark. He took it as a coincidence that the letter had arrived on June 15—the same day that Elnathan Gridley was to arrive in Boston to discuss his marriage and embarkation for the Mediterranean. What Evarts seemed not to notice was that the anonymous author also had some knowledge of his own movements, timing its arrival for the lawyer's return to Boston after several months in the South. It's unlikely that Silas Aiken, a mere college tutor, was privy to the travel plans of either man, but as a member of the Prudential Committee, Bennet Tyler surely knew. Did Silas worm that information out of the president in the course of a casual conversation? Or was any winkling needed? Had the tutor freely disclosed his plans to Tyler, perhaps even sent the letter with his blessing or at his instigation?

The bigger question is why a failed romance—even a broken engagement—meant so much to this middle-aged minister with a college to run. What made Tyler so set, as he expressed it, on "putting away" an aspiring missionary wife? True, he seems to have made a habit of meddling in the private lives of his students, but heretofore he had done so to secure their future in heaven, a goal rather weightier than this intervention in behalf of a lovelorn schoolmaster. Tyler himself explained his involvement purely as a means to avoid the "reproach" that the cause of missions would incur by sending abroad a female so manifestly unsuitable. But he had taken no steps to determine whether, in fact, she was. Relying on the word of Thomas Tenney—and possibly that of Elisha Jenney and Silas Aiken—Tyler had decided to banish Martha Parker from the mission field, and he saw in her spurned but still hopeful fiancé the perfect tool for doing just that.

What goaded him were the same anxieties that dimmed the horizons of Dartmouth's young men. Their worries beset its president, too, but even more intensely. That was because Tyler and many of his fellow religious conservatives were facing a crisis of authority within their own Congregational and Presbyterian churches by the mid-1820s as evangelical fervor prompted a growing number of women to make their voices heard during worship. Tyler's great friend Asahel Nettleton had always held the line, never permitting "females to pray and exhort in promiscuous assemblies"—not even when excitement peaked at his revival meetings. Their colleague Lyman Beecher agreed that women's "softness and delicacy of feeling" should make them shun "the notoriety of a public performance" including praying before audiences of both sexes. What could be more immodest, to say nothing of unscriptural? Only off-brand Christians outside the evangelical mainstream in New England like Methodists and Freewill Baptists had once allowed women to exhort and preach, but within recent decades their male leaders were cracking down on such practices. How unnerving to the likes of the Tylers and Beechers and Nettletons that differing opinions about the role of women in worship had now arisen within the ranks of the Congregationalist and Presbyterian clergy, the inevitable result of the evangelical message that women, by nature, were more religious than men.

It first appeared as a cloud no bigger than a man's hand, one arising not from a biblical sea but, rather more prosaically,

from miasma shrouding the newly dug Erie Canal. By the fall
of 1825, reports from upstate New York were filtering into newspapers back east about a series of revivals erupting in towns that
lined the canal route, all orchestrated with consummate skill by a
young Presbyterian preacher, Charles Grandison Finney. As congregations caught fire from Rome to Utica to Auburn, women
loomed ever larger in the religious excitement. For decades the
entreaty and example of pious wives, mothers, and sisters had
been bringing their menfolk into the churches, but now, for the
first time, some upstate women were taking on a more assertive
role in mainstream evangelical churches. They prayed and tes-
tified and exhorted at mixed gatherings known as "social meetings," sometimes publicly singling out certain individuals as "a
particular subject of prayer."

Finney did nothing to discourage such practices and even
preached against those husbands and fathers who kept their wives
and daughters from attending his meetings. A few of his supporters among the clergy went further still, openly advocating
for women's legal and political rights. By the spring of 1826, all
New England talked of these challenges. Some ministers invited
Finney to come east and preach in their churches, while others—
the more theologically and socially conservative—denounced the
revivalist and his "new measures." A conference at New Lebanon,
New York, convened in the summer of 1827, would reveal the
widening division between Finney's supporters and their adversaries, led by Asahel Nettleton and Lyman Beecher. Nettleton
denounced the "praying of females in the presence of males as
the greatest evil to be apprehended." Sharing his outrage, another
minister, citing Saint Paul, condemned any woman who spoke
"whenever the sexes are mixed up in an assembly for social prayer."
Too taboo even to bear his mention was the prospect of a woman's
preaching—that is, speaking from a text of the Bible. He dwelled
instead on those women who, "in the midst of a crowded assem-

bly" gathered for a revival "with a loud voice, began to pray for their husbands." Here was "a perfect revel of fanaticism." "Our mothers and wives and sisters and daughters" would surely "gain more respect and influence by keeping in the place which nature and nature's God assigned them, than by breaking forth as Amazons into the department of men."

What intensified the alarm over spiritually empowered women within the ranks of Congregationalists and Presbyterians was the beginning of a major shift in the religious allegiance of Americans. Between the 1820s and the coming of the Civil War, the number of Roman Catholics in the United States expanded steadily, largely but not entirely because of immigration, and with those believers came nuns who presided over convents and schools. For the first time, women invested with formal religious authority by their church figured as a significant and, thanks to their distinctive habits, a highly visible presence in the culture. The female religious virtuosity that nuns embodied and the institutional power they exercised both fascinated and appalled Protestants, among them Martha Parker's brother-in-law Isaac Bird. Before leaving Boston for Beirut, he had spent hours at a Catholic chapel, watching with rapt attention and deep uneasiness as two young New England women took the veil. Within a few years, many Protestants would go beyond silent dismay: in 1834, nuns became the first target of anti-Catholic mobs with the burning of the Ursuline convent in present-day Somerville, Massachusetts. It was a choice that betrayed misogyny as much as religious prejudice.

That attack inspired a telling prank played on Leonard Woods by the daughter of another Andover Theological Seminary professor. Woods's daughter Harriette recounted how, while the ruins of the Ursuline convent still smoldered, her friend Elizabeth Stuart, then nineteen, disguised herself in a nun's habit, burst into Woods's study, and begged him to save her from a pursuing mob. Then as now, the young have an unerring instinct for the jugular: present your elders with a knotty choice and watch them sweat. Would Leonard Woods succumb to his fascination with female sanctity and shelter the poor "sister" or act on his loathing of Catholicism and give her up to her pursuers? Harriette did not reveal her father's response, but Elizabeth Stuart's sly challenge speaks eloquently to the ways in which a gathering Catholic presence in the United States heightened tensions over women's empowerment and spiritual authority within Protestantism. So, too, did the complaint of Catharine Beecher, Lyman's eldest daughter, who was lamenting by the 1840s that "the leaders of the Catholic church understand the importance and efficiency of employing female talent and benevolence in promoting their aims, while the Protestant churches have yet to learn this path of wisdom."

Situating Martha Parker in this wider historical canvas tells us that her timing could not have been worse. She fell afoul of Bennet Tyler just as he and his allies were facing a crisis of authority within their own churches. In their view, the campaign by Charles Finney and his disciples to accord women greater scope in worship marked only the most recent and alarming sign of the evangelical movement's potential for radically reordering relations between the sexes. In a world where women were gaining ever more sway within churches and voluntary associations alike— and often with support from some leading men—female religious virtuosity seemed ever more dangerous. Small wonder, resonating as they did with these mounting anxieties in evangelical circles, that rumors about Martha Parker seized and shook places like Fairhaven and Hanover.

In this climate, Tyler believed, the American Board could not be too careful about what sorts of wives they sent to the mission field, lest that environment encourage even more women to exhibit entirely too much spirit. To him, Martha showed all the makings of such a person. Perhaps she would never have dreamed of praying in a mixed gathering of men and women, but the girl had made a spectacle of herself in other ways. Worst of all, she had held the whip hand in her dealings with his young men. How different she appeared to other evangelical men—to Elnathan Gridley and James Kimball, to Jeremiah Evarts and Leonard Woods. How fully they glimpsed her possibilities; how readily they took her part. Still, they surely recognized that women like her had the power not only to buttress but also to subvert the authority of men like them. How long could she count on their support?

That question among others weighed on Martha Parker's mind during the dark days after her fateful meeting at Townshend with Thomas Tenney, the point at which our story now resumes. His threats of the peril she would face in this world and the next had left her mired in despair and, as Elnathan Gridley feared, "deranged." It's the kind of crazy recognizable right up to the present for those women who confront an American culture that encourages them to excel but still finds so many ways to punish them for their success.

A Coquette?

Another woman would not have waited. Despite—or because of—all that the future threatened, the wedding would have taken place, as planned, in Dunbarton at the end of July. His loyalty alone would have won her over; his gallant resolve to stay constant and slay every dragon would have swept her off her feet. Another woman, too, would have calculated that once wed, he would fight all the harder to defend her—now also his—good name. And another woman—many other women—would have moved quickly to seal her connection to this respectable man and his prominent family. There would be disappointment, of course, if the marriage dashed their dreams of missionary glory, forced them to stay in America, and obliged him to settle for ministering to a church. But another woman would have consoled herself with the prospect of enjoying a comfortable life at home, especially after coming into his legacy of many fertile acres in the Connecticut River valley and all those feather beds.

Martha Parker was not that woman. Throughout the last week in July when they were together at Dunbarton, she resisted Elnathan Gridley's pleas to marry him then and there, "come what would." Friends and family pressed her, too. Her pastor, Walter Harris, urged her to go forward because "it will injure the cause of missions if you do not." Her mother and younger sisters agreed; according to Martha, they loved Elnathan and feared "people will talk should I never go to Wes[tern] Asia." Everyone in the village was talking already: *Was the bride backing out?* But none of them could move her: when Elnathan returned to Boston at the beginning of August, Martha stayed behind in Dunbarton, still unwed. Why? What held her back from marrying him?

Consider, first, her mother, Martha Tenney Parker Mills. So intent was she on squelching gossip that Madam Mills threatened to turn her daughter out of the house if she did not go through with the wedding. It's unexpected, that stark determination to keep up appearances. As the mother-in-law of two ministers and the wife of Lieutenant Thomas Mills, one of Dunbarton's leading citizens, this lady should have had a lock on respectability. Martha once described her mother and sisters as uncommonly "proud," the envy of their neighbors, because "we have had much happiness at home." She alluded, no doubt, to her then-widowed mother's matrimonial windfall back in 1821, a match allying her in middle age with the powerful Mills clan. But neither the envy of her neighbors nor the happiness of her children lasted for long. In the fall of 1824, the Reverend Walter Harris called upon Lieutenant Mills to rise from his pew and to make "an acknowledgment of unchristian conduct toward his wife" before all the congregation. At that time, Emily and Martha, both church members, were living in the village, and most likely they witnessed their stepfather's confession and public humiliation. Nor was this episode a brief, bitter interlude in an otherwise uneventful union. Little more than two years later, in December 1826, it would be Madam Mills who stood in church to acknowledge "hard and unbecoming words spoken concerning her husband," and a few months later, in the spring of 1827, Lieutenant Mills yet again admitted to "defaming his wife's character in various places, and at different times."

It was not uncommon for Dunbarton's Congregational church to effect reconciliations through such public confessions. Its members upheld rigorous standards for admission to membership and enforced a strict discipline on any who strayed, including confession before all the church of especially egregious faults. That ritual, they believed, would help to repair breaches between sparring spouses and estranged siblings or resolve quarrels among neighbors. Madam Mills and her children took pride in belonging to so discriminating a body of saints. They would have regarded their rigorous religious observance as enhancing the family's purchase on respectability—at least until Madam's second marriage imploded. That orthodox Calvinism set them apart from the majority of northern New Englanders who attended worship sporadically, if at all, and then many of them worshipped with those scruffy upstarts, the more theologically liberal Freewill Baptists, Methodists, and Universalists. But the Dunbarton church's efforts did not heal the broken union of Thomas and Martha Mills. The couple would battle into the next decade, and in 1835 the village's patriarch and Thomas's brother, John Mills, lodged a complaint with the church against his sister-in-law for "refusing to live with her husband." No wonder, then, that Madam Mills, her turbulent marriage already notorious in the neighborhood by 1826, wished to dispel any whiff of scandal involving Martha.

Her daughter felt the same pressure to save face, knowing that her mother and younger sisters dearly wished to prevent her from "becoming the subject of conversation." All the odder, then, that Martha put off marrying Elnathan. What was even more intolerable to her than being the talk of the town? To answer that question, recall that she had spent most of her youth watching her widowed mother struggle to support several children. Thereafter she had looked on, appalled, as a second marriage, which had seemed so advantageous, failed in a few short years. The same unhappy memories would have haunted her elder sisters, Ann and Emily, but the past had more hold on Martha because she, like her mother, was marrying above herself. By worldly measures, the Gridleys topped even the Millses, and here was their scion, Elnathan, ready to give up everything for her. If the Prudential Committee declared him unfit for the mission field because of marrying her, how soon would he come to regret that sacrifice—as inevitably he would? Would he and his family ever forgive her for his having made it? Still worse, would the marriage provoke Thomas Tenney into public revelations that besmirched her reputation and embarrassed the entire Gridley family? Martha could easily end up like her mother, despised by her husband and saddled with her in-laws' resentment.

Elnathan's willingness to give up too much for Martha would also spell the loss of what made him most attractive to her. He could satisfy her ambitions for this world and the next only if he remained a missionary. If he did not, she would pay a high price for marrying him. There would be no eventful life abroad as part of the Palestine mission, no reunion with her sister Ann, and no chance to shine as a spiritual virtuoso and missionary celebrity. It stayed with Elnathan, the recollection of Martha's telling him that "she could not bear the thought of preventing my going to the heathen." But what registered with him as Martha's selflessness we might read quite differently: the heathens' loss would be hers as well if she ended up in a mere New England parsonage, the disgraced wife of a cashiered missionary.

As she assessed her situation, then, Martha realized that she couldn't risk marrying her present fiancé until she could be sure of her former fiancé. She had to conciliate Thomas Tenney, thereby ensuring that he would make no damaging disclosures—not to Jeremiah Evarts, not to the rest of the Prudential Committee, not to anyone. She needed to stanch the rumors at their most lethal source to ensure that "Esquire Evarts can place perfect confidence in me." If she regained Thomas's good graces, perhaps he could silence Elisha Jenney as well.

Following Martha as she pursued that strategy through the late summer and the fall of 1826 leads us into the elusive, often inaccessible realm of sexual politics as it played out in this lost world. Watch the ways in which one young woman in the northern United States—and perhaps many others there and elsewhere in the early republic—understood and maneuvered to make her way in this patriarchal world. Note the array of influences within its evangelical culture that at once empowered and constrained her. Consider what differences the passage of two hundred years has made.

Martha proved remarkably resilient. By Elnathan's account, she returned from the meeting at Townshend so unhinged that her behavior left him "apprehending that she would become a maniac." Yet within days she regrouped, summoning her wits and resolve. The speed of that recovery leaves us wondering about whether, when first reunited with Elnathan at Dunbarton, she hadn't played up her distress. In view of her past with Thomas, it's easy to imagine Martha, even as she agonized over her future, reveling in the drama of the moment. Such stark despair would also have enlisted Elnathan's sympathies before he went to Townshend and heard the whole truth about her romantic history. Then again, the harrowing deaths of her father and elder brother and her mother's embattled second marriage might have toughened Martha to rebound quickly. What's certain is that her way of meeting this new crisis reveals the powerful ways in which evangelical teachings could sustain women under siege—as Thomas Tenney was soon to learn.

She set to work on a letter to him at the end of July while Elnathan was still at Dunbarton, perhaps unaware that she was taking matters into her own hands. "I feel, and more deeply than ever before, that I have erred," she began, "but I do not feel a submissive spirit." To the contrary, ever since he had confronted her at Townshend, "I have felt that God is a hard master," one who had "permitted me to commit faults." "I used to feel proud to think I could be flattered, caressed, and yet not be affected by it," she continued, but "now it must be known to many, that I once encouraged your addresses." Here, it seemed, was an unsparing self-appraisal, one acknowledging her past pride and her present inability to submit to God's will.

If Martha opened the curtain on her inner spiritual drama with this letter, a second, this one to his sister Sarah a few days later, offered the next act. She knew that Sarah would share it with Thomas, not least because he featured as the star player. "I have had a season of most distressing darkness," Martha began. "I told our family, that I should go immediately to hell." Thankfully, she had now regained that "submissive spirit" to the divine will that all believers should possess. She felt "humble before God," and she owed it all to her meeting with Thomas at Townshend: "His tenderness will never be forgotten. How could I ever pain his heart[?] But if I had not done it my pride might never have been humbled." Indeed, "God designed that he should suffer in order to bring me where I ought to be." It's a breakup line that echoes in our more secular present as "It's not you, it's me."

Besides stressing the fullness of her repentance and Thomas's role in bringing it about, Martha begged both brother and sister for "advice" about joining the Palestine mission. "I have usually wished to decide for myself, but now I cannot," she assured Sarah. So shorn was she of all selfish desire that Martha professed "to have no will of my own," but only to follow what God appointed as "the path of duty." Just as she was bound to obey God, Martha added, she must submit to Elnathan Gridley because "I am engaged to him, and must therefore do as he says." What a pity she had not acted on that principle when engaged to Thomas, she concluded, "yet what a <u>happy</u> thing it was; it was the greatest blessing I have ever received, and I will write it on the <u>tablet of my heart</u>." Lesson learned: she could not become his wife, but Thomas would always have the solace of having taught her how to be a proper spouse to another man. That should be satisfaction enough for any Christian—particularly a paragon like him.

Martha excelled at using religion to her advantage, drawing on the same arsenal that her former fiancé (among other men) used against her. If that tactic invites our cynicism, it shouldn't. She and he (and they) were true believers, so versed in their creed that they knew how to enlist its teachings to serve their purposes. For Thomas, that entailed telling Martha, as he had at Townshend, that by rejecting him without good reason, she "left him no reason to hope that she was a Christian." That thrust struck home: according to Elnathan, the "shock" of believing that she stood in spiritual peril had pushed Martha to "the brink of distraction." Thomas had counted on his words eliciting exactly this response: he expected that preying on her spiritual insecurities would make Martha buckle. It had always been his most powerful weapon, the one by which he hoped to possess her, body and soul. Imagine his astonishment when she rallied and returned his fire with ammunition forged from their shared faith. She credited Thomas with her reclamation and then dared him to match her godly selflessness by letting her go.

Listening to the exchange between these two "Redeemer's children" alerts us to yet another way in which evangelical Protestantism empowered women in the early nineteenth century. Besides sustaining the churches, voluntary associations, and academies that afforded venues for women to develop a civic identity, assert a public presence, and experience and express ambition, their faith provided them with the language and concepts that allowed them to challenge men in private as well as public settings. Far outnumbering men as hearers of sermons and regular churchgoers, women went to school on what their clergymen preached and the Bible taught, learning invaluable lessons. Someone like Martha Parker, steeped in evangelical culture since her childhood and schooled at Bradford Academy, proved more than a match even for a minister in training such as Thomas Tenney.

Another consideration, too, might have boosted Martha's confidence that she could prevail, and that was Thomas's palpable anxiety about any further investigation by the Prudential Committee of the American Board. Only days after his return from Townshend, he wrote to James Kimball that he "feared the result of their [the committee's] decision might be unfavourable to us all . . . and I felt disposed to do anything in my power to prevent the necessity of their interference." What accounts for his concern? Was it possible that Jeremiah Evarts's investigation would yield discoveries even more "unfavourable" to him than to her? All in all, it was enough for Martha to allow the lawyer to go forward.

By whatever promptings, her spirits lifted during the first week of August. Even though she had asked advice from both Tenneys, she had no intention of following it: her letters to them were overtures intended only to invite their assurance that all was forgiven. On the same day that she sought Sarah's help in bringing her brother around, she wrote to Elnathan, now back in Boston, announcing that her spiritual crisis had passed and "she had received forgiveness of her Maker." "Come [to Dunbarton] as soon as you please," she added. "I will be prepared to leave home this week—next, or any time you please." Provided, of course, that "Esq. Evarts can place perfect confidence in me." "If not," she told Elnathan, "let me go." No mission for her, no marriage for them. No wonder he was striving so hard on her behalf, prompting Evarts to complain that of late his conversations with Elnathan were "not entirely kind and friendly." Most encouraging of all might have been the sense that she had claimed the spiritual high ground from Thomas Tenney, using the weapons that her faith provided for the weak as well as the strong.

She had bested him. Bad enough that she had done it with his own tactics. Still worse, the more repentant she seemed, the more irresistible she became. His rival was about to vanquish him, too. Or so he heard from James Kimball, who warned him that "Mr. Gridley was determined to be married, and if the Board objected to Martha's accompanying him [to the Palestine mission], to turn his attention to some other field of labour." All in all, it was a new low for Thomas, miring him ever deeper in misery. His spirits did not lift even at the sight of Bennet Tyler's large frame suddenly filling the doorway of his lodgings. He told the president that his trip to Townshend had failed and "expected Martha would soon be married to Mr. Gridley."

"If she does," Tyler replied, "she is a <u>wretched woman</u> for life." A dire prediction and one delivered, as Tenney would long remember, "in a voice which almost made me shudder." Then the president demanded, "Will you, if the connexion does not take place with Mr. Gridley, take Martha to yourself?" The question tipped Tyler's hand, showing how he planned to move forward. The members of the Prudential Committee, he believed, would be loath to revoke their earlier approval of the Parker girl as a missionary, because to do so would be tantamount to impeaching her character. It might also prompt the impulsive Gridley to give up the Palestine mission, remain at home, and marry her, despite the blot on her name. But would she allow him to make so great a sacrifice—to choose her soul, slightly soiled as it would be, over those of the heathen multitudes? Not likely that even *her* conscience would tolerate such a blow to the missionary cause. How much better for all concerned, then, Tyler advised, for Thomas to step forward and renew his own offer of marriage. If it was accepted, both Evarts and Gridley would get off the hook, Thomas would get his heart's desire, and this "wretched woman" would get better than she deserved.

After weighing his visitor's question for some minutes, Thomas replied, "If I can see her feel as she ought, and it is in my power to make her happy, I can still love her." A bit dim, young Tenney, driveling on about happiness; fortunately, the Lord had provided Bennet Tyler to set him straight. "The engagement between her and Mr. G[ridley] and all she has done respecting going on a mission is <u>null</u> and <u>void</u>," the president decreed. "A previous engagement destroys its obligation. It is her duty to confess this to Mr. G[ridley] and all concerned. Her dismissing you in the manner which she has had <u>no effect</u>, in <u>weakening the obligation</u> of her engagement to you." There was the crux of the matter for Tyler: contract and obligation. Thomas insisted again, "I did not wish her to be bound to me, unless I could make her happy." The fellow was hopeless. Tyler tried again, this time resigned to speak the schoolmaster's language. He reminded him that it was Martha's "duty to go <u>back</u> where she was last spring, and begin in a proper manner." Propriety required her telling him "why she cannot be happy with you," in which case, "as an honourable young man, you will release her." Not that Thomas need fear that outcome, because "if she feels as she ought, there will be no such cause. This is the only way in which she can be happy; after what has passed between you, she will never be happy in a connection with Mr. G[ridley]."

Their minds met on one matter at least. *If I can see her feel as she ought. If she feels as she ought.* Those "oughts" sprang to the lips of both men from the hard-core Calvinism bred in their bones.

It taught that original sin had so disordered the workings of the will and affections that fallen human beings no longer desire what is right. Instead, they seek only to satisfy their own selfish wishes and whims. But if Martha was truly converted, as she claimed, God's grace within her soul would manifest its workings by freeing her from self-interest—meaning, the lure of exploring a wider world as Elnathan Gridley's wife—and awakening her to duty. That meant acknowledging the sacredness of the promise she had once made to Thomas Tenney and keeping her word. It was not that duty trumped feeling: to the contrary, following the way of duty caused men and women to have the *proper* feelings—to feel as they ought.

How strange to us in the present, this lost world of ironclad commitments and unacceptable emotions. No wonder, because it first came under fire from romanticism more than two hundred years ago, and it has been in retreat ever since, routed in recent decades by nearly every school of psychological and spiritual therapy. Even so, many felt its force throughout the nineteenth century and beyond. Consider the case of a young lawyer on the Illinois frontier in the early 1840s who promised his love to one woman, then fell for another belle and backed out of his engagement. But breaking his word—failing in his resolution—so battered the man's self-confidence and self-esteem that he plunged into a disabling, possibly suicidal, depression. Intellectually, he had rejected his evangelical Calvinist upbringing years before, but its emotive power over him persisted in this overwhelming sense of obligation to keep his word. Abraham Lincoln felt "honor bound" to wed Mary Todd.

Their contemporary Harriet Beecher Stowe explored the same emotional terrain in one of her justly less celebrated novels, *The Minister's Wooing* (1859). Only seven years younger than Martha Parker, Stowe came of age in the same rigorously Calvinist New England culture, and her novel's heroine, situated in a similar setting, struggles with the temptation to break her engagement to a starchy, middle-aged clergyman in order to marry a hot young mariner. Steeped in scripture (the just person is "he that sweareth to his own hurt and changeth not" [Psalms 15:4]) and devoted to a deity who's a stickler for keeping covenants, most of Stowe's characters agree, as one put it, that "to break the word that had gone forth out of one's mouth was to lose self-respect, and all claim to the respect of others." That was the world in which Bennet Tyler lived, and the world to which he was recalling Thomas Tenney. It was a world in which only certain feelings were warranted and in which promises once made—properly understood as legal contracts and sacred covenants—were absolute and binding.

It was all so simple, as Tyler saw the matter. Young Tenney need only stiffen his spine and press forward with his claim, renewing his proposal to Martha Parker. Once they learned of that offer, Jeremiah Evarts and the Prudential Committee as well as Elnathan Gridley would surely conclude that they could cut the girl loose without much damage to her reputation—nothing, really, that a swift marriage to the exemplary Thomas could not mend. There would be no need for anyone to look more closely into the matter, no opportunity for this misguided girl to tell her side of the story.

Thomas took Tyler's advice. Shortly after the president's visit, he wrote to Martha, again offering marriage. Included in that letter was his "transcript" of the conversation with Tyler, affirming the "correctness" of Thomas's feelings—and the incorrectness of hers. "You say 'I am engaged to Mr. G[ridley]—therefore I must do as he says,'" the schoolmaster wrote. "But did you not pledge yourself to another first? Have you ever stated <u>one</u> proper sufficient reason, why this pledge should be withdrawn? Have you ever requested me to release you from that engagement, as binding upon you at this moment as it ever was? True you have rescinded it, but in what manner?" In no manner that passed muster with

Thomas Tenney and Bennet Tyler, and men like them were, of course, the sole arbiters of what counted as satisfaction.

What was Thomas thinking when he set down those words and sent off his letter? From our vantage point, his confusions about marriage stand out starkly, a muddled mix of the old emphasis on "oughts" and obligation with the emerging ideal of individual happiness. He must have winced at the recollection of having always told Martha "in the <u>fullest</u> and most <u>unqualified</u> manner, my wish that no connection might even take place, unless she could give me her <u>undivided heart</u>." Why, without that "mutual esteem" and "mutual <u>attachment</u>" so essential to mutual happiness, he had assured the gathering at Townshend, "I would sooner roam the wood[s] with savages than subject her to an unwilling bondage." Now here he was, acting on the advice of a man who told him otherwise in a voice that nearly made him "shudder." His hypocrisy shamed Thomas—enough, at least, that he tried to shift the responsibility for writing the letter to Tyler himself. Wouldn't it carry greater force, the schoolmaster had pleaded with him, for the president to "state his opinion" in a letter to Martha or to her minister, Walter Harris? Ah, there would be no need of that, Tyler replied, now that he had manned up his protégé.

By the middle of August, Martha Parker knew that Bennet Tyler had pronounced her engagement to Elnathan "null and void." About the same time, she would also have learned—most likely from her brother William or her brother-in-law James Kimball—that rumors about her had traveled from Fairhaven to Hanover. More than a match for Thomas Tenney she might be, but for the president of Dartmouth College and the gathering force of public opinion? Realizing what she was up against unnerved her, at least at first. "I <u>now</u> believe that I was absolutely engaged to Cousin Tenney," she wrote to Elnathan. Her message mystified him, because, as he recalled, even when in "her deepest distress" upon returning from Townshend, a time "when her conscience was indeed awake," Martha had told him "that she had never at any time considered herself absolutely engaged" to her cousin. But now, Elnathan added, "in such a way was that claim urged that Martha feels it." Felt what—and why? Overawed by Tyler's rank and authority? Or recalled by her faith to keep a promise once made to her cousin?

Whatever she felt and thought, Martha acted within hours of reading the "transcript" of Tyler's advice that accompanied Thomas's proposal. She wrote back to her cousin, describing herself as "greatly <u>agitated</u>, but greatly relieved." She chided him for not having offered to marry her when they met at Townshend. What would her "emotions" have been had she wed Elnathan before receiving Thomas's most recent proposal? She declared that "I now feel decided to remain in America," even though it would make for "a trying scene" when she told Elnathan that "I cannot go to Western Asia." If he could "give me up readily," she added, "I should not be unhappy." There would be resistance from her family, too, but then their "<u>pride</u> must be humbled." She asked Thomas to come to Dunbarton as soon as possible to help mollify her mother and younger sisters, to whom her decision would "give <u>unpardonable offence</u>." Perhaps those Parker women, who were "constantly urging me to be connected with Mr. Gridley," would see matters differently if cousin Thomas were to "converse with them." "Pray that I may be <u>firm</u>, that I may keep my eye fixed on God," she told the schoolmaster. He had won her back, right?

Not even close. Martha had stopped short of promising to break her engagement to Elnathan—so far short that she assured Thomas that he "would love Mr. G[ridley]"—and then proceeded to list her current fiancé's many sterling qualities. She added that Elnathan would, of course, "feel unwilling to go on a mission alone"—to say nothing of the trouble he would have lining up another wife on such short notice. In fact, Martha was not at all "decided" about staying in America, announcing at the end of her letter that she intended to leave the final word about her future to Bennet Tyler and Jeremiah Evarts. She would write to Elnathan in Boston about "what the Pres. [Tyler] said about my obligation to you, and ask him to read it to Esq. Evarts." She felt certain that her fiancé would not be "unreasonable," that "he will wish me to do what is right, whatever might be his own suffering." Still, she added, "I am fearful I shall forget duty when I see him," because "his kindness and affection" could "destroy all my firmness."

Bumfuzzled by these mixed signals, Thomas headed to Dunbarton in mid-August, trying yet again "to find out as far as in my power, the real state of Martha's mind." What made the trip worth his trouble was the moment when, yet again, she professed to have loved him. She even produced as proof an extract from a letter (written to whom he did not say) that she had composed months earlier, at the time of her engagement to Elnathan. She had never confided her love for Thomas to any other person except her younger sister, Marianne, she explained in this extract, because "I was too proud to confess to any person, a truth, which I thought would injure me in their estimation." But how plain it was to her now, that pride had betrayed her, that she had feared losing face—as she need not tell him—with her sisters Ann and Emily and her brother-in-law James. After ending their engagement, Martha assured Thomas, she despaired that she "had forever lost [his] confidence and affection" and, in desperation, agreed to marry Elnathan because she "looked upon an exile from America as desirable. I thought I would give up earthly pleasures and live for God among the heathen." Yet "she had never felt so strong an attachment for Mr. Gridley, as she had done for me." In this telling, the Palestine mission had become not the beginning of her brilliant career but the place to bury her dreams of earthly happiness.

How Thomas yearned to believe that Martha had loved him once—and with more ardor than she now felt for Elnathan. But was she playing him? Did he wonder about the authenticity of that "extract" from her letter? He was unlikely to have forgotten that he had been a fool for her before, and it could not have escaped his notice that she spoke of loving him in the past tense and that she had given him no promise—said not even a word—about ending with Elnathan and beginning again with him. Nor could it have fallen softly on the schoolmaster's ears to learn that she had told no one else except Marianne about her affection for him because it would "injure [her] in their estimation." That stirred the memory of a letter sent to his sister Sarah only weeks earlier in which Martha declared that in rejecting him and accepting Elnathan, she had "suffered myself to be blinded by publick opinion; and the very step I took to preserve the good opinion of the publick was my means of losing it." Did he really compare so unfavorably with his rival in the eyes of so many? And would losing the "confidence and affection" of such a mediocrity as himself have driven Martha to seek "exile" among "the heathen"? No, the truth—however much of it Thomas admitted to himself—was otherwise.

As Martha knew it, the truth was that she ran a grave risk by keeping on the wrong side of Thomas Tenney. Dreading the future damage he and his friends could inflict on what was left of her reputation, she wanted the assurance that he would still come running when she whistled. No wonder his latest proposal left her feeling, as she admitted, "relieved." If scandal ended up rupturing her engagement to Elnathan, Martha's matrimonial prospects were bleak: she faced a future of spinsterhood, unless Thomas stepped forward to claim her. And if she were left on her own, the taint on her character would keep her from employment at any academy. Her only hedge against disaster, then, lay in stringing Thomas along, allowing him to hope, and keeping him quiet. That was what she sought to achieve by giving him, again, a little "encouragement" and a lot of equivocation.

Intent as she was on conciliating Thomas, Martha had not given up on her dream. Indeed, their week together at Dunbarton in August might have reminded her why she had so long resisted marrying this self-righteous bully, a fellow capable of promising, "If I am near her, I shall ever endeavor to correct her faults; I will treat them as my own." Throughout the month, she also kept up a correspondence with Elnathan, affectionate dispatches that betrayed no intention to break their engagement or to withdraw from the Palestine mission. Soon they would fall under the discerning eye of Jeremiah Evarts himself, to whom those letters "manifested strong attachment." Now that the shock delivered by Tyler's advice had worn off, Martha had begun to question whether he alone could prescribe her way of duty. Perhaps she could count on Esquire Evarts for a second and different opinion about to whom she was obligated and how she ought to feel. And if that great man took her part, he would silence Thomas and all of his allies, including Bennet Tyler.

Our tastes today run to heroines with more fire—to those who are unfailingly direct and assertive, secure in their right to self-possession. If Thomas reported accurately about what Martha told him, there's no escaping the conclusion that she was a master of feathers, resorting to flattery, false assurances, and downright deception. But she would not be the first or the last woman to discover that claiming power for herself could betray her into behaving in ways that compromised her conscience. And if manipulating Thomas—and maybe other men in her life— makes Martha Parker a flawed feminist by present reckonings, it does not diminish her daring. To the contrary, it deepens our awareness of the poverty of opportunity that her world presented even to those women armed with some advantages and of the paralyzing self-doubt and the treacherous cultural terrain that they struggled to navigate. In her way, if not in ours, Martha Parker was formidable, deploying personal and religious resources highly developed for other purposes to reach for something new.

By now, Thomas Tenney knew better than to underestimate her. It was not lost on him, her shrewd reckoning that to contend against Bennet Tyler would take someone even bigger and her hoping for such a champion in Jeremiah Evarts. How could Thomas object to entrusting her future—their future—to the two of them? That left him with only one way to outfox her—a long shot, but not impossible. On leaving Dunbarton, the schoolmaster did not head back to Hanover. He went straight to Boston.

I magine his surprise. "Tenny," as Elnathan misspelled his name, "came to me at Boston and spent a whole night in endeavoring to shew from Martha's letters to him and from a great bundle of communications which he had gathered, that she was a very bad girl, and would not do for a missionary." Even more maddening, he claimed that "M[artha] loved him more than she did me— then very <u>civilly</u> requested that I would relinquish my claims." "This I refused to do," Elnathan sputtered, "as evidently improper while the case was in a course of investigation by the Prudential Committee, and as it was Martha's wish I should abide their decision." Thomas served up a different story entirely about their encounter: the two rivals talked about Martha, nearly through the late August night, "in a very kind and friendly manner," "not an unpleasant word . . . spoken by either." Thomas produced the statement he had delivered at Townshend more than a month earlier, and Elnathan read it. When they parted the next morning, his host seemed "in a state of mind entirely tranquil," although he did appear "concerned" that Martha would remain in Dunbarton and marry the schoolmaster.

Elnathan himself admitted that "he had gained a new view of the subject from this visit." He could hardly have avoided it after comparing his understanding of Martha's past with Thomas's version. Her story to Elnathan had been that Thomas wore her down with constant letters and frequent visits, subjecting her to "a series of importunity the most pressing." A master manipulator, Thomas left untried "no art . . . that could operate on her feelings," and at last, weakened by a bout of bad health, she relented and reluctantly "encouraged" him. But here was Thomas himself with evidence—extracts from Martha's letters—that told a different tale. The first, dating from the summer of 1825, teased him for having lost his "confidence" and concealing his "feelings" from her. Only weeks later she signaled him even more directly to renew his suit, slipping him the note that asked if she could still confer on him "the highest earthly happiness," and in December she prompted another proposal by singling him out as "the only person she had ever loved." Martha had led Elnathan to believe that she had done nothing to invite the schoolmaster's attentions, but her letters revealed that Thomas had been a real contender for her affections.

What might have come as even more of a shock to Elnathan was how busy Martha had been during the same months that he and the Kimballs were promoting their courtship. Throughout that fall and winter, she had been lodging Elisha Jenney and taking his measure, pulling Thomas Tenney toward her, then pushing him away. *She* was the manipulator, adept at the "art" of arousing men's feelings and then beckoning or dismissing them as the whim struck her or other prospects arose. He had been, as Elnathan now realized, only the choicest of those opportunities.

There was a name for the type of "very bad girl" whom

Thomas was urging him to believe that Martha might be, a woman changeable and deceptive as the Lady Eve: a coquette. "Flirts" or "players" are today's terms of choice—the tamer ones anyway—but neither quite conveys the charge carried by "coquette" to evangelicals of two hundred years ago. Those who filled the ranks of their converts, they believed, were born-again Christians who shunned as vanity every sort of worldliness. Hence Thomas's utter astonishment when a friend, most likely Elisha Jenney or Silas Aiken, whose advice he sought after Martha broke their engagement "listened to all that had passed and confidently asserted there was something wrong—suggested the possibility that there was some coquetry." His Martha, a *coquette*? "I felt it was <u>impossible</u>." Surely not among the sober, pious "Redeemer's children": it would be as if a peacock had strutted into the henhouse. Elnathan responded similarly, perhaps with more gallantry than conviction but evidently in response to some gossip burning Martha's ears, when he wrote to her, "I can see nothing in the whole [affair] that looks at all like the Coquette."

His capitalizing the word was no misspelling. Elnathan was referencing the title of one of the most popular novels of the early republic. The work of America's first woman novelist, Hannah Webster Foster, *The Coquette* first saw the light of print in 1797. Its appeal proved so enduring that well-thumbed copies passed from one generation to the next, and publishers issued reprints until 1870. A target audience of young middle-class and elite white women raced through its pages, transfixed by the doomed protagonist, Eliza Wharton. A bright, lively young woman, she resists wedding a respectable but dull minister, the Reverend Boyer, succumbing instead to the seductions of Major Sanford, a dashing, amoral "rake"—vintage slang for a serial heartbreaker. So Elnathan's telling Martha that nothing in their situation resembled the plot of *The Coquette*—that there was "nothing that looks like [her] being engaged to two gentlemen at once"—not only signaled that people were talking but also captured what they were saying. They were using the novel to form their impressions and judgments about a romantic triangle in real life.

It should not come as a surprise that Martha and her circle were acquainted with this best-selling seduction novel, one of many churned out by presses on both sides of the Atlantic in the decades around 1800. True, evangelicals of this era disdained all novels as corrupting, but even by the second decade of the nineteenth century pious parents were christening their baby daughters "Clarissa," the eponymous heroine of one of the first and most famous contributions to this genre. Despite evangelicals' domination of print in the early republic, they were less insulated from exposure to the broader American culture than some of their counterparts in the present, who regard as reliable only the information that they and their children access through the filter of churches, Christian media, and religious schools.

More remarkable is the extent to which their reading novels turned even devout young women like Martha Parker into heroines of their own romances. "Shall I always be the means of making some one unhappy?" she gushed to Thomas. "Was it for this I was sent into the world? <u>Hard</u> as my heart is, I am not destitute of feeling. Yes, I do feel, most exquisitely feel." Did she. Still more striking is how faithfully Martha channeled the fictional Eliza. It was an identification with a character and an immersion in a plot made all the easier because, like her real-life admirer, this heroine is a fatherless young woman with brains and charm who is dissatisfied by the prospect of marrying a steady, pliant, but unexceptional paragon of piety.

Thus beckoned through the looking glass, Martha took the novel as a template, relating episodes from her own life in ways that echoed passages from Eliza's career. Remember her telling Elnathan that she was "accustomed to caresses"? Now listen to Eliza's boast of her "bewitching charms": "I am so pestered with these admirers. . . . I am certainly very much the taste of the other sex. Followed, flattered, and caressed." What consumed Martha, like Eliza, was trying to decide between two suitors and being, as the fictional heroine puts it, "loath to give up either; being doubtful which will conduce most to my felicity." And just as Eliza admits, without apology, to being "volatile" in her romantic preferences and to enjoying her conquests, Martha, even as she professed to take no satisfaction from attracting men's attention, indulged in the same rapid shifts of emotion toward her suitors. Rather than "volatile," she was "fickle," the homelier synonym favored by Yankees. She might also have found in the pages of *The Coquette* a plausible means of excusing her behavior toward Thomas, claiming that their engagement had been "conditional," Eliza's exact word to describe her shaky commitment to the Reverend Boyer. Like Eliza, Martha became "town talk" from a broken engagement, and she even experienced an emotional collapse that eerily mimicked the depression that precedes her fictional heroine's unwed pregnancy and early death. The novel appears to have made an impression on the men in Martha's circle as well: there is more than a little of Major Sanford, who swears to take his revenge on all coquettes, in Elisha Jenney and Silas Aiken.

It's not easy, finding out what people read in the past—even in the not-so-distant past of the nineteenth century. Trickier still is divining what individuals and groups made of what they read. What rare luck, then, that Martha Parker presents us with so rich an instance of life imitating art and in ways that suggest the fictional Eliza Wharton was at once a cautionary figure and, less expectedly, a model even for young evangelical women. Hannah Webster Foster's intent in conjuring her heroine might well have been to warn her female readers against coquetry—to teach them to feel and do as they ought. But paradoxically, Eliza also served to authorize the emotions and even (within bounds) the behavior that held out to them the possibility of making choices on their own and exercising power over men.

Readers in the early republic looked to novels—as many people today look to movies or television—to observe complex characters who are appealing despite (and because of) their flaws and vulnerabilities and whose experiences array the acceptable range of possibilities and expectations. Fictions often supply scripts for real lives, teaching their audiences what to feel and how to express those emotions. In this sense, Eliza Wharton was a model to young women in the first half of the nineteenth century—one all the more riveting and influential because of her ambiguity. Even though Hannah Webster Foster's coquette met with a tragic end in her bid for greater freedom, her character answered to something in many young women, Martha Parker among them. That it did so made her a "very bad girl" in the eyes of Thomas Tenney and Elisha Jenney, Silas Aiken and Bennet Tyler. Now even Elnathan Gridley was beginning to have his doubts.

The schoolmaster left Boston early the next morning of August 24 and arrived at Andover, some twenty miles to the north, without a moment to spare. He found Jeremiah Evarts just as he was boarding the stage headed north to Concord, New Hampshire, en route to Dunbarton. Mustering his nerve, he approached the lawyer and handed him a letter of introduction. It bore the signature of Elnathan Gridley, who had also directed him to where he would find Evarts. The letter referred to its bearer as "brother Tenney," as Evarts recalled, and included the assurance that "I might repose entire confidence in his statements." Thomas climbed into the stage alongside him, and together they rode to Concord, then took a chaise to Dunbarton, arriving around

nine o'clock at night. "We had several opportunities of conversing together," Evarts noted. Thomas Tenney's daring gambit had
paid off: even though he had not been able to stop the Prudential
Committee's investigation, he would have the ear of its leading
member all day and half the night.

They left behind in Boston a man bewildered. How, he wondered, had the Reverend Elnathan Gridley wandered into the plot
of a trashy—was there any other kind?—novel? True, Martha's
letters to him still "manifested a strong attachment." But perhaps
it was not strong enough, if it was true that only days earlier she
had invited Thomas to Dunbarton and talked to him about abandoning the Palestine mission and told him that she loved him
more. And then there were the falsehoods about her past, the
most egregious being her claim to have disdained flattery and discouraged all those "caresses." On the other hand, if Martha was
truly so bad a girl, why was the schoolmaster so eager to drive his
rival from the field and reclaim her as his own?

There had been no possibility of Elnathan's taking a seat in
that stage jolting toward New Hampshire. The Prudential Committee had prohibited him from seeing Martha since his return
to Boston at the beginning of August. That left him with only
his confusion for company. Even before his rival turned up at his
lodgings, Elnathan had confessed to Evarts, "I never was in such
circumstances before. I know not what to do—and have come to
a full stop." It took him a couple of days, but at last, matters sorted
out to his satisfaction, Elnathan paid a visit to the basement of the
Hanover Street Church, the headquarters of the American Board,
and there he found Rufus Anderson, someone his own age and
Evarts's right-hand man. Elnathan confided to Rufus the depth
of his disenchantment: "Martha intended to marry Mr. Tenney
unless she married himself; and that she was shaping her conduct
with that view."

Too harsh? Well, most likely those were her plans, even if

she hoped that it would not come down to cousin Thomas. But at least for the moment, Martha's hopes no longer mattered to Elnathan. By his reckoning, she had seized a power to shape destiny that belonged only to men—not to her or any other "very bad girl" who acted like a man. For her part, Martha had learned a different lesson from *The Coquette*—a warning about the grim fate that befell women like Eliza Wharton who played too long at courtship without securing a marriageable prospect. If, in the judgment of Elnathan Gridley, that made Martha Parker less than perfection, so, too, were the circumstances of women's lives, then as now.

CHAPTER SIX

You Belong to Me

When did regret find him? Not the day after. Not even a week after he and Thomas Tenney had talked through the night. Then he received a letter from James Kimball, who admitted to have been "waiting for some time in anxious suspense" for news from his old friend. James shared his fear that Jeremiah Evarts "would get Tenney's statement of facts"—the one Thomas had delivered at Townshend—and "get his mind biased before he was aware of it." Did the remorse start as his eyes traveled over those words? After all, it was he—angered by Thomas's claims, shocked by Martha's letters—who had put his rival and Evarts on the same stage to New Hampshire. Perhaps it had been bravado on his part—daring Thomas to do his worst. Maybe it was also Elnathan Gridley's way of testing which of her two lovers Martha truly preferred.

Candlelight would have been flickering from the windows of the Parker home farm when the two travelers arrived shortly after nine o'clock in the evening. Martha waited within along with her teenage siblings, Marianne, Hannah, and Daniel. Immediately, Evarts drew her apart and spoke with her alone. He asked her to "write her own views of the matter" and to do so without consulting anyone else before retiring for the evening. Off she went, "calm and collected," exactly as she appeared to him throughout the visit. She gave no sign of the astonishment she must have felt at seeing her former fiancé stride through the door with Esquire Evarts. She would have sensed then how matters stood. Still, she had not surrendered hopes of a different outcome.

On the following morning, Evarts listened as Thomas read aloud the statement he had delivered earlier at Townshend. Here was what James Kimball feared—that Evarts would take this version of events as the definitive account. Thomas also presented Evarts with written testimony from Elisha Jenney, alleging that Martha had given him "encouragement" during his months as a lodger at the Parker home farm, leading him on only to reject his proposal. Then Madam Mills, no doubt mortified that all the village was atwitter over the appearance of Esquire Evarts, arrived in answer to his summons and admitted that she had consented to her daughter's earlier engagement to Thomas Tenney. Thereafter Evarts spoke with Dunbarton's minister, Walter Harris. It was summer's end, likely a golden day, because for part of it Martha drove Evarts about the country roads in a chaise as they conversed privately.

She conducted herself with composure and dignity. She deferred, mentioning again that she entrusted her fate to Evarts and Tyler. She acknowledged past faults, in particular the pride that had prompted her to break off with Thomas, but she denied Elisha's accusations. As if to show she'd mended her ways, she told Evarts that "she did not think the advice of her mother and her younger sisters about marrying Elnathan could be relied upon at all," because, unlike her own humbled self, "they were actuated by feelings of pride." She accepted his criticisms of her past behavior gracefully, agreeing with Evarts wholeheartedly about the importance of stability in a missionary. And in the end, she performed to perfection the crucial part of feeling as she ought. "I think my obligations to Mr. Tenney greater than my obligations to Mr. Gridley," Martha confided, "though, if I had become acquainted with both at the same time, I should probably have preferred Mr. Gridley." From start to finish, it was a strategy calculated to assure him that she had the makings of a missionary.

It's hard to say exactly what Evarts made of her. He came to write his account of this visit to Dunbarton more than a year after it took place and principally with a view to vindicating himself and the Prudential Committee. If his recollections of that summer day are accurate, he told her that "according to her own admissions, she had been very fickle and changeable." When Martha replied that she had been "conscientious" about ending her engagement to Thomas, he responded, "Is it not rather true, Miss Parker, that you acted without any reference to your conscience, or without consulting your conscience?"

Did those misdeeds disqualify her from marrying a missionary? Not in the opinion of Elnathan's mentor, Leonard Woods. On his return from Dunbarton, Evarts stopped at Andover Theological Seminary to consult with Woods, who sat with him on the Prudential Committee. "My general views are in favor of lenity and forbearance towards Miss Parker," Woods advised. She need only to make a "proper Christian confession of her faults," which would be received by the committee "as satisfactory" and "the public will consider it so." As for young Tenney, she should "tell [him] the state of her heart, and he, if he is a man, will release her." There would be "difficulty" only if Thomas was "determined to hold her to her engagement," but that possibility was remote, surely. A real man—a Christian gentleman—would never compel a woman to marry him. Evarts heard him out, unconvinced. No, he warned Woods, "the matter was more serious than we had expected."

What made it "more serious" was not any discovery of what

Martha had done but what Bennet Tyler had planned. Evarts had left Dunbarton certain that the man would stop at nothing to gain his ends. The suspicion must have begun to creep up on him as he listened to Thomas reading his statement and to Martha admitting her greater "obligation" to the schoolmaster. Though absent, Tyler made his presence felt in their words. Then there was Evarts's meeting with Walter Harris, which left no room for doubt.

He tried to converse with the old clergyman about Martha, at least "so far as he [Harris] was inclined to converse," which turned out to be as little as possible. Yet from that reticence itself Evarts learned a great deal. Harris professed to know nothing about "the particulars of Mr. Tenney's courtship, nor [about] the circumstances of the engagement." And while he thought highly of Martha as a prospective missionary, he refused Evarts's invitation to return with him to Boston to meet with the Prudential Committee, or even to write in her behalf. Here was a man— the same man who only a few weeks earlier had urged Martha to marry Elnathan Gridley immediately—suddenly scurrying for cover. The reason could not have been lost on Evarts.

Throughout his long ministerial career, Harris, now sixty-five, had drawn women out of their households and into local religious and benevolent organizations. In sermons, he invoked biblical precedent to defend their new activism, and in his church records he noted with pride having nurtured the missionary aspirations of two young women in his church, Philomela Thurston and Ann Parker Bird. He had even composed a little memoir celebrating young Sally Ladd's sanctity. But by the mid-1820s, women's higher profile in the nation's religious life had become a lightning rod for men like Bennet Tyler. In such a climate, Evarts could well imagine him warning Harris that certain powerful men in New England—perhaps its almost-a-pope, Lyman Beecher, or its storied revival preacher, Asahel Nettleton—judged that Dunbarton's pious females enjoyed entirely too much encouragement. What a pity if those grandees should suspect that Harris had set himself—inadvertently to be sure—on the same dangerous course as Charles Finney, whose revivals were promoting such disorderly behavior among women in upstate New York churches. Would it not be prudent, then, for Harris to wash his hands of Martha Parker before an even greater scandal shrouded his latest protégée?

Bennet Tyler was a big man in New Hampshire, if nowhere else, and he had cultivated allies among much bigger men in evangelical circles. Holding the presidency of Dartmouth, too, had put some good things in his gift—or things good enough to be coveted by a small-town pastor like Walter Harris. The old man took pride in sitting on the college's board of trustees, and he would take even greater satisfaction from the honorary doctorate that Dartmouth conferred upon him the following year. Whether or not he earned that degree as a reward for doing Tyler's bidding, Harris now did as the president bade him. Impossible, he assured Evarts, for him to travel to Boston on Martha's behalf. His Dunbarton church was enjoying a revival. Why, the very next day President Tyler himself would arrive from Hanover to join in preaching throughout the weekend.

With those words, all the pieces fell into place for Evarts. Tyler had arranged that trip to have words—the last word—with this plucky young woman as soon as Evarts had cleared the village. The realization left no doubt in the lawyer's mind that to cross a man so cunning and resolute might dearly cost the missionary cause—to say nothing of Martha Parker and Elnathan Gridley. As he had warned Leonard Woods, here was a serious matter indeed.

❧

The time for halfway measures had passed. A month earlier, he had regarded writing to this headstrong girl as beneath him, nearly ridiculous. Surely it was sufficient simply to declare her engagement to Gridley "null and void" and to entrust the delivery of that message to young Tenney. Alas, she persisted in her obstinacy. It seemed nothing would do but that he, Bennet Tyler, confront this stubborn female, and bring the matter to an end.

Martha met with him at Walter Harris's parsonage on the last Sabbath afternoon of August, shortly after Evarts's departure. Neither left a record of their conversation, but a clue to what passed between them turns up in a letter she sent to Evarts dated two days later. Most of its contents echo her earlier statements, which suggests that she had written much of this letter in response to Evarts's request on the evening he arrived in Dunbarton. She had broken her engagement to Tenney in a manner that at first "satisfied my conscience," her letter began, but then realized that "proud feelings" had motivated her. Her emotions toward Elnathan had "experienced no change," and she regarded "a connexion with him" as "still desirable." Yet she feared that once her "errors, and that these, with deep coloring are publicly known," the scandal would "injure the cause of missions." She felt "bewildered"; she wished for others to decide what she should do; she would marry Elnathan and accompany him abroad only if she could "leave no reports in America prejudicial to my character."

Familiar sentiments, all, but then the letter's last sentence lands a surprise. Martha announced that she declined to serve as a missionary, "unless the Committee are decidedly of the opinion, that it is my duty to go forward." In other words, she was no longer awaiting the Prudential Committee's judgment: she was withdrawing from their service, pending their acceptance of her resignation. She was easing their way to letting her go; they needed only consent to her request. Too bad that the original letter does not survive, because it could confirm what the text strongly suggests—that the last sentence was a concession extracted from Martha by Bennet Tyler, one that she added directly after their meeting.

Here's how he must have wrung it from her: Tyler weighed in with his judgment that Elnathan and Martha would be committing "adultery" by marrying. A month earlier Tyler had declared their engagement "null and void," but now, as he and Martha sat together in the parsonage, he was giving Martha a foretaste of exactly how he meant to go about destroying both her reputation and Elnathan's. Besides accusing her of breaking a solemn vow and a legally binding covenant, Tyler was prepared to go public with the charge that the couple, by marrying, would stand convicted of what their culture regarded as one of the most shameful breaches of the commandments, a *Scarlet Letter* sin. Elnathan, who would later reveal Tyler's allegation of adultery in his correspondence, described it as striking "the fatal blow," because he had used "all his Rhetoric to convince the unhappy girl that she had committed a sin, pardonable only on condition of receiving Tenney's hand in marriage." Like Thomas, Tyler calculated that those tactics would play on Martha's spiritual vulnerabilities as a recent convert. She would have felt particularly susceptible to worries about getting right with God because Dunbarton was in the throes of a revival—the religious awakening that Bennet Tyler himself had come to the village to promote.

Evarts's warnings did nothing to shake Leonard Woods's confidence in a good outcome. Still sanguine at the end of August, Woods did not even plan to attend the meeting of the Prudential Committee to review the matter of Martha Parker. It was inconceivable to him that young Tenney would fail to act the part of a man and release her from their engagement, in which case, as

Woods assured Evarts, the Prudential Committee's "path will be plain." There would be a due show of repentance by the young lady, followed by her marriage to Elnathan, and then the two would set sail.

Bennet Tyler, too, felt confident of a good outcome—just not the same one foreseen by Woods. By August 29, he had made his way to Boston from Dunbarton, and almost certainly it was at his insistence that the Prudential Committee postponed its meeting to the next evening. Tyler had told them that a letter from Martha to Evarts was making its way by post, one that might figure in the deliberations. When the Prudential Committee convened at seven o'clock on the night of August 30, Evarts did indeed have in hand her offer to resign from the Palestine mission.

It came as no surprise to him. Nor did Tyler's account of meeting with Martha at Walter Harris's home a few days earlier. Tyler reported to the committee that the two had talked "on the subject of her duty and happiness; that he conversed with as much tenderness and as much seriousness as he was able;—that he endeavored to ascertain her real feelings and wishes." Then Tyler assured the committee "that he thought her affections were more deeply and permanently fixed on Mr. Tenney than on Mr. Gridley, and that her happiness would be promoted by a union with Mr. Tenney." Evarts would later recall Tyler offering these statements "with all the affection of a father." But at the time, the lawyer must have wondered: not even a week before, he had heard Martha express her preference for Elnathan. Perhaps something had compelled her to tell Tyler the opposite. Or perhaps Tyler was lying through his teeth.

Evarts's harboring those suspicions would account for why the Prudential Committee worked deep into the night, plowing through the documents he had collected. Those included the most recent letters Martha had sent to Elnathan, which manifested her "strong attachment" to him. Several hours later, the committee adjourned sometime after midnight without reaching a decision. Whatever transpired during that meeting troubled Evarts, and his letter recounting the group's deliberations alarmed Leonard Woods. "There is real difficulty to be disposed of," Woods responded to his friend. And on September 2, the committee dealt with that difficulty by disposing of Martha Parker, giving their "consent to her withdrawing from the service of the Board in accordance with her proposal."

The "real difficulty," of course, was Bennet Tyler, and the question is why he carried so much weight with the rest of the Prudential Committee. Besides Evarts, there were two other lawyers, both of whom also served as judges, and a Congregationalist minister—men not so easily impressed or intimidated as Walter Harris. Possibly some of its members shared Tyler's distaste for aspiring women or his convictions about ironclad obligations and unacceptable feelings. But most crucial in forging a consensus among them was a hypersensitivity to scandal. They all knew that Tyler and his powerful allies like Lyman Beecher and Asahel Nettleton could stir up trouble by spreading the story that the American Board had stood behind a young woman who played the coquette, broke her word, and lured one of their missionaries into committing "adultery." Their entire foreign missions operation would come under fire because of yet more bad press about women. And lately there had been a lot.

All the while he was dealing with the matter of Martha Parker, Evarts had been turning over those other troubles in his unquiet mind. There was the controversy brewing over Charles Finney's female followers and, of more immediate concern, the fallout from two other romances for which the American Board bore responsibility. At the epicenter of that public relations disaster stood the Foreign Mission School in Cornwall, Connecticut, founded by the board in 1817 to educate a diverse group of students from indigenous nations and abroad, young men of piety and promise recruited principally by its missionaries. Among them were John Ridge and his cousin, Elias Boudinot, the mixed-race sons of two prominent Cherokee leaders. Both wooed and won white women whom they met in the village of Cornwall: Ridge wed Sarah Northrup in 1824, and two years later Boudinot married Harriet Ruggles Gold.

The first of those unions provoked public outrage—along with a significant drop in contributions to the American Board. The Cornwall school's governing authorities quailed, pledging that another such marriage would never take place. But only two years later, they found themselves contending against a determined Harriet Gold, who defied both them and her family by marrying Boudinot. Her Cherokee husband's "color is nothing to me," she declared, "his soul is as white as mine." Well, color must have been something to Harriet, but her early-nineteenth-century heart was in the right place.

Becoming acquainted with diversity, then as now, has a way of giving people new ideas—or encouraging them to follow out the logic of older ones. And living in a community created by missionary zeal, where they studied, played, and prayed with young men from around the world, had made Sarah and Harriet firm believers in the foreign missions movement's most fundamental tenet: the equality of all souls, every single one of them worth saving. That universalist outlook made all the world "kindred," members of what Leonard Woods once called the "great family of immortals." It followed, at least for these two couples in Cornwall, that people of different races should feel free to marry and that women were entitled to speak up as forcefully as men about the meaning of equality.

For his part, Jeremiah Evarts admired Harriet Ruggles Gold and her principled stand. "Can it be pretended at this age of the world that a small variance of complexion is to present an insuperable barrier to matrimonial connexions," he wrote, "or that the different tribes of men are to be kept forever and entirely distinct?" Even so, Evarts saw disaster looming in the charges that years of missionary preaching had "poisoned" Harriet, like Sarah before her, and that Cornwall's scheme was to create "a nursery of Indian marriages." He knew that the American Board could not afford more episodes that drew attention to these strong-minded, independent young women being cultivated in missionary circles. Much as it galled him to capitulate to his racist critics, Evarts closed the Cornwall school in the fall of 1826.

Only a few weeks earlier, he had met with another defeat, one he might have found as bitter. Evarts wrote to Martha Parker, informing her that the Prudential Committee had judged it "expedient" to accept her offer to withdraw from their service. He advised her that she "did right in not wishing to go on a mission, unless, all things considered, there was fair prospect of your promoting the cause of Christ, and of leaving no just ground of anxiety to the friends of missions at home." Thinking to soften the blow, he assured her of Elnathan Gridley's "cheerful acquiescence in their decision." He also asked her to convey his greetings to Thomas Tenney.

So many devils beset Elnathan Gridley. There was his disgust at how cavalierly Jeremiah Evarts had delivered the board's decision, telling him that "I might feel myself free." Free from his engagement, the lawyer meant, as if Elnathan wished to be rid of the woman he loved. There was his shock and hurt at learning that Martha had resigned from the board's service—that the committee had simply consented to her request. How could she have given up their dreams? There was his jealousy, already aroused by Thomas's revelations and now deepened at what the committee called her "<u>indecision</u> of <u>character</u>." This fig leaf of language made it all the worse, a studied vagueness meant to conceal that Martha had kept two lovers in play, gaming to cheat spinster-hood. It enraged him, having to "relinquish his claim" to so infe-rior a rival, and that loss only strengthened the passion he felt for her.

Writing to Martha about a week after the Prudential Com-mittee's decision, Elnathan admitted that the whole episode had been "painful in the extreme" because "no one ever did, prob-ably no one ever will, have that place in my affections which you have had, and which you seem likely to retain." Nonetheless, he knew that she could "never be made happy by all the kind atten-tions, which the love of one detained on her account from Mis-sionary service could bestow." At first glance, that line reads like a compliment to Martha's devotion: conscience could not allow her to cheat all those heathen souls of Elnathan's ministry. On second reading, it sounds like more of a kiss-off: *Don't expect me to stay home in order to marry you.* But the third time through, yet another meaning emerges: he was telling her that he knew that her interest in marrying him had depended on their going abroad together. If that made her the model of a self-denying Christian, it also made him less than the love of her life.

Miserable as he was, Elnathan acquitted himself as he believed a Christian gentleman should. He was generous, telling Martha that Thomas loved her and adding—perhaps a barb lurked here—that she would reciprocate the schoolmaster's affection. After for-mally releasing her from their engagement and bidding her an "affectionate farewell," he added almost playfully, "And now Miss Parker, permit me as a friend to have a little friendly conversation with you, and to request you hereafter to favor me occasionally with a friendly letter." He assured her that "my estimate of your character is lessened little, if any, by all that has been disclosed." He repaid her many falsehoods by insisting that he found nothing in her behavior that "looks like lying or deceiving." He encouraged her to take heart and strove to restore her confidence. "Your character is not lost," he felt certain, and in his estimate she would always be a remarkable woman. "Few indeed, can fill the place which you are capable of filling," he reminded her, and because of those strengths she would live down all the "calumnious reports" and "shame every one who has circulated them."

Kind words, most of them, but they raise the question of how fully, if at all, Elnathan grasped the perils of Martha's position and her limited options for self-rescue. After he left her at Dunbarton at the beginning of August, had she confided in him about her efforts to counter the campaign to force her to feel as she ought? When did he learn about Tyler's meeting with her at Dunbarton and his threats to charge the couple with committing adultery? Did he recognize the narrow scope of her life choices and the price she would pay for making the wrong choice? Did he feel sorrier for her than he did for himself?

One week after writing that letter, Elnathan Gridley boarded a vessel bound for the Mediterranean. He did not visit Dunbarton before he sailed, admitting, "I wish to be spared such a scene." That hasty departure also spared him unwanted attention from the public at large: Jeremiah Evarts got it instead as the board's dooming of this romance began to draw critics.

It started with a twentysomething heckler named Homan Hallock. The son of one minister and the younger brother of another, Homan had gained entry to Amherst College on the strength of his pious pedigree but lasted only one term. Poor health appears as the official reason for his departure; more likely, that evangelical fold held no charms for a black sheep. Thanks again to family connections, he landed in Andover, apprenticing at the firm of Flagg & Gould, which specialized in religious pub-

lishing. Before long, this printer's devil gave in again to wander-
lust, and he opened negotiations with the American Board to run
their missionary press at Malta, an operation that was blanketing
the Mediterranean rim with tracts and books. By March 1826, he
was negotiating his salary with Evarts and admitting—without
apology and probably not for the first time—that his character
was "far from what it ought to be . . . and if I have any true piety,
it lies almost concealed in a mass of sin." Too bad if the young
man's wicked ways bothered Evarts, because he needed Homan
more than Homan needed him: without his talents as a printer,
the young man observed drily, "the heathen must all perish unaf-
fected by any light or truth."

Unaccustomed as he was to such insouciance about sin, to
say nothing of perishing heathen, Evarts gritted his teeth and
kept bargaining. Then, only days after Elnathan Gridley's departure, Homan sent Evarts a letter that mocked the Prudential
Committee—remorselessly—for prying into the private lives
of prospective missionaries. He had learned that inquiries were
being made to various people in different places about his own
marriage prospects—to which Homan took great exception: "If
my bare word is sufficient, I can very soon set all this matter to
rights; if it is necessary that other testimony should be heard, I
may as well plead guilty." Warming to his subject, he declared his
plan to postpone marriage until he turned thirty "for the satisfaction of all who have any business to know." "I swing clear for all
that the fair can say or do," the printer added, because "there is
not a soul west of the Atlantic that I cannot leave forever, without
a sign or a wish; and that, as I have said before the most amiable
and desirable female that any country can produce, would present
no fascinations, allurements, or, temptations which could make
my mind waver at all." No, not even if "she could, at the same
time, make me chief, lord, governor, and potentate over the most
excellent Kingdom under the light of the sun." So there.

A few days later, Homan's older brother, the Reverend William Hallock, waded into the fray. He advised Evarts that he'd written "a blunt letter" (one beginning with the line "O tempora! O Mores!" [O, the times! O, the manners!]) to his brother after hearing gossip that the young printer was "about forming connexions with a little snub of a damsel." In return, Homan served up the same sarcasm to his brother that he'd dished out to Evarts, prompting William to conclude that the Prudential Committee's investigations into matrimonial plans were "rather a ridiculous concern in the whole of it." O, the times, ever since the scandal over Martha Parker and Elnathan Gridley.

The Hallocks' letters signal that even the devout wondered whether the American Board overstepped its bounds by meddling so directly in private lives. As for the less than devout, the Parker scandal would only have confirmed their suspicions that evangelicals were intent on curtailing the personal liberty of all Americans. Managing their missionaries' romances was only the latest assault on individual freedom from these believers who also campaigned to stop dueling and drinking and swearing all week long and doing business on Sundays. Homan's reactions to the board's oversight also suggest that Elnathan himself—the man who "relinquished his claim" to a woman in response to his sponsors' pressure—had become as much an object of ridicule as of sympathy. No way, this young man's letters almost shouted, would a proud Amherst dropout and almost master of the printing craft truckle to a bunch of pious snoopers. The red-blooded Homan Hallock would have no psalm singers sticking their long noses into his love life. Too bad poor Gridley hadn't shown the same gumption.

But Rufus Anderson, for one, was unruffled. He kept his head down, handling the mail that came into the Missionary Rooms during one of Evarts's long absences from Boston. On the backs of both the Hallocks' letters, Rufus scribbled that they required no response. A tempest in a teapot, he felt certain, a little squall, soon becalmed now that Elnathan Gridley was gone.

Elnathan had hoped to leave regret behind in America, only to find it awaiting him abroad. His new city—Smyrna, today's Izmir—offered no shortage of attractions. It commanded a sweeping harbor in the Mediterranean ringed by cloud-robed mountains, their hillsides planted with red-roofed dwellings, cypress, fig, and olive trees. For many centuries the resort of European merchants and mariners, this seaport on Turkey's southwest coast had been the most Westernized spot anywhere in the Ottoman Empire. When he arrived in January 1827, some five thousand Europeans and Americans resided there amid a Muslim majority and large enclaves of Armenians, Greeks, and Jews. Yet neither the place nor its expatriates—even the Protestants among them— were much to Elnathan Gridley's liking.

The British consul set the tone for the little society of English speakers, greeting this new missionary with the sally "Well, well, every trade must live, and s'pose you have good salaries and come here to see the world and live off the fat of the land." Indignant, the young man shot back "with some warmth" about "the prospects I had left, and the prospects I had before me here, and assured him that it was not the expectation of any earthly good that had brought me hither." That exchange quashed Elnathan's prospects of being invited to the gay whirl of balls and card parties that caught up most of Smyrna's Western residents and visitors— diversions that he would, in any case, have declined. Even his fellow New Englanders were an unappetizing lot, most of them engaged in a thriving opium trade to China. For company, he turned to the Greeks, visiting their schools, distributing tracts in their communities, and hiring a tutor in modern Greek.

That still left plenty of time to dwell on the past and to nurse his grievances, often assisted by another unhappy bachelor missionary, his partner, Josiah Brewer. He, too, "came out single" to Smyrna, but in this case because the parents of his intended bride had refused to risk their daughter's life in the missionary cause. The disappointed Brewer preferred a different explanation, one that blamed his bad luck on the American Board, and Elnathan did not discourage him. Together, the two men worked each other into a frenzy of resentment over their unmarried state, and Elnathan began sending letters brimming with self-pity and simmering with dissatisfaction to his mentor back in New England.

Leonard Woods must have dreaded the coming of every post. Long the patron of his former student, he had supported Elnathan's decision to marry, admired Martha Parker for the "loveliness of her character," and defended her to the end. Underestimating Bennet Tyler had been a mistake, but what was to be done about it now? After the committee accepted Martha's resignation, Woods did his best to buck up Elnathan, praising him for behaving with "propriety" throughout the whole sorry business. But these letters from Smyrna warned that propriety's hold on the young man was slipping the longer he dwelled on his loss. How painful, Elnathan recalled, being told by some members of the Prudential Committee that he had been "deceived in regard to the affections of my <u>dear</u> friend, and that acquaintance had been so short that my own affection could not be strong." Parted forever from Martha, he found that sorrows "steal away my [hours of?] study, they break in on my devotions, and haunt my repose." Despite his efforts to "rise above it," he was "thrown back again on myself and all my sorrows return." Yes, that description of a man in misery's thrall does bring to mind Thomas Tenney, raising the unanswerable question of whether Martha Parker brought out this behavior in her men or whether men hardwired for obsession were drawn to her.

What made Elnathan even more reluctant to let go of Martha was his failed quest for another wife. No sooner had he dispatched that heartfelt farewell to her than he asked the Prudential Committee for time to form "a new connexion." In other words, he wished to find and marry another woman before setting sail from Boston. We shake our heads at this news: he's the lovelorn friend, desperate for a balm to wounded pride and broken heart, whom we've all advised not to rush into another relationship. Maybe so, but keep in mind the marrying ways of many of his fellow missionaries. Passion—at least for one's partner—did not top their priorities: what really mattered in a mate was a shared commitment to converting the world. And so luxuriantly did the romance of foreign missions flourish among early-nineteenth-century evangelicals that Elnathan could feel confident that some pious young woman would quickly step forward, so keen to join the Palestine mission that she would ignore the torch he still carried for Martha. Most likely he would not love this "new connexion," nor she him, but that wouldn't matter much to either of them. The couple would set aside mere romance to collaborate in pursuit of their shared spiritual aims, which, once married, he could pursue with much greater safety than did those bachelor explorer missionaries.

Then, too, there was something that Elnathan wanted even more desperately from a partner than a boost to his self-esteem or a reprieve from greater risk. It is a desire less familiar to many of us looking in on his life two hundred years later, but one revealed in full when the Prudential Committee denied his request. Accustomed though they were to their missionaries' rushed courtships, the committee members "severely reprimanded" Elnathan for this "disgraceful" haste, advised him to postpone marrying for a couple of years, and hustled him, unwed, to the other side of the world. Why the scolding—to say nothing of the hurry? No doubt Jeremiah Evarts wished him to "go out" a bachelor explorer missionary, as originally planned. Perhaps, too, he and other committee members feared that a second, hasty engagement on Elnathan's part would only keep the scandal over Martha Parker in the public eye or draw yet more unwelcome attention to the mating practices of missionary couples.

Whatever the reasons, their response astonished and then infuriated this eldest son and heir. His letters erupted with denunciations as worrisome to Leonard Woods as the young man's obsession with Martha. "I feel myself to be an injured man and that the injury is utterly irreparable," Elnathan wrote, having been robbed of the "rights granted me by my God, and guaranteed by the laws of my country." Had he known that the committee would dictate "the matrimonial concerns of missionaries," he would sooner have "been a galley slave, than thus have hazarded the dearest—most sacred right that God has given." What stoked Elnathan's outrage at being deprived of this liberty was his concern about inheriting property: at stake were all those valuable acres of Gridley land back in Farmington.

Recall that according to the terms of his father's will, if one of the sons died childless, his portion of the landed estate would revert to the survivor. Recall, too, Elnathan's desire to deliver on the hopes of his mother, Hannah, to give her grandchildren and thus secure his patrimony. Didn't the members of the Prudential Committee realize that enforced celibacy would imperil fulfilling the obligation owed to his family and that the risks of being stationed in the Ottoman Empire might cut short his life expectancy? How could they deny his desire to procreate as soon as possible, he demanded, these men to whom he "had transferred that confidence, that trust, and almost all that love which a dear earthly Father, now laid in the grave once possessed"? These men, too, who had not found so "disgraceful" the haste with which other missionaries often mated.

As the scion of an old Yankee clan, Elnathan keenly felt the obligation of continuing the male line to carry forward the family name, a duty reinforced by the republican principle that owning property endowed men with political independence. That patriarchal ideal's powerful hold prompted him, immediately after ending his engagement to Martha, to seek another bride. And when his sponsors refused, Elnathan felt that his masculinity was under attack. The spiritual fathers at the head of a powerful evangelical institution—men whom he had hoped would enable him as a patriarch—had instead shamed him and stood in his way.

The entire episode attests to evangelical Protestantism's vexed relationship with ideals of manhood in the nineteenth century. Elnathan Gridley's anxieties about being barred from marriage display the same touchiness about male autonomy conveyed by Homan Hallock's antic promises to stay single. All that's missing from the writings of both young men is what stands out so prominently in the words and actions of others who felt their manly prerogatives imperiled: misogyny. The Tenneys and Tylers, the Jenneys and Aikens, responded to the challenge of changing gender roles by attacking those women who dared to compete with them—and might beat them—at what had been exclusively a man's game. But even men who gave no sign of resenting women slipped easily into the suspicion that the evangelical movement was capable of betraying male believers by curtailing their ability to control their lives. Surfacing in the sensitivities of Elnathan and Homan was the same haunting sense that their faith could compromise manliness.

Did that cross the mind of Leonard Woods? We imagine him cosseted in his book-lined study back in Andover, shaking his head over Elnathan's letter. Fondly he recalled the days when they would sit together in this room and talk "with the freedom which [he] was always accustomed to use" with the young man who was like a son. He remembered the high hopes that he and other members of the Prudential Committee had harbored for

Elnathan, how after a few years in the Palestine mission he would return in triumph to the United States and star on the lecture and fund-raising circuit.

Now he feared for him. There was his hostility toward the board, couched in all of the defiant blustering about liberty. But even more alarming was Elnathan's threat, one that arrived at the end of the letter, to leave the mission field entirely unless he was allowed to return home and find a wife. The committee must not only bring him back to the United States but also "leave me to the free exercise of the rights which God has given me, by laying upon me no restrictions which it would not be thought proper to lay upon a Minister of the Gospel at home." By that he meant that any future candidate for his wife should not be subjected to the same scrutiny by the committee that Martha Parker had endured: "Could I ask a lady to subject herself to all this, and assure her that if she passed the trial, she might hope to become my wife?" No, of course he could not. Or would not. That's what Leonard Woods glimpsed between the lines: the very real prospect that Elnathan Gridley meant to return to the United States and reclaim Martha Parker.

Maybe so. It appears they kept in touch—that she sent him those "friendly letters." Their correspondence would have been slow and spotty, because it took several weeks for letters to make their way between New England and Malta, where Elnathan had stopped and spent the fall of 1826. It would have taken even longer—four, five, even six months—to travel between Dunbarton and Smyrna. But that need not have kept the two from writing, and it's hard to imagine Martha, with her flair for epistolary self-dramatization, resisting this opportunity. Letters to an old lover, a man pining away for her in exotic places: What could be more romantic? Telling, too, is that following his departure, Martha wrote to Elnathan's friends and family in Farmington. The letters themselves have not come to light, but a neighbor who saw them reported that Martha expressed to Hannah Gridley the "particular attachments" she felt toward her son and his family. The most suggestive evidence for some ongoing correspondence comes from Elnathan himself, who confided in Leonard Woods that after he sent his farewell letter, "Martha said to her Sister, 'Marianne, never shall I love another as I love Gridley.'" Those sentiments could have reached him by letter in Boston immediately before he sailed for the Mediterranean, but also thereafter at Malta or in Smyrna. Whenever he received that "friendly letter," he might well have taken it as "encouragement"—at least to keep writing.

And why not? Much to the surprise of her relatives, Martha made no move to marry Thomas Tenney. Shortly after the Prudential Committee accepted her resignation, the two did engage in a public reconciliation through the Dunbarton church just as her mother and stepfather had done and would do again. Martha might well have performed her repentance by standing before the congregation and acknowledging her sins. Or she might have submitted only the written confession, repeating her earlier admission that she "did not dispose of the engagement with Mr. Tenney, in a Christian manner," and that "had I been governed by right feelings, I should not have wished to be released from this engagement." Thomas, too, submitted a brief statement to the Dunbarton church, allowing, "I have no reason to suppose that, at the time she received proposals from Mr. Gridley, she felt that her obligation to me was still existing." Here was hardly the sort of reconciliation to rekindle a romance—and yet another reason to suspect that Martha might have hoped for, even encouraged, Elnathan's return.

CHAPTER SEVEN

Like a Virgin

For weeks she had watched for white sails on the horizon. Every vessel that entered port might bring her long awaited, her beloved. She envisioned their embrace, imagined that moment of holding each other tight again after so long a separation. Time went by, and still she waited, anticipation deepening to anxiety, then darkening to dread. Would there be no reunion, no memory of the moment when Martha, perched on the shoulders of an Arab striding through the shallow waters—just as she herself had been borne into Beirut years before—came ashore and fell into the embrace of her sister Ann? Had death stolen her heart's desire?

The truth was nearly as bitter. It was early February 1827 when the large packet of letters arrived in Beirut. War, piracy, and bad weather always slowed the mails in the Mediterranean, and this winter was especially wretched: it had taken nearly two months for these letters, some sent from New England, to make their way from Malta. The morning the packet arrived, Ann had her hands full, dressing their small children, so it was Isaac Bird who broke the seal on Elnathan Gridley's letter and read it aloud to his wife. There was a long account of the events that had ended with his landing in Malta alone, leaving Martha behind "in disgrace and grief." "It was because I loved her that I bade her farewell," the letter concluded, his "settled conviction that Martha's happiness demanded it," even though the "sorrows" of losing her "will go with me to the grave."

Stalwart Yankee that she was, Ann waited until night fell and the household slept before sobbing her heart out. It wouldn't do, breaking down in front of the Arab servants in her household or the Armenian scholars who assisted her husband's translation of the Bible. As she wept, perhaps she recalled a small tombstone—a stone tablet no bigger than a man's hand—unearthed in Beirut not long ago. The relief depicted a Roman couple, the wife seated, signifying her as the deceased, the husband standing at her side, clasping her hand. The discovery of this exquisite artifact set abuzz the town's small circle of Western expatriates. Ann must have heard it described, perhaps had even seen this powerful image of lost love. Its memory would have returned when Elnathan Gridley wrote of what he would take to his grave.

Staunch Calvinist that she was, Ann brushed away her tears and resigned herself to God's will. As a member of sinful humankind, she knew that she deserved "still sorer chastisements" than the loss of her sister's company. But don't be fooled: the same deity that had taught her never to get too comfortable had also impressed upon Ann the importance of making sure that no one else did either. For the faithful, all things were possible, just as for the wicked, there was no escape from a reckoning. Anyone who doubted it had only to look around Beirut to see how low, how hard, and how fast even the mighty could fall.

Situated on a spit of land stretching into the Mediterranean and nestled among groves of mulberry trees and well-tended gardens, the little town sheltered several thousand Muslim Turks, Greek and Maronite Christians, and Jews. Its port boasted a lively commerce and well-stocked bazaars. But stick a spade in the ground almost anywhere in the warren of narrow streets and brick dwellings, and some vestige of a glorious past—like that small grave marker—would rise from the dirt. Centuries before, a Roman city had flourished on the same spot where Beirut now modestly stood, and imposing reminders of its ancient magnificence abounded. Stroll around town to admire three fine gray granite columns, now shorn of their pedestals and capitals, the ruins of a bath, cisterns and wells, and a sarcophagus adorned with wreaths and a bull's head. Head down for the harbor to survey the main pier, faced with the same gray granite, and to search along the shore for the remains of mosaic floors. Climb into the hills to gaze at what was once a spacious amphitheater.

To Ann, the humbled city of Beirut was an emblem, signifying what her deity could make possible. A splendid outpost of pagan Rome lay buried under the rubble of this sleepy seaport now ruled by the Muslim Turks, but soon, as Christian believers like her interpreted the Bible's prophecies, the town of Beirut, the Ottoman Empire—indeed all the world—would embrace evangelical Protestantism. Her sovereign God could effect astonishing reversals of fortunes, and Ann expected them, prayed for them, and worked to make them happen in great and small matters alike. That included the future of her sister Martha.

Ironically, the power of those religious convictions for Ann Parker Bird—beliefs shared by all evangelicals—would lay bare the divisions among them over womanhood, manhood, and sexuality. The resistance that she organized in Martha's behalf would imperil their movement's continued expansion in the United States and throughout the world. Jeremiah Evarts and the rest of the American Board might have thought it fortunate, at first, that an ocean lay between them and this holy woman. Soon they realized it was not far enough.

❦

It's unlikely that Elnathan Gridley had met Ann before she left for Ottoman Syria at the end of 1822, but her reputation seems to have preceded her. Whether from Martha, James and Emily Kimball, or others, he knew that the lady was formidable. So formidable that upon arriving in the Levant, he opted to settle in Smyrna rather than Beirut. He feared her wrath for abandoning Martha to her fate and referred, with studied vagueness, to "the relationship in which I stand to Mrs. Bird." Yet he need not have worried. The same packet containing Elnathan's letter to the Birds included several letters from Ann's women friends back in New England, reporting news of the broken engagement, deploring Martha's disgrace, but blaming the American Board rather than Elnathan.

Accordingly, Ann wrote back to him immediately, assuring Elnathan of her "warmest sympathy." She expressed her hopes of soon giving him "a cordial welcome" to Beirut. She invited intimacy, urging him to share his feelings with her. She even expressed her regret that he had released Martha from their engagement. "She might have remained <u>your widow</u> or affianced bride, until Providence opened a way for her to become entirely yours," Ann suggested, and then held out the hope that—well before the couple met in heaven—"my dear sister will still be the partner of your cares and the sweetener of your toils." For her, there could be no doubt about the "relationship" in which they stood. Elnathan was family now, and Ann would "never own any other person as a brother than yourself," even though "our <u>Christian friends</u> in America should not sanction the appellation." Some friends (and Christians) they had turned out to be, she thought, starting with Jeremiah Evarts.

Among that great man's many failings was what Ann took to be his low opinion of missionary wives. Included in the packet of letters that had at last reached the Birds in February was one from Elnathan's missionary partner, Josiah Brewer, who disclosed

Evarts's advice to the bachelor pair that "you will enjoy better health, possess better spirits, accomplish more labor, and do more for the cause of Christ" by remaining single for a few years. Ann read that remark as an indictment of missionary wives, evidence that Evarts considered them "not merely <u>useless lumps of baggage</u>, but rather, <u>dead weights</u>, that will by and by, press into the grave the poor infatuated men who brought us hither." Contempt for women like herself meant, she told Elnathan, that Evarts was "evidently displeased" that the young man "did not choose to come out alone." It must be either that Evarts and the rest of the Prudential Committee "were determined you should come to this country unmarried, <u>let happen what would</u>, or that my sister has been guilty of some great crime, which you all determine should be hidden from me." Her words answered to his darkest suspicions—that an unscrupulous organization and its leader were bent on sacrificing a young man's happiness and a young woman's reputation.

Even more gratifying to Elnathan was Ann's disdain for his rival. She lambasted Thomas Tenney as a tool of Bennet Tyler and a "wretch" who did not deserve Martha's forgiveness, let alone her hand in marriage. She insisted it was impossible that her sister "ever gave Tenney <u>that encouragement which amounts</u> to a promise of marriage." And even if Martha had, couldn't a woman change her mind? Since settling in Beirut, Ann had kept up a correspondence with "two of the first young ladies in the circle of my acquaintance" back in New England, both of whom had broken their engagements to clergymen and thereafter married pious, respectable men "of great promise." Yet Ann had "never heard that either of them were censured for having changed their minds," nor had any scandal spoiled their chances at landing even better marital catches. That would be because women were "usually treated by the public with greater lenity than men, if found wavering on the subject of matrimony." Besides, she added archly, "as the whole female sex has sometimes been styled fickle, it would seem they were entitled to a little extra lenity on account of their infirmity."

Her observations echo the defenses of Martha once voiced by Jeremiah Evarts, Leonard Woods, and other members of the Prudential Committee. At first, they had found no great fault in her breaking an engagement or even in being less than forthcoming about her reasons for rejecting Thomas Tenney. But Ann proceeded to press well beyond the argument that women deserved society's indulgence when it came to dismissing their fiancés. If the Prudential Committee wished to make past love lives of perfect constancy the rule for prospective missionary wives, she declared, they must apply the same standard in selecting the men they sent abroad. Had Evarts enforced such consistency in the past? No one knew better than Ann that he had not. Her several years at Bradford Academy as understudy to its preceptress, Abigail Hasseltine, had made the younger woman privy to some choice gossip about the romantic lives of many missionary couples. The women back in New England with whom she corresponded no doubt added to that stock of stories, and now she dished them all to Elnathan Gridley. When it came to "fickle," her sister Martha had nothing on the men in their circle.

The worst offender in Ann's annals of romantic perfidy was none other than Rufus Anderson, whom we have encountered before in these pages. As a college student, he had dreamed of partnering with Harriet Newell's sister for missionary work in India. Years later, he dreamed of succeeding Evarts at the head of the American Board and, to boost his bona fides, published a popular biography of the Cherokee convert Catharine Brown. Never far from Boston's Missionary Rooms, he was working there on the day that a despairing Elnathan stopped by to confide his romantic woes. But back when Rufus still yearned to become a missionary—in fact, to join the Birds in the Palestine mission—he had selected a prospective wife, one Miss Cleaves, to share in this venture.

That young lady lacked the advantage of being kin to Harriet Newell, but Rufus set about making her the woman of his fantasies. "She was introduced to me as a sister missionary," Ann recalled. Rufus "sent her to our best female seminaries, had the entire direction of her studies and expressed his wish at the Seminary with which I was connected, that in all her studies her ultimate destination might be kept in view." Then, after three years of preparing this "particular friend" for the honor of becoming Mrs. Anderson, Rufus abandoned her, "and the young lady is represented as meekly bearing her disappointment, and only weeping at the ill treatment she had received." As poor Miss Cleaves endured this public humiliation, her former intended, far from being "thrown into disgrace," was placed "in a station where the churches look upon him with high expectation." Ann was alluding to his position at the American Board, where predictions that Rufus Anderson would rise to the top were amply justified: he had thrown over his "particular friend" in order to court the sister of Henry Hill, that organization's treasurer and the heir to a considerable shipbuilding fortune. Ever alert to the ways in which the right woman could be the making of him, Rufus wed Eliza Hill at the beginning of 1827. A love match, surely.

Ann Parker Bird's full-throttle assault on this variant of the double standard suggests that a trend was under way among some evangelicals to curtail the freedom that women claimed in contracting marriages. In the United States that she left behind, Ann recalled, women could break engagements without getting a reputation. To the contrary, a majority of the public regarded women as entitled to the freedom to change their minds. But only a few years later, here were Bennet Tyler and his Dartmouth acolytes bent on depriving her sister—and perhaps others—of that liberty. Still more worrisome—as Ann might or might not have known—even some of Martha's defenders sounded a little shaky on a woman's right to choose. One of the questions that Evarts went all the way to Dunbarton to answer was whether, in fact, Martha's engagement to Thomas had been "conditional" on her family's approval. Once he decided it had not, he deemed her withdrawing consent to the marriage a reflection on her character. Similarly, Leonard Woods's insistence that a gentleman release a lady from an engagement she no longer desired implied a commitment that carried an obligation until the gentleman decided otherwise. Then there was James Kimball, who, after disclosing Martha's previous engagement to Elnathan, could muster only the tepid defense that she "was not so bad a girl." That's what she was up against.

In this milieu, Martha Parker was also up against herself. By her account, she had called off her marriage to Thomas without any worry that doing so raised questions about her character. Yet she had not risked telling Elnathan anything about that engagement until compelled by events and then produced an array of excuses to explain it away. She had pitied the smitten schoolmaster and accepted his proposal when she was "low in health," she explained, her "head disordered to that degree which would have rendered doubtful the legality of a will." And so forth. That suggests backing out of her commitment to Thomas burdened Martha even before she was bombarded with messages about obligation from Bennet Tyler. True, men could meet with reproach and even with lawsuits for failing to wed their fiancées, but if they were willing to endure the gossip (and pay any court-ordered damages), no one challenged their right to renege on a promise of marriage. Not so, at least in some evangelical circles, for women who changed their minds. They received the message that they were not free to control their bodies and their destinies. But not all of them believed it.

Some twenty years would elapse before the authors of the

Ann Parker Bird, Isaac Bird, and William Goodell, members of the Palestine mission, protested the American Board's treatment of Martha Parker.

Seneca Falls Declaration denounced the "false public sentiment" created "by giving the world a different code of morals for men and women." Ann Parker Bird had come to that position two decades earlier in distant Beirut. As she saw the matter, whatever her sister Martha had done, Rufus Anderson and other men had done far worse and with no consequences, thanks to their "Christian friends." Such injustice, all the ranker because it was compounded by hypocrisy, outraged her. She subscribed to the homespun credo—one that has echoed down the years since the sixteenth century and maybe earlier—that what's sauce for the goose is sauce for the gander. And by the beginning of 1827, some notion was taking shape in her mind of how, all the way from Ottoman Syria, she would serve up a fitting revenge to the men who had wrecked her sister's life. Far from restraining her, Ann's piety encouraged and empowered her to call out the double standard.

⤬

She took her case to Jeremiah Evarts himself—but not by herself. Both Ann and her husband, Isaac, feared that they would lose command of their feelings and fire off an intemperate letter to Boston that would do more harm than good. To strike the right note called for a natural diplomat, their friend William Goodell. His bottomless fund of finesse would make William the American Board's man in Constantinople for more than thirty years, but in the mid-1820s he and his wife, Abigail, were partnered with the Birds in the Palestine mission at Beirut. Raised in a dirt-poor family on a small farm in central Massachusetts, he had worked his way through Bennet Tyler's Dartmouth and then Andover Theological Seminary, perfecting along the way the droll wit that disarmed both his peers and his superiors. Now aged thirty-five and well launched on his career, he confronted Evarts not only out of sympathy for the Parker sisters but also from concern— even alarm—about the direction of foreign missions. William had his own agenda, broader goals shared by Ann Parker Bird and other members of the Palestine mission, and he seized on this opportunity to advance their cause. To listen closely to William Goodell's words—and, as important, his silences—is to discern the mounting conflict among evangelicals over the influence of women within their movement.

He began his letter to Evarts in mid-February 1827 with some smooth talk. "Being too sad to joke, and too young to rebuke, I propose . . . to intreat in behalf of my suffering fellow countrymen who are driven <u>vi et armis</u> [with force and arms] to monkhood." Without mentioning Martha, his letter proceeded to offer a defense of the women already stationed in the Palestine mission. "I fear, Sir, you think, that we have not got very good wives," he began, echoing Ann's sentiments. "But I assure you, that Mr. Bird thinks he has got <u>a very good wife</u>, and I think I have got <u>a very good wife</u>, and we would not willingly exchange them for any body we know of." He then assured Evarts that married men were far more effective than "explorer missionaries," bachelors who traveled from place to place. William had learned that "a residence of <u>more than months</u> is necessary to inspire confidence in those, who . . . cannot be persuaded at once, that we have no self interested unworthy views in our professed regard for their good." True, the reports from explorer missionaries filled the religious press with colorful copy, but wives did not keep their husbands from traveling occasionally to those locales so entrancing to American readers. He had voiced similar views in an earlier letter to Evarts. Married men could not "run away in time of danger," and together with their wives they provided a model of American domesticity to inspire the rest of the world. Besides, he riffed, "a good wife is better than ten soldiers to keep a house in order; better than ten washer women to preserve one from the filth and vermin of Syria; better than cordials in sickness, or fire places in cold weather." That being the case, he concluded, "we <u>pray</u> you to send out <u>wives</u> with your Missionaries, if you can possibly <u>prevail on the young men to take them</u>."

Nice touch, ending with a joke—or so William thought. Everyone knew, none better than he, how eager, even desperate, most men headed for the mission field were to find wives. On one occasion which he recounted with breathless excitement in his memoir fifty years afterward, the members of the Brethren, Andover Theological Seminary's secret society of future missionaries, had pooled their resources to track down a partner for one of their number. They rented a fine horse, one fast enough to carry William quickly from town to town in New England, and after failed overtures to several women he finally interested a shirttail relative. An engagement quickly followed, whereupon William rode to Boston, purchased enough material to provide the affianced bride with "a complete stock of clothing for a whole lifetime," then returned and enlisted "every praying widow in the young lady's neighborhood" to "make up these garments." The couple wed within weeks and went off to the Sandwich Islands. To William's mind, such pairings seemed the stuff of pure romance—the romance of the foreign missions movement. No wonder the blasted hopes of Elnathan and Martha had stirred his sympathies.

Part of what prompted William's support for bringing as many women as men into the field was the conviction—one shared by Jeremiah Evarts and Leonard Woods—that missionary wives helped to build support at home for the American Board's endeavors. The women who dominated local missionary organizations in the United States and shouldered the burden of drumming up enthusiasm and collecting contributions in their communities could not read enough about the likes of Harriet Newell and Ann Judson. What better way to hold and grow that audience than by introducing new heroines into the drama of the world's conversion being scripted monthly in missionary publications? And who could have been better cast for that role than the pretty, accomplished, winning Martha Parker?

But there was another consideration, too, something that William and his fellow missionaries in the Ottoman Empire kept discovering, much to their dismay. All of their observations confirmed that female sanctity inspired profound admiration among Eastern Christians of both sexes. It was a fascination shared by American evangelicals, but the two faiths differed sharply over the Virgin Mary, the holy woman most compelling to Eastern Christians. Missionaries' letters and journals abound with amazement and disgust at the veneration she inspired, yet even as they ridiculed Mary as the "God-Mother," they acknowledged her power. Pliny Fisk noticed that "all classes of people" in Ottoman Syria accepted the tradition that Mary had died on Mount Zion before ascending into heaven, which occasioned many challenges to a tract he was distributing that placed her death on the Greek island of Patmos. He took it to heart when "they demand of me proof," and he finally asked for the offending assertion to be omitted from future tracts. Protestants had nothing in their theology even close to a virgin "God-Mother," but missionary wives like Ann Parker Bird were better than nothing if the goal was to appeal to the religious sensibilities of those drawn to holy women.

Two powerful arguments for missionary wives, yet William Goodell's letter raised neither with Jeremiah Evarts. To the contrary, what's striking is his resort to praising the Palestine mission's "very good" wives for their domestic service as washers of clothes and killers of vermin. It was a compliment that his own spouse, Abigail Davis Goodell—speaker of Arabic and teacher of adults and children—would have spurned. Like most missionary families, the Goodells had servants, and Abigail, an academy-trained woman like Ann, cultivated connections with important women in Lebanon. On one occasion, she gamely sipped coffee with a local prince's harem, shrugging off a warning that the hostesses might have poisoned her cup. Among her earliest impressions of Beirut's natives was the disapproving notice that "the women perform a great part of the servile labor, such as bringing burdens upon their heads or backs, laboring in the fields, light their husband's pipes, etc." On one occasion, she and Ann Parker Bird ganged up on a Maronite priest, lectured him "on the impropriety of living separated from his family, and told him that he ought to love his wife [as the] apple of his eye." As those two believed—and the rest of the missionary community agreed—an important purpose of wives' work abroad was to elevate the status of native women through education and conversion to Protestant Christianity.

William knew that his wife was no household drudge, and like her he was an ardent advocate of education for women both in the United States and abroad. Why, then, didn't he defend missionary wives by pointing to their impressive accomplish-ments? Why did he resort to jokes instead, a rhetorical strategy signaling his—or his sponsors'—discomfort with the whole sub-ject? His studied reticence suggests William's recognition that some evangelicals—perhaps a growing number—did not wish to hear about women's attainments outside the household. He had left the United States before the advent of female believers who asserted their spiritual authority in Charles Finney's revivals, but the newspapers and correspondence he regularly received in Bei-rut would have alerted him to the blowback.

William knew, too, that his vision for the future of missions in Syria would meet with resistance from the American Board back in Boston. In the early summer of 1826, Evarts had written confidentially to William, making clear his preference for sending more unmarried explorer missionaries into the Ottoman Empire. It's easy to understand their appeal, both to Evarts and to the male audience whom he hoped to cultivate. The earliest explorer missionaries in the Middle East projected an image of masculine daring, and their tales of exotic travels, physical risks, and har-rowing confrontations held the promise of appealing particularly to men, a distinct minority in evangelical churches. But William had decided that the explorers' day was done, at least in Ottoman Syria: "By travelling about we could tell you wonderful things of rooks and roads, and khans, and Bedouins which might please the literary; but our appropriate business is certainly very wide of this; and this should only come in by the by."

By contrast, his ideal missionary was a fellow "who will sit down quietly with a family in some place" and serve as an exam-ple of "charity, patience, and all goodness," thus "drawing silently" the affection of a few admiring locals. That fellow sounds a lot like the model evangelical wife and mother—the "angel of the household" who subtly, almost imperceptibly, exercised her spiri-tual and moral influence over children and spouse. It was a strikingly feminized rendition of the missionary's role—and one that no doubt owed much to the influence of Abigail Davis Goodell and Ann Parker Bird. Indeed, because of their wives' insistence— immediately after William learned of Evarts's "confidential" preference for explorer missionaries—he and Isaac Bird wrote back, informing their superior, "We are fully convinced, (and our wives are <u>more than fully convinced</u>,) that for Syria <u>married</u> missionaries are at present decidedly the best." For all four members of the Palestine mission, then, the doomed romance of Martha Parker and Elnathan Gridley meant not only a personal loss but also a missed opportunity for their vision of the mission to prevail.

It was an ideal remarkable for its high valuation of women, an esteem underscored by William's willingness to partner with Ann Parker Bird in pursuit of justice for her sister. These more egalitarian views had gained some currency among their fellow evangelicals in the North before the firestorm stirred up by Finney's revivals drove many believers to join those like Bennet Tyler. Their lives in Syria had led the Goodells and the Birds in the opposite direction. The more familiar they became with Ottoman cultures that venerated a few women while denying the rest formal education and legal protections, the more the missionaries' commitment deepened to demonstrating the superiority of the Christian West in that regard.

Not a word of his letter to Evarts, William felt sure, would ruffle the feathers of any cock of the walk back home, even those most loudly crowing claims of patriarchy. Then, a few days later, he added a postscript in an entirely different tone. "The general ground you have taken in regard to all Missionaries in Syria is improper," William erupted, and "the measures you adopted in regard to Gridley to maintain your ground were <u>illegal, unjustifi-</u>

able, and (do pardon the expression, my dear Sir for I love you) very, very unchristian." He was way out of line, and he knew it, but William could not stop himself, because "we feel for Martha more than you will ever know in this world. . . . My dear sir, do pardon me if I have used any improper expression I love you, and pray for you. But we all feel." Felt what—besides anger? And why did those feelings so suddenly overwhelm this practiced—and usually self-possessed—broker?

It had to have been the arrival of another missionary, a weedy young fellow named Eli Smith. He was then unmarried and, intent as he was on mastering Arabic by traveling throughout the Middle East, likely to remain single for many years. His turning up in Beirut—only days before William added his postscript— confirmed the worst fears of the Palestine mission. Those worries included the prospect of a marriage uniting Martha with Thomas Tenney, and Smith arrived with the news—mistaken, as it turned out—that they had probably wed. Even more upsetting to the Birds and the Goodells—something borne out by the bachelor Eli Smith's appearance—was the American Board's evident determination to create a cadre of celibate missionary clergy. Just as Josiah Brewer had warned them, Evarts seemed "bent on sending as many single men as possible," which would, as William put the matter, drive missionaries to "monkhood."

That apprehension was not far-fetched. According to Jeremiah Evarts, "The Christian public are by no means united, as to the expediency of missionaries of the present day being generally married." The risks to wives and children and the burden of supporting families abroad made some donors so disgruntled "as to withdraw their connection with Foreign Mission Societies for that alleged reason." Celibacy had also found advocates among the founders of the missions movement. Little more than a decade earlier, as William could recall, the young men who first organized the Brethren had required its members to renounce matrimony, inspired by the example of those pioneering missionaries, the Jesuits, and determined to surpass them. But by the 1820s, all missionaries in the Mediterranean littoral had a horror of anything that might confuse them with their rivals among the Roman Catholics and Eastern Christians who maintained an unmarried clergy of priests, monks, and nuns. That concern only fortified most in their opposition to bachelor missionaries.

Dread that the American Board disagreed prompted William to dash off his frenzied postscript, which he sent to Evarts accompanied with what he called a "memoir." He attributed the work to Gregory, one of two Armenian translators who assisted him in composing a Turkish-English grammar. Before entering his employ, Gregory, then a priest or vartabet, had spent several years at a monastery in Jerusalem before leaving the Armenian Orthodox Church and taking a wife. William had urged Gregory to set down his recollections of monastic life and then translated the memoir from Turkish, doing some editing of his own. "You are also at liberty to alter any of the language," he advised Evarts, "which may appear to suggest too offensive ideas for the public. I have softened it down wonderfully from the original."

It's a loss that Gregory's original does not survive, because William's expurgation could still quicken the pulse and pop the eyes of most readers. It piled on salacious stories about how the monastery's resident bishops preyed on the wives and daughters of pilgrims and kept boys for "the most unnatural and detestable purposes." The place "became a perfect brothel," so bad that the priests at last implored Gregory to expel the boys, because "we are so filled with carnal thoughts, that, when we go to church, we cannot pray." With its tales of adultery and pederasty abounding among the Armenian clergy, the memoir anticipates those Catholic-bashing antebellum novels with their lurid array of seductions, rapes, and infanticides taking place behind the walls of nunneries.

William's hope was that Evarts would pay particular attention to the memoir's conclusion. There Gregory weighed in at length with his judgment that the prohibition of marriage among Armenian monks "gives strength to our passions, and works in us all manner of concupiscence." Such were the perils of a bachelor clergy. But curiously, what's missing from all that "concupiscence" is any mention of monks' partnering for sex either with each other or with adult male visitors to their monastery. "I have suppressed some things," William explained, "which were not only too gross to be written even to a friend, but too gross even to be hinted at—<u>abominables</u>, which, I am sure, never entered the heart of the most impure and lewd debauchee, that can be found in America." Did those unmentionable "abominables" include sex that involved adult men? It seems unlikely: after all, propriety did not prompt William to omit pedophilia from the memoir. Instead, his silence on the subject of intimacies between adult men alerts us to the surprising diversity of attitudes among evangelicals not only about women but also about same-sex relationships during their movement's formative decades.

During his first years in Beirut, William came to admire the senior member of the Palestine mission, Pliny Fisk. One of the Brethren's charter members in youth and a lifelong partisan of bachelor missionaries, Fisk had never married, and in the fall of 1825 he had written to Jeremiah Evarts, urging him to send more single men to the Middle East. "The whole business of itinerating seems to lie on me," Fisk wrote, adding, "These men who have wives and babies to take care of I find are not very fond of rambling." He alluded, of course, to William Goodell and Isaac Bird. Yet their different visions of the Palestine mission's future did not embitter Fisk toward the two and their wives. To the contrary, he invited Abigail and Ann, when the two held back at Malta, to join their husbands in Beirut, writing that he was "exceedingly anxious" to see the Goodells and the Birds "established with your families" and expressed his wish that "I may soon have more such sisters, nephews, and nieces in Syria." According to William, "Mr. Fisk always expressed to us his thankfulness that we came out married and he, and we regretted, that as the work of pioneering was over here, he had not himself a wife." He told the two couples that marriage was "a very comfortable way of getting through the world . . . though but a poor monk myself."

The truth about Fisk's "monkhood" was more complicated, and William knew it. Fisk repeatedly put off returning to the United States to find a wife—despite overtures from the American Board—and mocked his prospects for attracting someone suitable. He joked to William that "all the good girls" he once knew back in the United States would be wed by the time of his return. And because "all America" would know his "object" in coming home, "every modest girl will veil her face, while all the rest will put their hands out of the window, as much as to say, 'Here I am, take me.'" Worst of all, ministers and deacons throughout New England, "rejoicing at the opportunity of shipping off to the heathen some maiden lady whom they have long pitied," would "give her ample credentials of her character for her youth up almost to old age."

So many reasons—and so often rehearsed within earshot of others—for this "poor monk" to stay put and keep single. But the heart of the matter was that Pliny Fisk's sole romantic attachment, one of passionate intensity, had been to his partner and fellow explorer missionary Levi Parsons. Their profound bond, one that began in college, the two sealed in a "covenant ceremony" before they left the United States. Meeting privately, they pledged with "sincerity of heart, and with earnest prayer for divine assistance, [to] give ourselves to each *other*." They exchanged promises

Pliny Fisk and Levi Parsons, partners in the
Palestine mission

"to live in love; to maintain the most perfect harmony of feeling, of design and of operation; to unite our strength, our talents and our influence, for the conversion of the heathen." They vowed never to separate unless duty demanded, "having our hearts knit together as the heart of one man." No surviving evidence suggests a sexual relationship between the two. The possibility exists that they censored such references from their letters and journals, but whether or not it had any erotic component, the emotional and spiritual intimacy between them is indisputable. After Parsons's death at Cairo early in 1822, Fisk formed no close relationship with another man or a woman, perhaps remembering his partner's promise that their "union" would "be lasting; it will be immortal."

If Fisk often mentioned the possibility of marrying to protect himself from gossip and innuendo, he had nothing to fear from William Goodell. The sound of someone's protesting too much would not have escaped his sharp ears, but he was content to play along and even to pass along Fisk's assurances to the American Board. Only months before Fisk's death at the Goodells' home in

Beirut, William had informed Evarts that this lifelong bachelor was "contemplating a voyage to America for the sole purpose of getting a wife." Fisk's choosing a man as his lifelong loving partner did not trouble William. It bothered him so little, in fact, that he shielded Fisk. A few years later, William made his views plainer still in a letter to Rufus Anderson, alluding to a fellow missionary sent to the Levant by a British society who had married "a woman more than ten years his senior." What prompted this union, in William's opinion, was the groom's desperation for what we would call "a beard." The man had "suffered, for a considerable time a species of persecution, not uncommon in England," he explained, "but from which the young gentlemen of America <u>have been</u>, and it is hoped <u>still are</u> most hopefully exempted." At the time of this writing, Fisk had been dead for three years, but if the fear of that "persecution" had haunted his friend, William had nothing but sympathy for the other "young gentlemen" whom it stalked.

True, the embrace of evangelicalism by a growing number of Americans often counteracted the trend toward greater sexual freedom and experimentation ushered in by the Enlightenment. Yet the same potent combination of romanticism and revivalism that encouraged heterosexual couples like Thomas Tenney and Martha Parker to explore and share their feelings seems to have promoted a similar curiosity and candor among evangelical men—and women—who experienced attraction to one another, whether spiritually, romantically, erotically, or in some combination. One Virginia Methodist preacher wrote to his fellow itinerant and "covenant brother," "I love you with a pure love fervently . . . I dream of you; I dream of Embracing you in the fond arms of Nuptial love, I dream of kissing you with the kisses of my Mouth. I am Married to you."

Those attachments met with acceptance by some evangelicals. If his protectiveness of Fisk attests to the prejudices of some believers, William Goodell also praised Americans for being more tolerant of such relationships than were the British. Confirming that estimate is the description of the covenant ceremony uniting Pliny Fisk and Levi Parsons, which does not lie buried in the men's private papers: Parsons's brother-in-law featured it prominently in a pious memoir of the missionary he published in 1830. Then there were Charity Bryant and Sylvia Drake, two contemporaries of Fisk and Parsons, fellow northern New Englanders and conservative evangelicals, who lived openly as a loving couple in Weybridge, Vermont. Valued by neighbors for their skills as tailors, esteemed for the piety that made their home a venue for religious gatherings of other devout evangelicals, they gained acceptance as husband and wife from both their relatives and the wider community.

The complexity of the evangelical past reveals itself in these relationships and the responses they elicited, a legacy challenging those among today's believers who hold that gay sexuality is a sin to be condemned or a sickness to be cured. It also raises the possibility that as many evangelicals came to resist their movement's empowerment of women over the first half of the nineteenth century, the same decades might have witnessed their retreat from the liberal views of same-sex partnerships expressed by William Goodell.

Sometime in the spring of 1827, William Goodell made extracts of his letter to Jeremiah Evarts and sent them to Elnathan Gridley in Smyrna. It was a gesture of support, letting his fellow missionary know that he had joined forces with Ann Parker Bird. Elnathan placed William's letter inside his portable writing desk, leaving it, like those from Ann, unanswered. It was only Daniel Temple who knew enough to worry. The American Board's printer stationed in Malta, Daniel enjoyed the confidence of all the Levant's missionaries despite his Eeyore-like way of seeing the gloomiest side of every situation. By early summer of 1827, he felt "very great anxiety" because Elnathan had informed him of plans to return to the United States in the spring of the following year. "I fear the Board was altogether in the wrong," Daniel warned Rufus Anderson, "and dread the consequences." Oh, well, Rufus shrugged: that was only Daniel's way, lugubrious fellow that he was.

In fact, there was cause for his concern. Two weeks earlier, Elnathan had dispatched another letter to Leonard Woods. It repeated his complaint that the Prudential Committee had infringed his liberty ("What, has not a free and independent citizen of the U.S.A. a right to select his own wife?") but went further. He charged that the committee had plotted to end his engagement "with the express design of sending me to my field of labor a single man." He believed that the committee thus revealed their "predilection" for "Monkhood in their Missionaries." (In one draft of the letter, he referred to it as "truly Popish.") He described himself being injured "no less sensibly than had they, by an assassin's hand plunged a dagger to my heart." He dwelled on Martha, too, praising her many gifts, reviling the committee's treatment of her, and declaring that he now regarded her as his "true and lawful wife." Had she jilted him, Elnathan continued, he "could have given her up without a sigh." "The lineaments of that face which I used to trace with delight" would long since have faded from his memory; the sound of Martha's name would have "ceased to send a thrill to my soul." But his feelings were not those of "disappointed love," he insisted: they were "the feelings of a loving husband torn from his loving wife."

Those were exactly the emotions that Ann Parker Bird's letters to him had encouraged. Once back in the United States, he told Woods, he intended to find a spouse—or better still, as Ann's letters had led him to hope, Martha would be "restored" to him as his lawful wife. Regret having found and claimed him long ago, Elnathan had acquitted Martha of any wrongdoing. He had known even before leaving Boston, he now insisted, that she "still stood ready to accompany me wherever duty might call, and that her wish for a release was entirely through the influence of the [Prudential] Committee and President Tyler," who "had urged her as she hoped for the salvation of her soul, to become the wife of Tenney." A day after he wrote to Leonard Woods, Elnathan also drafted a letter to Dunbarton's pastor, Walter Harris, expressing the same sentiments. "The world <u>must</u> know the arts by which and the men by whom she was torn from her rightful husband, and given to another." True, he had "sinned" by giving her up, yet he had done so only because he believed "Martha was already lost to me, and that by that act I might give relief to an innocent sufferer which might snatch her from the grave."

But perhaps she was not lost to him after all. He had warned Leonard Woods that his next appeal to his former mentor would "probably be in person" and, following that, to a much wider audience who had known and admired him as a fund-raiser for the American Board. Why, if he hadn't submitted so tamely to the Prudential Committee's decision several months earlier, "a single word" from him about the injustice being done him and Martha would have "arm[ed] the whole Christian public in my favor." It was true, what Rufus Anderson had once said about Elnathan—that "the partisan mode of warfare" was "best suited to his genius." Once back in America, he aimed to make as much trouble as possible, having been armed for that battle by Ann Parker Bird.

He would first spend the summer in Caesarea (today's Kayseri), a city of close to 100,000 inhabitants, most of them Turks, in a region that he referred to as "savage Cappadocia" (central Anatolia). His plan was to learn Turkish, an acquisition that would make it harder for the American Board to force him from the field. At the back of his mind, too, was the promise of distraction in a spot offering greater opportunities for adventure than did Smyrna. It would arouse the suspicion of Ottoman officials, an Englishman—so they deemed any English speaker—turning up so far inland, so Elnathan took precautions. He "assumed Greek dress, and shaved my head after the manner of the Greeks and hope to pass the summer here in quiet, unnoticed by the Turks." The locals quickly saw through his disguise: everyone in town took him for a British spy but cultivated his acquaintance when the young man's brief medical training came to light. Elementary as his skills were, they impressed his neighbors enough for Elnathan to complain that they pestered him constantly for consultations.

Some distraught lovers would have found diversion enough in those doings, but he sought out even greater risk to hold misery at bay. By the end of September, he had found it more than twelve thousand feet above Caesarea, the summit of a volcano that he called "Mount Argeus," known today as Mount Erciyes. He made it nearly to the top and descended, tired and sweaty but safe. Shortly thereafter, chills set in, followed by fever. Josiah Brewer would later attribute the illness to the strain of the ascent, even as he lauded Elnathan's exertion as a bracing reproof of the "Asiatic disinclination to bodily exertion." More likely, the reluctant physician had picked up a virus from one of his patients. A trader named Abraham who had been attending Elnathan and teaching him Turkish nursed him during his sickness. As the missionary lapsed in and out of delirium, Abraham believed that there was "something on his mind which he wished to communicate," but "either through weakness or reluctance he forebore [*sic*] to speak." What did it mean that once, toward the end, "he sprang from the bed very forcedly and fell, stretching himself from east to west"?

Elnathan Gridley was dying but didn't know it. Nor was he aware that months earlier, sometime in April 1827, Thomas Tenney had made Martha Parker his wife.

CHAPTER EIGHT

The Butterfly

It took them all by surprise. So "hasty and unexpected" was her sister's decision that even Emily had known "nothing about it until the engagement was made." "I think her intentions were good in consenting to become his wife," Emily wrote to the Birds, and Martha, now the bride of one year, "has a little daughter and appears happier than I ever thought she would in any situation." Emily's words leave us wondering. Was she defending her sister from Isaac and Ann's objections to the marriage? Was she implying that this new baby, Mary Eliza, had reconciled her mother to a marriage entered into with those "good intentions" that might pave the path to hell? All that's certain is that none of her intimates had foreseen this outcome, which raises the question of why Martha Parker married Thomas Tenney.

What played some part was the religious revival that had swept Dunbarton and surrounding New Hampshire towns during the fall and into the winter of 1826–1827. Her brother-in-law James Kimball reported that Martha "forgot all her trouble" once caught up in the excitement and "seemed much as usual" during those months. Perhaps in this atmosphere of heightened spiritual fervor, she came to accept Bennet Tyler's judgment that she could show herself "governed by right feelings" and reconciled with God only by keeping her promise to Thomas. Marrying him might have seemed to her again, as it had before, a means of proving her spiritual mettle through self-sacrifice. With the mission field closed to her, she would have needed all the more to allay anxieties about the state of her soul, fears that would have gripped her with even more force in the wake of the scandal. Her emotional fragility concerned Walter Harris enough for him to warn Emily Kimball that her sister "must be treated with the greatest degree of tenderness or she may yet be a maniac." Despite any assurance about her salvation she had experienced during the revival, Martha might still have needed protection from herself. Perhaps she hoped to find it by marrying the man who had long insisted that he knew how she ought to feel.

Practical considerations also played some part, chief among them Martha's need for employment. The female academy at Boscawen over which she once presided did not renew her appointment for 1827, which suggests that even her participation in the revival had not restored her reputation. Being rejected as a missionary's wife by the American Board was not the ideal recommendation for a schoolmistress. Then there was future peril forecast by Elnathan's letters. She would have known—either from him directly or from his other correspondents—about his intention to return to New England. Whether he meant to try to claim her or to wed another woman, his appearance would engulf her again in gossip. Faced with that threat, Martha might have seen marriage and motherhood as a hedge against fresh disgrace, especially if she could count Thomas and Tyler among her allies.

It's likely, too, that a dearth of emotional support from her immediate family made Martha incline toward "cousin Thomas." The whole sorry situation had left relations strained among the three eldest Parker sisters. For her part, Emily assured Isaac Bird that like his wife, Ann, she had been "exceedingly distressed" on Martha's behalf. "I have not as she supposes been insensible and indifferent to what has been passing," Emily insisted, even though "after weighing everything I have decided it was not her duty to go to Asia." Those words conjure images of a dispirited Martha, seeking out her sister for sympathy, and Emily, crisply replying that she should pull up her socks and accept the dispensations of providence. Or worse, after "weighing everything," Emily might have told her outright that the "duty" of saving all those "Asians" belonged to someone other than—perhaps less compromised than—her sister. She felt certain, too, that Martha "would not have been happy to have married Mr. G[ridley] and remained in this country." Her sister was pining not for the missionary himself, she implied, but for her own lost missionary career.

Ann Parker Bird's letters surely would have offered Martha greater solace and encouragement. But news of her broken engagement did not reach Beirut until the beginning of 1827, and it would have taken about six months—well after her marriage to Thomas—for any response from Ann to arrive in Dunbarton. Thereafter, family members took care to keep certain letters from Martha. As late as the fall of 1828, according to Emily, Martha had "never seen one line of Ann's writings in which she blames Mr. T[enney] and the Board, etc." A good thing, too, in Emily's view, because "I think it would be the height of imprudence for her to see the letters." "Our good Dr. Harris," still worried about Martha's becoming a "maniac," agreed with her.

It seems heartless, their depriving Martha of the knowledge that Ann took her part. But to that objection, Emily would have asked what good it would do for Martha to know, now that she had married a man Ann despised and become the mother of his child. Besides, even though she acknowledged that the Prudential Committee "had a false view of things," Emily admitted that she could not "feel towards the American Board as Ann does." "I have not one doubt but that they sought the best good of the missionary cause," she wrote to Isaac. Indeed, so deep was her trust in the American Board that to mourn her daughter, Martha Ann, who died one year after the Prudential Committee had accepted the resignation of her namesake, Emily made a contribution in the little girl's name. Notwithstanding their differences, her family and friends all hoped to keep their dear Martha from going insane.

Meanwhile, back in Boston, Jeremiah Evarts was realizing that he faced a formidable challenge. The Parker scandal, he feared, held the potential not merely to diminish the standing of the American Board but to splinter the evangelical movement itself. If the complaints he was receiving from the Palestine mission were to circulate among a wider audience, how many people in what evangelicals liked to call "the Christian public" would continue to share Emily Parker Kimball's trust in the organization that he headed?

It was bad enough, William Goodell's letter with that outlandish postscript condemning the board's treatment of Gridley as "illegal," "unjustifiable," and "very, very unchristian." The fellow went too far—even before sharing that filthy "memoir" about Armenian monks and urging its immediate publication and wide distribution among evangelical readers. Had the man lost his senses? Still worse was the outrageous screed that had followed shortly thereafter from the Birds—a letter signed by both him and *her*. It had come in response to Evarts's letter informing them—as soon as the matter had been resolved in the fall of 1826—that the board had accepted Miss Parker's resignation. It was a simple matter, he had explained: the young woman had been so "fickle in her feelings" that the Prudential Committee "could not tell what her real mind was in regard to the two suitors" and feared that she "would want stability on missionary ground." And at the end of his letter—a small, thoughtful touch to ease their disappointment—he added his expectation that Miss Parker would marry Mr. Tenney, "who has conducted himself extremely well during the whole transaction."

When this letter from Evarts had reached Beirut in March 1827, anyone within earshot would have heard the sound of Ann Parker Bird's fuse being lit. No longer would William Goodell alone speak in her sister's behalf. It was rare—nearly unheard of— for the wife of a missionary to write jointly with her husband to the American Board. But the response to Evarts, sent by the couple in mid-April 1827 and received by him in the fall of that year, bears every sign of being as much Ann's work as Isaac's. And unlike William Goodell, who held his burst of fire for a postscript, every line of the Birds' letter let loose a fusillade.

The two leveled an unsparing indictment against everyone who had played a role in Martha's ruin. Why had the Prudential Committee credited slurs against her from an anonymous accuser? Shouldn't they have considered whether ulterior motives prompted William Gould to impugn the character of his once-admired employee? What right had Bennet Tyler to declare Martha's engagement to Elnathan null and void? Who had gained anything by the couple's disgrace and heartbreak except for that "fawning, deceitful lovesick youth," Thomas Tenney? Pointed questions all, but the sharpest—unmistakably Ann's contribution—focused on the Prudential Committee's singling out Martha for breaking an engagement. "Why has not this principle of judgment been acted on before?" "Why make choice of a fatherless girl as the first to make the experiment upon? Let us ask if you have not, and never had, any persons of the stronger sex, in the missionary service, who have been fickle in their love concerns. Why were they so easily pardoned?" Evarts would have winced at that last swipe, thinking of Rufus Anderson.

Nor could the lawyer have missed the Birds' inclination to couch the entire matter in legalistic language, especially those ominous references to "our view of the case." Recalling earlier charges from both William and Elnathan that the American Board had acted illegally, Evarts thought it entirely possible that the members of the Palestine mission might go to law and sue for damages. At the very least, they seemed headed for the court of public opinion with some choice gossip guaranteed to explode the American Board's claims that their missionaries abroad—to say nothing of their administrators at home—modeled domesticity and respectability.

As troubling as these letters from Beirut was the prospect of Elnathan Gridley's coming back to New England to plead his cause—and maybe Martha's, too—in person and in public. Evarts would have learned from Leonard Woods that this event was in the offing, and he dreaded the publicity that would ensue. Even among evangelicals—as Homan Hallock's taunting letters attested—anxieties were mounting that powerful corporations like the American Board infringed on their employees' individual liberties. As for other sorts of believers and nonbelievers, some of them Jacksonian Democrats in the making by the late 1820s, Elnathan's grievances would only inflame their conviction that evangelicals were intent on curtailing the personal freedoms of white American men.

Here was Evarts's worst nightmare. As he catastrophized the possible future, the opposition to the American Board galvanized by Ann Parker Bird would travel from Ottoman Syria to the United States. The Palestine missionaries' charges would gain even greater traction because the newly famous Isaac Bird—whose gripping dispatches about the persecution of a young Protestant convert by the head of the Maronite Church dominated the religious press for most of 1827—vouched for their truth. Then Elnathan Gridley himself would return, launching his tell-all tour. Taken together, their revelations would spell disaster for the board's finances, choking off the contributions that funded missionary operations. Still worse, it would make even more men in the United States suspicious of evangelicalism. Already a hard sell, it would get harder still if Elnathan became the poster child for all of America's unhappy patriarchs and their sons. Perhaps worst of all, it would expose and aggravate the deepening divisions within the evangelical movement over the role of women within their churches and the world beyond.

To head off this looming crisis, Jeremiah Evarts set straight to work. Throughout the year 1828, he committed hours to composing a long, detailed narrative of the Parker scandal, referencing throughout a thick sheaf of documents compiled to support his version of events. It was a lawyerly labor, bristling with logic and evidence. If the members of the Palestine mission meant to see him in court—any court—he planned to be ready for them.

I trust there are none of my brethren in the Mediterranean who are in any peculiar danger of <u>mutiny</u>," Daniel Temple wrote from Malta to Rufus Anderson, "tho' you seem to have some fears of that kind." Did he. Those fears and worse had haunted Rufus and his boss for more than a year, and once Evarts decided to compose a narrative of the Parker scandal, his able subordinate set about collecting documents that would support the actions of the American Board. Rufus pitched in eagerly, knowing that his own future was at risk if the matter was not resolved. From the outset of Martha Parker's troubles, Evarts had consulted him on the appropriate steps to take, and as early as the spring of 1827, Rufus had written to William Jowett, the head of British missions in the Mediterranean, defending the board's decision as a providential stroke that "the King of Zion probably designed [as]

nothing more than a severe moral discipline to both parties (who doubtless needed it)." A day later, he expressed the same bracing sentiments in a letter to Elnathan Gridley.

That made Rufus the ideal person to undertake the unpleasant business of visiting the Tenneys, now wed about six months, in order to gather copies of the letters that Martha Parker, as she was then, had written to Thomas. Off he went in early November 1827, just as the winter was closing in on Hampton, New Hampshire, where Thomas now served as headmaster of an academy. "Fearing that Mrs. Tenney might be rendered unhappy, should she know I was in the place for such a purpose," Rufus took lodgings at a public house and wrote to Thomas, requesting a meeting there. But Thomas insisted on Rufus's spending the night at the couple's dwelling, where he conversed with them "till rather a late hour" and again in the morning. Martha, now about four months pregnant, treated her husband in ways "commonly considered proof of genuine attachment; and I was peculiarly gratified to see it," Rufus noted in his report to Evarts. He considered that "there <u>might</u>, it is true, have been an <u>effort</u> on her part; but if there was, it was made with a great deal of address, for there was no appearance of it."

Still, how could he be sure with a woman like her, one so practiced at concealing her emotions? She might find the devil himself settled at her fireside and never bat an eye. Something like those reflections must have prompted Rufus to take "the liberty of making in private some free inquiries of Mr. Tenney respecting the state of Mrs. Tenney's feelings." Thomas replied that "he had no doubt of her affection for him, nor that she regarded her marriage to him as a desirable and happy event." The only downside to the entire episode, in her husband's view, was that Martha "had been much humbled by the mortifications through which she had passed, and was consequently backward to take the lead in religious efforts." Understandably, she would have had little enthusiasm for joining Hampton's chapter of a female foreign missions society.

At Rufus's behest, Thomas also composed a letter reprimanding his new in-laws, the Birds. See here, he lectured those two, Gridley had submitted himself to the Prudential Committee's decision and had given up Martha easily. How dared they "believe it <u>possible</u> that the <u>best men</u> in this happy land, men, who are called by the christian public to direct the appropriation of their charities, are capable of artifice and deception, and can practice the most <u>base hypocrisy</u> with those, whom they send out as missionaries!" Why, the Prudential Committee "have only to speak, and the whole christian public would rise in their vindication." Of course, if Jeremiah Evarts had shared that certainty about "the whole Christian public," he would not have sent Rufus Anderson to New Hampshire.

Perhaps, too, both men, knowing all that they did, felt some concern—even guilt—about this marriage that they had done so much to bring about and now felt obliged to defend. Rufus assumed that Martha would be "rendered unhappy" by setting eyes on him, and he turned up in Hampton without writing to Thomas to announce his intentions. Paying a surprise visit to a man he had probably never met before was an odd lapse of etiquette in this age of easy communication by post. Did he wish to catch Thomas off guard? Rufus also took time to interview one of Martha's younger sisters, most likely Marianne, who was living with the couple while she attended the academy in Hampton. She "certainly gave" him "no reason to suppose she was otherwise than pleased with the relation, she sustained to Mr. Tenney."

Evarts liked Rufus's report on his visit to the couple—so much that he included it in his roster of supporting documents. But in fact, it tells us nothing about the marriage of Thomas and Martha. As we've seen, she had the ability to rein in her emotions even under intense pressure, and she would not have wished to give Rufus the satisfaction of witnessing her unhappiness. But the report does disclose what her visitor wished to hear. Rufus made an express inquiry about Martha's "feelings" for her husband, looking for confirmation that despite the strife preceding this union, the two had after all achieved a companionate marriage. Maybe he sought that assurance to soothe his own conscience; most certainly he knew that his report would help to disarm critics among their age peers, including the Birds and the Goodells. It helped, too, that in a brief postscript at the back of her husband's letter, Martha confirmed that even though she slept while he wrote, his words were "in accordance with my own feelings." The sentence bore the signature "M. P. Tenney."

That is the last scrap to survive from the hand of Martha Parker, now Tenney. Yet again, finding her in full eludes us. Evarts would exclude her several letters to Elnathan Gridley from his documentary record, and neither that correspondence nor her many letters to Ann Parker Bird in Beirut have ever come to light. We can discover Martha through her own words only in her statement to the Prudential Committee, the extracts of her letters chosen by Thomas Tenney, and this brief farewell to history's record. It saddens but does not surprise: Martha's final declaration that her feelings conformed to those of her husband—a single sentence to attest that she felt as she ought. It leaves us wondering whether, like many women before and after her, "M. P. Tenney" had decided that her sanity, even her survival, lay in near silence.

It took nearly a year for Jeremiah Evarts to complete his work and the American Board to weigh in with their approval. At the outset of the narrative—which he billed as "a standing memorial of the fairness, candor, and integrity of the Committee"—Evarts announced his purpose as "preserving a permanent record, which may be needed to prevent misunderstanding hereafter." Privately he was more candid, admitting that he wrote a "full account of this business" to prevent "public exposure." In other words, he aimed to stop the likes of Ann Parker Bird and William Goodell and Elnathan Gridley from litigating their case in the court of public opinion and igniting an uproar. How very Catholic, how truly "popish" of the American Board, he could hear people murmur, cultivating a missionary clergy committed to celibacy, with poor Elnathan Gridley as their first, unwilling recruit. How highhanded and unrepublican, their scheming to end his engagement, even enlisting Bennet Tyler as their henchman to ruin the "fatherless" Martha Parker's reputation.

It was Evarts's great good fortune that those particular suspicions were, if not implausible, unfounded. In fact, the board had neither intended to encourage lifelong bachelorhood among any of its missionaries nor plotted to keep Elnathan unmarried. But the Palestine missionaries' certainty that the board was guilty of such gross misdeeds opened the way for Evarts to focus his narrative on disproving those false charges—something easily done— and to avoid the subject that he hoped to keep from "public exposure." What this doomed romance revealed—and what he wished to keep under wraps—was the widening division over the role of women within their movement among evangelicals. In the latest round of this mounting conflict, it had been conservatives like Bennet Tyler who claimed a scalp—Evarts's own. Seeing how sharp the knives of his adversaries were, Evarts strove to conciliate them and to heal this dangerous breach. He produced a narrative that pounded home the message that the Prudential Committee, guided solely by the facts of the case, reached a just decision. Martha Parker had deserved her fate.

That meant her defenders—among whom, don't forget, Evarts had once numbered—received short shrift in his narrative. He dismissed out of hand Elnathan's testimony that William and

Charlotte Gould, Elisha Jenney, and Thomas Tenney had many and varied motives to take part in Martha's undoing. So much hearsay, the lawyer shrugged, charges proving only that Elnathan's "powers of reasoning were affected by his feelings" and "his imagination was much heated." That freed Evarts to say as little as possible about all of Martha's accusers, insisting only that neither he nor other members of the Prudential Committee knew anything about any of them or wished to know more. They had not troubled to look into the Goulds' history with Martha. As for Silas Aiken, the author of the anonymous letter, Evarts did not even recall his name, "nor have I ever seen him; or had any communication with him." It sufficed that this young man was "stated to be a professor of religion and a man of good character." He had no curiosity about Elisha Jenney either. He'd "never seen him," and mentioned only that Elisha, like Silas and Thomas, was studying for the ministry. These passing references raise more pointedly the question of why Evarts had not attempted to learn more about the people who had conspired in Martha's disgrace. Perhaps he had, but realized that to include those findings in the narrative would not have served his purposes.

Discounting Elnathan's defense of Martha—and his fingering the authors of her misfortune—became even easier when news of the missionary's death reached Boston in February 1828. That cleared the way for Evarts, who had just begun to compose his account, to make Thomas Tenney his star witness. This young man—who had at first inspired Evarts's mistrust—presides over the narrative's pages as a disinterested, dispassionate chronicler in full command of "the facts." Indeed, Evarts asserted, "the case has very rarely occurred, in which the principal witness had so good opportunities as Mr. Tenney of knowing the truth; or in which a witness commanded more unhesitating confidence of all parties." Interviewing the schoolmaster in person, Evarts found him "perfectly frank and unreserved," ready to answer any question "without any wish to disguise, conceal, or color, the facts of the case." His written accounts, too, bore "unquestionable marks of a noble and disinterested spirit." What's more, when Evarts visited Dunbarton with Thomas in tow, he found that Martha and her sisters received their cousin "with as much kindness and friendship, as would have been expected in the case of a successful suitor, where nothing unusual had taken place." Why, even Elnathan Gridley liked the fellow, so well that after their long conversation in Boston the two rivals "left each other with mutual respect, confidence, and affection; and not an unpleasant word was spoken by either during their conversation." With Elnathan dead, who could say otherwise?

Still more remarkable are the many suspicions about Thomas that Evarts's narrative refused to entertain. This jilted suitor had composed the account he read at Townshend with no ulterior motive, Evarts declared, but rather with "the full expectation, that Martha would marry Mr. Gridley, and without any intimation having been made to him, that objections could be preferred against her to the Committee." Not likely, given that Bennet Tyler had directed Thomas to write it. Then there were the many extracts of other people's letters sprinkled through Thomas's narratives of events. Evarts never so much as raised the possibility that the schoolmaster might have carefully selected or even edited other people's words to advance his cause. Nor did it trouble him that both Thomas and his friends were not above making threats. During their visit to Dunbarton, Thomas presented him with an "account" in which Elisha Jenney attested that he had been "making addresses" to Martha in December 1825. Thomas left the lawyer with no doubt "that Mr. Jenney and his sister might make a plausible statement, which, in case Martha went abroad in a public capacity, would be likely to be extensively circulated." Yet Evarts did not include Jenney's "account" in his collection of documents, most likely because it did no credit to its author.

Bennet Tyler benefited from the same airbrushing. Evarts studded his narrative with assurances that his adversary had played a part "entirely honorable to his character," showing "rare judgment" and "great benevolence." Only at one point did the facade of collegiality crack, Evarts's contempt for the man flickering in a few words. He could not stoop to defend Tyler's bullying—his telling Martha that her engagement to Elnathan was "null and void" and that their union would be adulterous. That was "strictly and wholly his _own_ advice; and for it he only is responsible," Evarts declared. But then, perhaps recalling what the man was capable of, the lawyer added that Tyler "doubtless felt able to justify himself for the part he took, for he is not apt to act hastily or unadvisedly." Certainly not without the advice of his powerful friends like Lyman Beecher and Asahel Nettleton.

That left Martha. The narrative's "nothing to see here" strategy—one designed to draw attention from her accusers— ruled out any chance that Evarts would try to imagine them through Martha's eyes and then entertain the possibility that fear of those men had influenced her behavior. To the contrary, as Evarts insisted at several points in the narrative, she showed "unbounded confidence in the upright intentions and genuine friendship of Mr. Tenney," as well as complete trust in Tyler's counsel. We had hoped for better from the man who had once lectured Thomas about the board's responsibility to shield its missionaries from "unjust accusations" and to protect their "intimate and sacred" rights. Instead, as Martha, now a wife and mother, receded into the privacy of her Hampton household, her younger self emerged from Evarts's narrative reinvented as, if not quite a coquette, still the daughter of Eve: fickle, deceptive, and entirely too free with her "encouragement."

Evarts pressed that conclusion on his readers by insisting—as did Thomas—that Martha had accepted the schoolmaster's proposal "unconditionally." Both men ignored a good deal of evidence to the contrary, including some supplied by Thomas himself. His extracts from Emily Kimball's letters implied, as Martha claimed, that she had agreed to marry Thomas pending her sister's consent. Not only did Emily write to Thomas about withholding her approval of the marriage, but Martha's letter breaking their engagement informed him that "her [Emily's] consent cannot be obtained, and I regret that I expressed to you so much [meaning that she would agree to the marriage] before seeing her." Evarts himself did nothing to get to the bottom of this matter he judged so important. He neither interviewed Emily nor solicited written testimony from her, nor asked Martha and Thomas about their differing recollections of the engagement's terms during his visit to Dunbarton.

Even if Martha had agreed unconditionally to Thomas's proposal, why did Evarts come to regard breaking that promise as damning evidence that she had been "fickle in her feelings to a fault"? After all, he and other members of the Prudential Committee had earlier expressed the view that her ending "engagements more or less sacred" did not disqualify Martha from becoming a missionary. To Leonard Woods, Martha's changing her mind about which suitor to favor was "a mere girlish freak" that did no damage to her "moral or religious character." And if Evarts had interviewed Emily, he would have discovered that Thomas himself had once spoken lightly of *his* breaking a promise of marriage. At some point in his pursuit of Martha, he wrote to her, "If I should be engaged to another, and you will then let me know [that you can marry me] you will make me the happiest of men." Here was "sufficient proof," as Emily saw it, of the "mutual understanding" between Martha and Thomas "that a dismission from either party in case of courtship was sufficient to break off an engagement."

❧

In Evarts's new willingness to condemn Martha, we can see the long shadow cast by Bennet Tyler. The narrative signaled Evarts's recognition that placating Tyler and his allies would come at the cost of agreeing that women could not change their minds about whom to marry and that they should instead be brought to "feel as they ought." He was obliged to abandon his earlier conviction that women deserved protection from men who felt entitled to control them. Announcing his surrender, he wrote that if the Prudential Committee had sent Martha abroad as a missionary, "it would have been saying that she was under no obligation to Mr. Tenney, and that there was nothing in the way of her marrying Mr. Gridley." This chipping away at a woman's freedom of choice, as we in the present can readily grasp, was no small concession, and one that revealed how imperiled Evarts felt by Tyler and his partisans.

Just as Evarts's narrative echoed conservative views about women's rights and obligations, it reflected the growing pressure from that quarter to clip the wings of those in search of broader horizons. That concern surfaces in his close inquiry into why Martha refused to marry Elnathan—despite pressure from her family and Walter Harris—at the beginning of August 1826. "Mr. Gridley pressed her vehemently," the narrative reads, urging "that, if the Committee should not send her out [to the mission field], he could enter into other employment, or take her with him to Connecticut." But no: that did not satisfy her, as Evarts pointedly observed, because "it was with a view to missionary employment, that she became connected with Mr. Gridley." There it was: her ambition convicted Martha. Indeed, her own words, explaining why she broke with Thomas and accepted Elnathan's proposal, betrayed her. "Where I thought my motives were pure," she wrote in the letter of resignation wrung from her by Tyler, "I can now perceive, that I was governed by proud feelings." Martha meant that she deserved better than Thomas Tenney. That she felt inspired to pursue her dreams. That she believed herself capable of making a difference in the wider world. Known today as self-esteem, those "proud feelings"—when exhibited by a woman—registered as sin to many in Martha's world. That made her letter of resignation Evarts's prize exhibit: he clinched his case by citing her confession to this fatal flaw, like a lepidopterist pinning a butterfly.

Martha Parker was hardly the first person, female or male, who sought marriage to become a missionary. But the changing climate of opinion respecting women's scope within evangelical circles, one prompting stricter oversight by the American Board, made her the first to pay a high price for her choices. Evarts frankly acknowledged and defended this new order. The Prudential Committee had every right to judge the prospective wives of missionaries, he wrote to Elnathan Gridley in Smyrna, because such women were "public characters," just like those who taught in female academies. Any women permitted to occupy positions so public must, of course, understand and accept the need for their being judged and monitored by men.

That shift had not escaped Ann Parker Bird's notice. Only five years had passed since she and her husband, Isaac, had left the United States, yet women like herself now faced new and formidable challenges. "How amazingly have their [the American Board's] views altered since we left our native country," she wrote to Elnathan in the spring of 1827. When she had entered the board's service a few years earlier, "I know not that any inquiry was then made respecting the wife of a missionary." Its rules had not even required her "to furnish testimony of having made a public profession of religion, or of possessing a hope, that I had been born again." In fact, she had once conversed with Evarts himself about "the propriety of examining those, expected to be the wives of missionaries," and he remarked, "<u>That would never do</u>." How to account, then, for "why he was led to adopt measures

in my sister's case so contrary to all former ones, and so contrary
to his views of propriety or expediency"? Ann felt sure that it was
all about achieving what she took to be "his darling object"—the
creation of a celibate missionary clergy.

Jeremiah Evarts did indeed have a "darling object" in view,
but not that one. When he allowed Bennet Tyler and Thomas
Tenney to have their way with Martha's future and then made a
case to justify their actions and his acquiescence, what he hoped
to accomplish was healing the rift over women among evangelicals. To do so as quickly as possible was essential, he believed,
because their movement faced daunting challenges by the late
1820s, matters he regarded as far more pressing and important
than any contest over the rights of women.

So many worries crowded upon Jeremiah Evarts's mind by 1828,
among them the fear that his body was wearing out. Con-
sumption, the disease that would kill him three years later, was
withering his lungs. But as his body wasted, he drove himself all
the harder, as if desperate, before dying, to make all the difference
he could. He felt the greatest urgency about the growing demands
of Southern whites for the forced removal of Native people across
the Mississippi, nations among whom the board had established
missions. He attended congressional debates on that issue in the
spring, gathering the information to be marshaled in the "William Penn" essays, moral and legal arguments against both slavery
and Indian removal that he published in newspaper installments.
There was also the new campaign inspired by Lyman Beecher
to promote the strict observance of the Sabbath. Evarts figured
as one of the major organizers of this movement, rallying public opinion to halt travel and mail delivery on Sundays, in yet
another bid to shore up his standing with Tyler's camp.

That activism—as well as other evangelical initiatives to end dueling and to curb drinking—had begun to attract sharp criticism by the end of the 1820s. Among the critics were other Christians—typically not evangelicals but liberals like Unitarians and Universalists—whose most prominent public intellectual was William Ellery Channing. By the end of the 1820s, he was warning that all evangelical voluntary associations were "perilous instruments" that "ought to be suspected" because they constituted "a kind of irregular government created within our Constitutional government." "Let them be watched closely," Channing advised, for "a dangerous engine is at work among us." In other words, he feared that Lyman Beecher's moral majority was seeking to impose its values on everyone else in the United States. Channing's alarm was not misplaced: their domination of print media allowed evangelicals extraordinary opportunities to shape public opinion, raise money, and mobilize popular support. Then as now, their collateral efforts to spread evangelical beliefs throughout the rest of the world drew less unfavorable notice. But for a few critics, the American Board—now with about fifteen hundred missionary associations and auxiliaries—made an irresistible target. Evarts himself came under attack for his large salary and constant soliciting of funds.

The message that evangelicals threatened democracy in America caused even more of a sensation by the late 1820s because it was being promoted by two women. The first, Frances "Fanny" Wright, was a Scots intellectual who toured the United States presenting her radical views on labor, love, equality, and religion. At the ready to denounce any encroachment of church upon state, she skewered revivals for giving the evangelical clergy an outsized influence over their converts, particularly women. An intellectual powerhouse and an eloquent speaker, Wright knew how to command a crowd, but Anne Royall outclassed even her when it came to grabbing attention. She didn't look like a contender for celebrity, this stubby, chubby, fifty-and-then-some Southern widow. She had picked up a pen to support herself, writing about travel and politics, even composing a novel. Fans and critics alike described her, variously, as sharp-eyed, abusive, impertinent, impudent, "a complete bully in petticoats," and "destitute of every attribute that belongs to a *lady*." The woman was "a virago in enchanted armor," John Quincy Adams marveled. By 1828, the year that Evarts was composing his narrative of the Parker case, she was sticking her pikestaff into evangelicals.

Anne Royall would already have come to his notice. She had taken her first tour of New England a couple years earlier, gathering material about its history, towns, and most prominent citizens for another book. She sought out the acquaintance of other women writers—the poet Lydia Sigourney in Hartford and the scholar of world religions Hannah Adams in Boston—and she strove to ingratiate herself with the region's liberal religious leaders, praising the Unitarians and Universalists as "the most humane and benevolent" of all Christian believers. In the summer of 1827 she came back to New England with another book in the works—her "black book," she called it—and evangelicals squarely in her sights. Passing through Manhattan, she praised the city for improving its "female High School" and added that "if the money bestowed annually on useless, and I might add pernicious societies was devoted to the improvement of the rising generation, its effects on Society would soon be felt." "These missionary, tract and all societies connected with them, instead of enlightening the people, are plunging them into greater ignorance," she warned. Fortunately, "the American people" would not "tamely stand still, and suffer these sleek pampered blackcoats, to bridle, saddle, and *ride them.*"

Farther north, Royall met incoming fire from the Boston *Gazette,* whose editors sneered at "this genius of the quill and ink-pot." She shot back, calling its editors "a set of cut throat scoundrels" and leveling what would become a familiar threat: "They tell me you are missionaries. I'll have you all in my black book." "Missionaries" quickly became her pet name for all evangelicals, and she would make their foreign missions movement the object of biting ridicule in her next publication, titled, as warned, *The Black Book*. Although not a freethinker like Fanny Wright, Royall shared her concern about evangelicals' efforts to gain cultural and political ascendancy and their clergy's influence over women. And Royall was far more dangerous. Wright's open contempt for all religions—to say nothing of marriage and monogamy—marginalized her, but the professedly Christian Royall was not so easily sidelined. She also had a positive genius for antics that stuck in people's minds, like challenging a gentleman who took issue with her opinions to "mortal combat with pistols." Such brazen encounters made Royall the butt of endless jokes—and obsessive media attention. Constant newspaper coverage of evangelicals coming under attack from this clownish but publicity-savvy character—rarely seen without a pipe of tobacco clenched in her teeth—had the effect of lowering those "sleek pampered blackcoats" in the estimate of some Americans.

These well-publicized attacks by two high-profile women impressed upon Jeremiah Evarts the importance of promoting unity within the evangelical movement. Their celebrity added to the reasons that believers like himself and Leonard Woods had chosen not to die on the hill of women's rights or anywhere close to it by the late 1820s. How easy for more conservative believers to point to Fanny Wright and Anne Royall as a warning of where things might be headed if their own movement persisted in encouraging those women who raised their voices in churches, in voluntary societies, in print, and from the mission fields abroad. No wonder, then, that in composing his narrative of the Parker scandal, Evarts capitulated so completely to Bennet Tyler. Or could it have been that Evarts was beginning to see Tyler's point?

Did it cross his mind that evangelicalism itself was incubating progeny like the Parker sisters, young women who could emerge from the chrysalis of their faith to become beings far more free?

Imagine Jeremiah Evarts in the summer of 1828, reading newspaper reports of yet another of Anne Royall's rabid attacks on "missionaries." Imagine him imagining what this harpy might do with the Parker scandal. Worst of all, he could easily imagine that doomed romance becoming a cause célèbre even without her assistance. Elnathan Gridley could no longer defend himself or Martha, but with friends like the Birds and Goodells this dead missionary would become even more dangerous as a martyr. His ghost seemed to warn as much even from the grave with the haunting words of a letter that Leonard Woods received after his death. If "savage Cappadocia" snuffed out his life, Elnathan wrote, his grievances would be known, because "I sorrow not alone—there are sorrows at Dunbarton—there are sorrows at Farmington—sorrows at Malta—sorrows at Beirut." Sorrows enough to make evangelical leaders like himself the sorriest of all, Evarts decided, unless drastic steps were taken. Their agitation could metastasize the Parker scandal from its nodes at Fairhaven and Boston, Hanover and Dunbarton, into a cancer capable of destroying the entire foreign missions enterprise. The American Board stood to lose the support of the "Christian public," and the whole business would give ammunition to those Americans who mistrusted evangelicals' prominence in the public sphere.

There was only one way to head off catastrophe. Evarts told Rufus Anderson to pack his bags again, this time for a trip that would take him farther than New Hampshire. His orders were to meet with the members of the Palestine mission, sharing with them Evarts's narrative and all the supporting documents. That should spike their guns—or so both men hoped. Rufus set sail for Malta in late November 1828, carrying along with him what Evarts described to Thomas Tenney as "a complete vindication of our conduct, in the affair of Mr. Gridley." Evarts also directed Rufus to size up the prospects for missionary work in Greece, now fighting for independence from Ottoman rule. "How is the female sex treated?" the lawyer wished to know. "What is the state of morals among women? Whether the people are desirous of having their daughters educated?" American evangelicals had so much to teach these people.

Rufus, of course, had every reason to dread a close encounter with the Palestine missionaries. He would have dreaded it even more had he seen those letters to Josiah Brewer, the disconsolate bachelor missionary once partnered with Elnathan, in which Isaac Bird offered his—and, presumably, Ann's—view of events. "After long doubt between two lovers sometimes off and sometimes on," Isaac scoffed, Martha "at last musters decision enough to make choice of Mr. G., consents to have her intended marriage to him publicly announced, visits the whole country under the name of Mr. G.'s intended wife, but, after all, this committee are not able to say that the girl loves Gridley a whit better than the other man. What a dilemma sure enough!" To Isaac and others in the Palestine mission, the committee's decision still remained "a most dark and unaccountable action." Martha "is now in a sense lost to us, as well as disgraced before the world," and "she is cast off into the arms of a man whose character never prepossessing, had now become detestable. And who are the authors of our sister's ruin?" Well, one of them—the man who must have thought himself the most unfortunate of the lot—was headed for the Mediterranean at the end of 1828.

Yet again, Rufus Anderson's luck held. He landed at Malta and found all the Palestine missionaries assembled there, refugees rattled by their near escape from the chaos engulfing Beirut.

It had started two years before in March 1826, when Greeks in revolt against the Ottoman Empire began pillaging the coast of Syria. Its regional potentate, the pasha of Acre, dispatched troops of Bedouin Arabs who, instead of providing protection for Beirut, plundered dwellings, including those of the Goodells and Birds. Abigail Davis Goodell delivered a child while her husband warded off a party of marauders storming their home. William later wrote to Rufus that "the missionary ladies especially have exhibited a courage during this whole affair which is truly wonderful, and which has called forth the admiration of the Frank [Western] inhabitants of this place. But I assure you a Missionary in this country needs a set of nerves made of iron not to be perfectly unstrung in such a time as this." Their trouble had only begun.

Some was of the missionaries' own making. As Eli Smith observed, both the Birds and the Goodells had engaged in "open and sharp controversies with the ecclesiastics, which had provoked their rage," and they were "all too ready" to engage in "disputes with the people." Their aggressive evangelism principally targeted other Christians in the city, the Greek Orthodox and the Maronites, and by the beginning of 1827 the clergy were forbidding members of their churches to associate in any way with the missionaries. Beirut's governor informed William that "whatever violence was done to us, he would not intervene to protect us." Only the onset of the plague in the spring of 1827 calmed opposition enough for William to again feel safe "sitting by the window" of his dwelling.

That calm did not last, and by late summer of 1827, when the Bird family sought refuge at a village on Mount Lebanon, a mob beat the local sheikh who had offered them shelter. Ann Bird herself rushed to the scene of the attack, helped to bandage the wounded man's injuries, and then remained in the village with her children for weeks thereafter while Isaac tried to find a place for them elsewhere. It was a long wait, especially the day that "a large stone came thundering down the chimney into the room" where she and her children were staying. The Birds' plight prompted William to inform the board that "in case of war with England, which has been seriously talked of daily for a long time, our lives would be in danger; for it seems now pretty clearly ascertained, that we could not, like other Franks, 'flee to the mountain'; and if we could not find means to leave the country, it is impossible to say what would be our fate."

That crisis came. The Battle of Navarino in October 1827—a naval victory in which Britain and other European powers destroyed the Ottoman sultan's fleet—made all Westerners unwelcome in Beirut. By January 1828, Bird reported that the consuls had ordered their flags struck, and "many Christians are leaving the city under new apprehensions." By the beginning of April, both the English and the French consuls had left town, with William remarking, "We are now at the disposal of a capricious Pasha, who is more than half a madman and half a rebel; and we cannot trust to the mountains. We are surrounded by wicked Patriarchs and princes, and priests, and people; and we have no protection." "We know not whether we are free or whether we are a sort of privileged prisoners under watch," Isaac agreed, "to be reserved for some closer confinement whenever it shall suit the Pasha's pleasure." Oh, yes, and the plague had returned. On April 29, 1828, the Birds and Goodells fled to Malta, joined shortly thereafter by Eli Smith.

They were still recovering when Rufus Anderson arrived early in January 1829. By now nearly two years had passed since William, Isaac, and Ann had written those letters challenging Jeremiah Evarts and the Prudential Committee, and all that they had endured in that time left them physically exhausted, emotionally drained, and apprehensive about the future. The last thing they wanted was another battle, which made Rufus's task easier than he'd thought possible. After reading Evarts's narrative, the missionaries composed a "memorandum" vindicating the Prudential Committee from any misdeeds and praising its members' "great tenderness" toward Martha when they set out to "ascertain the nature of the complaint against her." They did register objections to the "improper bias of the Committee" in favor of Thomas Tenney, as well as the "very doubtful propriety" of "some of the opinions etc." of Bennet Tyler. Even so, Evarts's narrative dispelled their suspicions that the board had plotted to fill missionary ranks with lifelong bachelors or to ruin Martha's reputation. "In releasing Miss P. from her engagements to the Board," the memorandum concluded, the members of the committee "acted conscientiously, according to their best judgment and on the facts before them, of what was demanded by the highest interests of the sacred cause of missions." William and Isaac, no doubt at Rufus's urging, wrote obsequious apologies to Evarts and the Prudential Committee, perhaps feeling a little foolish about some of the charges they had leveled. If no sinister conspiracy was afoot, what remained to be done? Elnathan was dead, Martha was married, and perhaps the Palestine mission itself—as its demoralized members feared—was no more.

That resolution did not satisfy everyone. "As every severe tempest leaves behind its marks of desolation, so this also has not passed away without some unhappy relics of that character," Isaac Bird observed. "Some hearts have probably received from it a chill which it will require much of the sunshine of divine grace to restore." Isaac's own heart might have numbered among them, belying Rufus's upbeat assessment of his "simplicity of character" and "disposition to be pleased with all the world, (except the Maronite patriarch and Thos T[enney])." Of greater interest to Rufus was another person, one whose chilly heart was never likely to warm toward him.

We imagine him studying her at Malta—taking her measure—

and Ann Parker Bird eyeing him back, both wondering what she might dare say to his face. She was no Abigail Davis Goodell, a lady, in Rufus's estimate, of "a most amiable disposition" and "good common sense," intelligent and kind. Though "amiable" enough, Ann was "susceptible of strong excitement" yet, much to his surprise, "without those liabilities to depression which are common in such cases." And whereas "Mrs. G. must be a pleasant companion to almost any person" and "possesses a large share of patience," which made her inclined to "suffer cheerfully," the take-charge Ann "will resolutely act." Letters she had written to his brother-in-law Henry Hill's wife—which came into Rufus's hands—had caused him to imagine Ann "a creature of feeling, romantic, desponding [?], and unlikely to sustain herself in a self-denying and dangerous situation." How wrong he had been: by all reports, she looked after the safety of her husband and little children "with heroic courage." Indeed, as Eli Smith had told him, "she scarcely knows fear," despite having had ample opportunity to make its acquaintance.

Ann might not have known fear, but Rufus did. How disappointed he sounds, finding no way to diminish her. He had to concede that Ann and Abigail had both "sustained the cares, labors, privations, and vicissitudes of the last two years of their residence in Syria," which "entitles them to the respect, affection, and confidence of us all." How well they would serve the American Board as heroines of the missionary cause, perhaps even as martyrs in the making. Still, there was a price to be paid for allowing women so much public notice, and by Rufus Anderson's calculations there would be no counting the cost if Ann Parker Bird—intense, determined, and brave—became the avatar of the new evangelical woman.

⁂

Back in New England, James Kimball—ever the Greek chorus commenting on the drama of Martha Parker's life—sounded a note of resignation. Writing to Ann and Isaac Bird at the beginning of 1830, he reported receiving a letter from Martha, now in Standish, Maine, where Thomas Tenney had lately taken a position as minister. The couple had made yet another move—from Hanover to Hampton to Standish—and with many more over even greater distances to follow over the decades. James judged that Thomas's "hasty temperament has led him astray sometimes," a fault that could account for his troubles holding a job. Yet "I think he ought to be forgiven by us as he seems disposed now to do right." Affection for Thomas Tenney, it seems, was still wanting among many in Martha's family. "Tho he was never a favorite of mine," James continued, "I think he will be useful as a minister and will make Martha happy—to some extent and it is possible under all circumstances as happy as any man could."

CHAPTER NINE

The Sorcerer's Apprentice

She wrote as "Mary Irving." After her work drew praise from readers, the editors asked in the magazine's pages whether the author would disclose her true name to the wider public. They kept asking; she kept mum. The pen name stayed. The little mystery served so many purposes. It must have daunted this young teacher, just turned twenty when her pieces first appeared in 1848, joining the company of luminaries who also published short stories, poetry, and nonfiction pieces in *The National Era*. There was Lydia Maria Child and Harriet Beecher Stowe, Nathaniel Hawthorne and John Greenleaf Whittier. Armed with the last name of another celebrity author—Washington Irving—"Mary" might have found it easier to slip into their company.

Did she fear, too, that her father would disapprove of publishing under her own name? Even though he had drilled her in Latin and Greek like a gifted son, would he frown on putting herself forward in this way? Did she disapprove as well? Should any lady—let alone a devout evangelical—make herself so conspicuous? Only once had her own mother's maiden name seen the light of print. But no matter. By whatever name, her daughter had won a modest fame, and once she'd picked up her pen, she could not put it down.

Her output was stupendous. Nearly every issue of *The National Era* included something of her authorship, as if this novice meant to show her editors that she could command any form, tackle any subject. There were sentimental poems, each rendered in inexorably rhymed couplets. The title of one, "Spray from the Tear-Fountain," might have been the title of all. Fans of that treacly poetry might have had less enthusiasm for her earliest forays into short fiction, which featured tales of Native people attacking white settlers on the Maine frontier. She had picked up a taste for blood and thunder during her early youth in that far north, haunting the old graveyards of Standish and summoning their dead. Thereafter her family moved on, first to Ohio's Western Reserve, where she spent her adolescence. She did not follow a few years later when they moved to southeastern Wisconsin but paid at least one long visit, which yielded material for her many tales of "Quabosha," a raw settlement swarming with recent immigrants. In all her writing, religion was the reigning theme, and she skewered evangelicals' rivals—Catholics, Mormons, and spiritualists—with abandon in prose and poetry, fiction and nonfiction. She cultivated younger readers, too, providing short pieces for magazines such as *The Friend of Youth* and *The Little Pilgrim*. And when it came to reform movements, she ran the table: reformed drunks, worthy poor, diligent students, and pious slaves packed her pages. Every good cause of the mid-nineteenth century won her endorsement—except women's rights.

Promising as her literary career was, writing didn't pay well enough. By 1850 she was supplementing her income by teaching at a school in Hartford, Connecticut, founded by her aunt Ann and uncle Isaac. Two years later she was in Bradford, Massachusetts, living with other relatives and attending her mother's alma mater there, an academy offering more rigorous course work than her earlier schooling in Ohio. Thereafter she spent more than two years in Thibodaux, Louisiana, at a female academy headed by another uncle, and finally she worked as a governess for a year in Washington, D.C., while stepping up her game as an author. She wrote stories of novella length serialized over several issues, hoping perhaps to match the recent success of Harriet Beecher Stowe's *Uncle Tom's Cabin,* a blockbuster first published in installments in *The National Era.* Why not aim high? "Mary Irving" remained one of the magazine's most popular contributors, and she knew all the right people from lodging with the family of its editor in chief, Gamaliel Bailey. A mecca for the young and ambitious then as now, the nation's capital fizzed with excitement, and Bailey, an antislavery activist, threw parties that filled his home with prominent reformers and a pride of literary lions and lionesses.

Somehow, it was not enough for his star boarder. She was waiting for something better, but that something was not marriage. Now in her mid-twenties, she professed to have no regrets about being single. "Many a one who 'marries for a home,' as the phrase is, finds only an aching void," she wrote shortly after leaving Bradford Academy. "The sensitive school-mistress worn with duties and cares that torture her aching brain and lonely heart may grasp the offer that promises a home, and find, too late, that it was but a mirage on the desert of life." But this sensitive school-mistress suffered no such regrets, and sometime during that year in Washington a real oasis beckoned. Aunt Ann and Uncle Isaac Bird had been lobbying in her behalf with the American Board, aided, no doubt, by Abigail and William Goodell during their return visit to the United States. It worked: at the end of 1855 she decamped to the board's mission school at Tokat, a city in northern Anatolia near the Black Sea about three hundred miles north of Kayseri, where death had claimed Elnathan Gridley. From that distant spot, she sent *The National Era* occasional dispatches about her travels and her new life. "Mary Irving" disappeared four years later when the woman behind the pseudonym, Mary Eliza Tenney, the eldest daughter of Martha Parker and Thomas Tenney, married Cyrus Hamlin, a twice-widowed missionary more than twenty years her senior.

Are the daughter's choices a measure of the mother's disappointments? Did Mary Eliza pursue her brilliant career as a counterlife, a redress for Martha's regrets? Had the mother confided in the daughter, lamenting her lost possibilities? Did other relatives—her aunt Ann Parker Bird, perhaps—relate the tale of her mother's doomed romance with missions and Elnathan Gridley? Or could those stories have come, less sympathetically, from a grandmother, the one whom Mary recalled saying, "I wish she'd leave her books, and mend her clothes; I thank *my* stars, I know not verse from prose." It's easy to feature this young woman taking in all their tales, choosing among them to construct her own preferred version of the past, and then deciding to strive for and gain what her mother had lost. Easy, yes, but can we make that leap of imagination?

Among the historian's occupational hazards is projecting onto past actors present-day assumptions about how people think and feel. Martha Parker's story lends itself to that kind of malpractice because she left so little direct testimony of any kind, and almost none after her marriage. Then again, even if, like Mary Eliza, words had spilled from her pen and every scrap of that record survived, how revealing would it be? Often those in the past who chronicled their lives in the greatest detail can prove the most elusive among historical subjects. It should come as no surprise: think of those in the present with whom we are most intimate, yet who still remain unknown to us. Doing history keeps us humble by teaching, time after time, that human beings are unfathomable.

Yet we can say with certainty that some of "Mary Irving's" own leaps of imagination, especially her earliest short stories, involve saving characters who bring to mind her mother. The eponymous heroine of "Bessie Lindsay," for example, is a "little Amazon," a wild child who, after having settled down and found religion during a stint of teaching at a female seminary, marries her handsome, high-minded cousin and heads off with him to their mission in "Hindustan." It's Martha Parker's fantasy, fulfilled in fiction. Then there's "The Return: A Leaf from Life's Volume," in which an industrious young Yankee woman without any better options marries an "unprepossessing" fellow. It's the author's parents, even more unmistakably when this fictional couple decamps to a frontier resembling southeastern Wisconsin. (Recall that both James Kimball and Isaac Bird had described Thomas Tenney as "unprepossessing.") Decades later, the wife's adventurous brother, whom she had thought long dead, returns a wealthy man eager to "make her a lady," as he had always promised. Disguised as male, the hero who fulfills this worn old woman's girlhood dreams could only be Mary Eliza herself.

Through the entwined lives of Martha Parker and her eldest daughter, we can trace the transformation overtaking evangelicalism in the North over the nineteenth century, all that it offered women and all that it withheld. If her mother's life course reveals the forced retreat of many in that movement from nurturing women's aspirations, Mary Eliza's career reflects the determination of some of their daughters to press forward even in the face of mounting opposition. Among them were the growing number of single women who, like Mary Eliza, strove to enter the foreign missions field. Their ranks slowly increased after the late 1820s, and by the 1850s some thirty unmarried women had taught school in missions that spread from Ceylon (Sri Lanka)

to Liberia to Greece to Persia and all the way to China. By the end of the nineteenth century, they would dominate Protestant foreign missions, outnumbering married missionaries of both sexes.

The future would not have brought that change if Rufus Anderson's preferences had prevailed. After Jeremiah Evarts's death in 1831, Rufus realized his long-cherished ambition and took the helm of the American Board. Among the signatures of his tenure, which lasted until 1866, was a new rule that all men serving in foreign missions "must go out" accompanied by wives. But if he banished bachelors from the board's ranks, thus increasing the number of married women in the field, Rufus opposed opening the door to more single women. It was only the expanding number of mission schools for girls that defeated his wishes, creating a demand for teachers that outran the supply of missionary wives, and unmarried women seized that chance for a career promising fulfillment, adventure, and possibly even fame. More and more of those spinsters clamored to enter the mission field, bided their time until an opportunity arose, and then seized the moment. For them, Ottoman Turkey, not Texas, was the land of opportunity.

That was Mary Eliza Tenney's strategy. In her mid-twenties, she had enrolled at Bradford Academy, seeking not only the training that would prepare her for teaching abroad but also the imprimatur of its venerable preceptress, Abigail Hasseltine, who was now more than ever a powerful figure in the foreign missions movement. Thereafter Mary Eliza waited for two years, and when the board's mission in Tokat came calling, she knew what to do. She wrote to Rufus's subordinate, a clergyman charged with vetting candidates, to request an interview. Her letter performed to perfection all of the cardinal virtues desired in a female missionary: benevolence, humility, and deference. "I believe I have a real desire to do good to the extent of my ability, to the great world of perishing souls abroad," Mary Eliza wrote, yet she would not be "unwilling, should it be thought really best by those wiser than myself—to stay in the already wide field of usefulness which Providence has been pleased to open to me." She did not mention that this "wide field" included being a popular contributor to a national magazine.

Both Uncle Isaac and Aunt Ann lent their support with letters to the board. Ann in particular lavished praise on the young woman who "has been in our family so much, that she seems like a daughter." Not only an excellent teacher, one who "became the mainspring" of her uncle's Louisiana academy, Mary Eliza also had "quite a talent for the acquisition of languages." No wonder so many sought her services, from Thomas Tenney's younger brother, who hoped to "engage her as teacher in a new Female Seminary on the Mt. Holyoke plan" at Oxford, Ohio, to Catharine Beecher, who had offered a position at her Hartford academy. There was also support from abroad: an American missionary in Ottoman Syria had assured the Birds that if Mary Eliza "does not go to Tocat, she must consider herself booked for Mt. Lebanon." But even Ann stopped short of lauding her niece's literary achievements, a silence that speaks eloquently about why Mary Eliza chose to remain anonymous to her readers.

There's no missing Ann's satisfaction that her niece had "long felt" that she was "loudly called" to "missionary ground," but not all members of the family shared her sentiments. The opposition of some of her relatives had, as Mary Eliza admitted, "kept me from taking any decided steps heretofore" to realize her dream. Among those who objected—who "think I am taking unnecessary pains to find a path of usefulness"—might have been her father. True, Thomas Tenney supported the education of young women, even "drilled" his daughter in Latin and Greek. Yet even though both Mary Eliza's and Ann's letters to the board make mention of his training her, neither includes any mention of him encouraging his daughter's missionary aspirations. Of course, many parents objected to their daughters' going abroad on missions, especially if they went out to the field as single women. But Thomas would also have seen in Ann Parker Bird's promotion of his daughter's missionary prospects a strategy to savor that incomparable delicacy, revenge served up cold. How it must have galled him, realizing that the life he had stolen from Martha, Ann had restored to Mary Eliza.

It miffed Rufus, too, sending out yet another single woman, but what could he do? What would irk him even more was another significant change under way by the middle decades of the nineteenth century. By the 1840s and thereafter, the women who led female academies played an ever more prominent and powerful role in shaping the foreign missions movement. Their emergence ended the days in which evangelical men enjoyed exclusive control over the selection of missionary women, a transfer of power that seems to have taken hold without some of them noticing. Among the clueless was Justin Perkins, who for decades headed the American Board's mission in Persia.

In 1842, Perkins returned to the United States, intending, among other business, to recruit two single women to work as teachers at his school in Urmia. At first, he approached personal acquaintances, young women whom he had taught in New England many years earlier, but no prospects appeared after a search of several months. He did succeed in persuading a newly ordained minister, David Stoddard, to join his mission, and then, at the end of his visit in December, he discovered that a teacher at Bradford Academy, one Harriet Briggs, had expressed an interest in going abroad. Indeed, so smitten was she with the romance of missions that Harriet had asked her minister to get Perkins's autograph for her collection. Perhaps she would be game to teach at the Urmia school—perhaps even amenable to marrying Stoddard.

The two men slogged through a snowstorm to Bradford Academy, where Harriet instantly made a good impression on Perkins, especially because "she appeared ready to meet the self-denial of going out <u>single</u>." Then who should join the company but Abigail Hasseltine, "the venerable sister of Mrs. Judson," as Perkins gushed in his journal, "who, between thirty and forty years, has been the principal of this school of the Prophetesses." That lady quickly took control of the negotiations. To Perkins's suggestion that Harriet go out as a single woman, "she stoutly objected, considering her age, delicacy, modesty, etc. calling her <u>a little chicken</u>, but she at the same time volunteered her entire willingness that she should go out as a <u>married</u> missionary." Perkins believed that neither woman had "any idea of what was afoot," but Hasseltine had been managing such matches over many decades of training her "Prophetesses." A glance at David Stoddard shivering in her unheated parlor told her all that she needed—enough to tell Perkins on what terms the Persia mission might have her "little chicken." It was Hasseltine, too, who, after an interview with Stoddard's elder brother about the family's finances, sealed the deal that resulted in the couple's marriage.

That still left Justin Perkins short two single schoolteachers, so he "resolved as a last resort to make a trial at Mount Holyoke Seminary." Like Bradford Academy, Holyoke was becoming a "rib factory," as evangelicals joked, supplying wives for missionaries. Its founder, Mary Lyon, asked for volunteers in response to Perkins's request, and when some forty of her female students and faculty submitted their names, it was she who chose the first, her protégée among the teachers, Fidelia Fiske, and the two women together selected the second candidate. When Fidelia's mother objected to her daughter's decision, "Miss Lyon, who entered very deeply into the case," accompanied Fiske to her mother's home "to arrange the matter with her friends." Fidelia not only taught in Persia for the next fifteen years but also became the subject of the first memoir to celebrate a single woman in the mission field. The tombstone marking the grave of this "Prophetess," one who found honor in her own country, towers over all others in the Fiske family plot, including those of her male relatives. There was a sight to unsettle Rufus Anderson. To say nothing of that popular memoir of Fidelia, *Woman and Her Saviour in Persia,* implying that the two title characters enjoyed an especially tight relationship. But really, what did Rufus expect? His fellow evangelicals had been insisting for decades that women were the spiritually superior sex.

All in all, the emergence of the foreign missions movement as a magnet for single women of ambition and talent leaves us wondering whether Rufus missed a bet. Would a shrewder fellow have taken the opposite tack, actively recruiting—with the complicity of dynamos like Abigail Hasseltine and Mary Lyon—and then exporting abroad the boldest female spirits like Mary Eliza Tenney? What better way to rid evangelical ranks in the United States of those women committed to vocations other than motherhood and more equal treatment of their sex in the rest of the world? But if that was a lost opportunity, the course taken by events throughout his long life, which lasted until 1880, would not have left Rufus Anderson too deeply disappointed.

They were such operators, these women in the nineteenth century. It's a pleasure to look back from the present and watch them in action—the academy preceptresses and the missionaries, the members of benevolent associations and reform societies. Even as they gained more knowledge about, experience of, and influence in the world beyond their households, most of them insisted that their efforts posed no challenge to traditional roles. Why, they were up to nothing more than making the most of women's God-given talents and superior virtue, their special ability to elevate morals and heighten religiosity, all skills that they practiced and perfected as wives and mothers. Especially slick when it came to marshaling such justifications were evangelical women, a gift endowed by speaking from sincere conviction and in the face of increasingly stiff opposition. They got plenty of opportunities.

Their being in the vanguard of American women's entry into public life arouses our curiosity. With that past as prologue, why did most evangelicals of both sexes hold back from or even oppose the agitation to accord women greater civil, legal, and political rights in the United States? So much about northern evangelicalism suggests that it should have nurtured feminism. Under that faith's auspices, significant numbers of white middle-class women attained literacy, acquired more formal education, entered the nation's civic life through voluntary associations, and discovered within themselves new inner resources. Why, then, didn't more find their way to Seneca Falls in 1848 and into the women's rights movement thereafter? Why did so few women among the leading lights of mid-nineteenth-century feminism hail from evangelical backgrounds? It was not the women who flocked to Bible, tract, and missionary societies, not even those who organized to combat intemperance and prostitution, who then came to fill the ranks of the women's rights movement. To the contrary, the most conspicuous in early feminism's forefront were Quakers like Lucretia Mott and liberal Christians like Lydia Maria Child.

A closer acquaintance with the early life of Mary Eliza Tenney only deepens the mystery. When her family moved to Ohio's Western Reserve, her father became the principal of an academy known as the Grand River Institute, and there the adolescent

Mary Eliza fell under the spell of a charismatic teacher, Betsy Mix Cowles. The Oberlin-educated, never-to-wed daughter of an evangelically minded Congregationalist minister, Cowles served as the head of Grand River's Female Department for most of her thirties, all the while lending her pen and her organizational skills to the cause of abolitionism and women's rights. Mary Eliza modeled herself on this remarkable woman: she embraced the single life and honed her writing skills to oppose slavery and advocate for women's education. But like many of her evangelical sisters among the "Prophetesses," Mary Eliza took no part in the organized movement for women's rights and even published under a name not her own. Something held her back—or induced her to hold herself back—a reluctance shared by many other women with evangelical sympathies. Among them, surprisingly, was Cowles herself, a radical reformer who, despite pouring her energies into organizing against slavery and in favor of women's rights, refused to speak in behalf of either of those causes before public gatherings. For all their prominence in evangelical circles, Mary Lyon and Fidelia Fiske also refused to speak publicly—not even in support of missions.

Perhaps the most poignant figure of them all was Catharine Beecher. The eldest child of Lyman Beecher, Bennet Tyler's patron, she founded a female academy in Hartford, Connecticut. Early in 1826, a revival started at that school spread throughout the city, and Catharine claimed credit for kindling the fervor. She also tried to enlist recognition of her achievement from Hartford's evangelical clergymen as well as from her brother Edward, also a minister, and from Lyman Beecher himself. They held back, with the most devastating rejection coming from her father, who scolded her for assuming religious leadership within the community and rebuked her for even thinking "of such a thing." Crestfallen, Catharine suffered her disappointment during the same months of 1826 that scandal, building through similar channels

Betsy Mix Cowles, teacher and reformer, inspired her students and promoted women's rights and the abolition of slavery. Date unknown.

and for similar reasons, overtook Martha Parker. Well connected as she was in evangelical circles, Catharine surely heard of Martha's plight, perhaps sympathized with her as someone who shared the bitter experience of being put in her place by men determined to maintain their privileges.

Burned but not beaten, Catharine made another bid to imitate her famous father only a few years later. This time she strove to match Lyman Beecher not as a revival leader but as a reformer. Inspired by a lecture delivered by Jeremiah Evarts in behalf of the indigenous nations threatened with removal, Catharine orga-

Catharine Beecher, author and
educator, the daughter of Lyman
Beecher and sister of Harriet Beecher
Stowe and Henry Ward Beecher,
in 1848. She aspired to match her
father's successes as a revivalist and
reformer.

nized a petition drive in 1829, a national campaign that targeted
women. Supporters of her "Ladies' Circular" not only signed peti-
tions to Congress but also called public meetings to rally more
women to the cause. Participants justified their new activism
as an extension of evangelical women's long support of Indian
missions and schools, but in the end that did not prove warrant
enough to set Catharine's mind at ease. Still haunted by memories
of her father's disapproval of what she called "her revival," she
dreaded being found out as the campaign's organizer. So intense
was her fear of being discovered as the circular's author that she
swore the printer to secrecy. But nothing could keep anxiety from

overwhelming her: Catharine suffered an emotional collapse, one that she described leaving her "utterly prostrated" and experiencing "such confusion of thought as seemed like approaching insanity." After a long recovery, she would advise the members of her sex to keep to their "domestic and social circle," ignoring "the promptings of ambition, or the thirst for power." She specifically condemned those women who, like her former self, petitioned Congress, a political act that "seem[s] IN ALL CASES, to fall entirely without the sphere of female duty."

The fate of Catharine Beecher—like that which befell Martha Parker—announced the resolve of culturally conservative evangelical leaders to patrol the boundaries between the sexes ever more closely. So committed had they become to that surveillance by the 1830s that their ministers denounced even those Christian women outside evangelical ranks who spoke in public settings. Among their first targets were the Quakers Sarah and Angelina Grimké and Abby Kelley, who took to addressing "promiscuous assemblies"—that is, audiences including both men and women. First radicalized by abolitionism, they came to recognize the oppression of women through their sympathies for the plight of slaves.

Confronted with this spectacle, many evangelical ministers recalled women from their own churches praying and exhorting in Charles Finney's revivals only a few years earlier. They promptly prohibited their female members from praying aloud, lecturing, or preaching. In July 1837, for example, the General Association of Massachusetts Congregational Churches issued a pastoral letter denouncing "those who encourage females to bear an obtrusive and ostentatious part in measures of reform, and countenance any of that sex who so far forget themselves as to itinerate in the character of public teachers and lecturers." Methodists and Baptists, insurgent evangelical denominations rapidly gaining in membership, also voiced their opposition to female preaching. This message from the pulpit, one often echoed in the popular media, that women should shut up and sit down or suffer the consequences would hold back many in Mary Eliza Tenney's generation.

That backlash had been building for a long time within the evangelical movement. The rise of abolitionism and women's rights in the 1830s did not mark the first moment that the radical potential of their faith had dawned on believers. As the blighted ambitions of Martha Parker and Catharine Beecher attest, the widening scope of women's activism had aroused concern in some quarters at least since the mid-1820s. And nothing did more to steel the determination of those critics to stop its progress than the recognition of their own movement's role in enabling it. Because evangelicals stood in the vanguard of educating and empowering women, they became the first to face its consequences. The men who pioneered the foreign missions movement in the United States back in the second decade of the nineteenth century had not in their wildest imaginings foreseen the celebrity and influence it would bestow on missionary wives and preceptresses of academies. Neither could they have envisioned the self-esteem it afforded fund-raising agents and female missionary society members, nor the sense of owning the movement that it promoted among the wide circle of rank-and-file donors. It came as a shock to some, a pleasant surprise to others, the ways in which not only missionary societies but all such voluntary associations made women aware, for the first time, of their competence, their collective power, and life's possibilities.

It was astonishing, too, for all evangelicals, to discover how divisive to their movement those challenges to traditional understandings of womanhood and manhood had proved. Astonishing and dismaying, because their churches, which had long struggled to attract more men into the pews, faced new obstacles to that goal by the middle decades of the nineteenth century. The upstart Mormons, with their promises of patriarchy in the present and for all eternity, had entered the religious free market in the United States and already shown strength in the competition for male adherents. By then, too, Catholic nuns, set apart by raiment signaling their special religious authority, were becoming familiar sights in many American settings and giving even more daring ideas to Protestant women. Could it be that the attacks on Mormons and Catholics mounted in intensity after 1830 due in part to evangelicals' suspicion that their own movement's empowerment of women had, in different ways, fostered their competitors' success?

Maybe so. What's open to no doubt is that a sense of guilty complicity in fostering feminism lurked in some quarters of antebellum evangelicalism. One of Mary Eliza Tenney's fellow contributors to *The National Era,* Lydia Maria Child, captured that faith's contradictions when it came to women by comparing the evangelical movement to the sorcerer's apprentice, a figure from folklore. This hapless fellow enchants a broom into bringing buckets of water from a nearby river but then cannot command the counter-magic to make it stop. "Thus it is with those who urged women to become missionaries and form tract societies," Child wrote in 1841. "They have changed the household utensil to a living, energetic being; and they have no spell to turn it into a broom again." A delicious comeuppance, by the reckoning of this author, who embraced a liberal form of Christianity, supported women's rights, and wrote under her own name. But much to Child's disappointment, if evangelical women would never turn back into brooms, neither would most of them become enchanted enough to carry water for the women's rights movement.

That's because so many had fallen under another spell. It was an enchantment often intoned by culturally conservative evangelicals, but one that resounded in many quarters of antebellum American society. The public square, the churches, and the literary marketplace all rang with the incantation that God and nature had designed women to keep within the confines of their households. To come under its thrall was to accept that women did themselves and their sex a favor by holding back—by staying off the public stage and out of the public eye. It was keeping within a narrow compass—avoiding any behavior that bespoke self-esteem and ambition—that endowed women with sanctity and ensured their safety, granted them their special powers and privileges as a sex. To stray outside those bounds would compromise them both socially and spiritually. Hence Thomas Tenney's warning that by breaking their engagement to pursue her dreams, Martha Parker had lost her claim to numbering among the "Redeemer's children." So pervasive had that message become by the middle of the nineteenth century that women in the rising generation of evangelicals, like his daughter Mary Eliza, had listened and heeded as their own inner voices played it over and over. Such was their romance with evangelicalism: it filled them with dreams but then doomed their full realization.

When incantation failed to work its charm, coercion came into play. The means by which constraint was brought to bear on women who did not fall into line—pressures that were all the more powerful for being informal and subterranean—we can only glimpse in the case of Catharine Beecher. But the record so carefully compiled about Martha Parker brings into the light what usually stays hidden in the shadows of the past and often remains concealed even in the present: the social networks mobilized and the cultural weapons marshaled to cut women down to size. Centuries before the invention of social media, conservative evangelicals dabbled in the dark art of character assassination with anonymous letters and gossip, threats and blackmail, the promise of punishment in this life and the next. That makes them no worse than many other Americans, then and now. The difference is that as their protean movement first gathered force in the early nineteenth century, evangelicals seemed poised to offer women a world of new possibilities. By breaking faith with that promise, their most progressive leaders abandoned their movement's fundamental principles. That betrayal continues into the present among those believers who resist reckoning with or even acknowledging evangelicalism's rich and complicated historical legacy with respect to sexual politics and sexuality.

Acknowledgments

Some of the people thanked below might not wish to have their names connected with a book titled *Doomed Romance*. Too bad and too late. Luckily, the two scholars who bear the greatest responsibility for encouraging its author stand above reproach. For a long time, I have felt privileged to count among my colleagues Anne Boylan and Rebecca Davis, distinguished historians of religion, gender, and sexuality, and I cannot begin to repay their many readings and astute criticisms of this study in all its incarnations. Other learned friends have also stimulated my thinking (and corrected my mistakes) on a number of matters. I've received expert advice about the development of nineteenth-century print culture from James Brophy, the history of sexuality from Richard Godbeer, the provisions of wills from Bruce Mann, the meaning of Middle Eastern antiquities from Steven Sidebotham, the finer points of Calvinism from Robert Schoone-Jongen, and the heroines of the foreign mission movement from Grant Wacker. Lisa Keamy, physician by profession and grammarian by hobby, has sustained me with lunch, shopping trips, and the unvarnished truth about whether anyone outside the academy would have the remotest interest in reading my latest chapter. My splendid nieces, Kyla Hart and Rachel Speer, divert me with play dates during which history is never discussed. I count myself most fortunate to have enlisted Geri Thoma as my agent and Victoria Wilson as my editor at Knopf. I also thank my copy editor, Ingrid Sterner.

The greatest debt for *Doomed Romance* I owe to my late husband, Thomas Calvin Carter. He banished my early doubts about the significance of Martha Parker's story, and his confidence (to say nothing of his expert genealogical research) sustained my efforts to capture in these pages its message to the present. I can't imagine writing a book without him, and the memories of our many years together have such power to sustain that I won't have to try. I can also count on Anne Heyrman-Hart, who has always read my stuff and this time around sent me flowers with cards bearing messages such as: "Dear Martha, Nobody does it better!!! Kisses and Congrats, Elnathan." For your wit, whimsy, and so much more, dear sister, this book is for you.

Notes

ABC   American Board of Commissioners for Foreign Missions Archives, Houghton Library, Harvard University
IBP   Isaac Bird Papers, Manuscripts and Archives, Yale University
JEN   Jeremiah Evarts's Narrative, in ABC 74
MH   *Missionary Herald*

CHAPTER ONE: THE WORLD BEFORE HER

4   Through it all, her faith: No. 26 Elnathan Gridley's Statement, no. 21 Thomas Tenney to Evarts, July n.d., 1826, no. 12 William Gould to Evarts, Fairhaven, June 19, 1826, no. 13 Evarts to Gould, June 24, 1826, [unnumbered] Leonard Woods to Gridley, Nov. 3, 1826, all in ABC 74; *Merrimack Intelligencer* (Haverhill, Mass.), Sept. 30, 1809; *Farmer's Cabinet* (Amherst, N.H.), Sept. 16, 1815.

5   And she would reach out: No. 28 Martha Parker to Evarts, Aug. 29, 1826, Extract of a letter from Martha Parker to Sarah Tenney, Aug. 2, 1826, in no. 33 Continued Narrative of Thomas Tenney, July 5, 1826, 6–7, both in ABC 74; Dana L. Robert, *American Women in Mission: A Social History of Their Thought and Practice* (Macon, Ga.: Mercer University Press, 1997), 1, 3, 32, 37, 55, 82–83, 120. The American Board did not send a single woman abroad until 1827, nor did it designate wives as full-fledged missionaries until the twentieth century.

Both Martha and Elnathan counted among the many adherents of the Edwardsean or New Divinity movement, which dominated New England Congregational churches during the opening decades of the nineteenth century. His education at Yale and Andover, both New Divinity educational strongholds, points to his affiliation with that movement, while her family's church upheld the rigorous standards for church membership characteristic of New Divinity practice. Excellent coverage of this conservative Calvinist evangelical faith appears in William Breitenbach, "Unregenerate Doings: Selflessness and Selfishness in New Divinity Theology," *American Quarterly* 34, no. 5 (1982): 479–502; William Breitenbach, "The Consistent Calvinism of the New Divinity Movement," *William and Mary Quarterly*, 3rd ser., 41 (1984): 241–64; David W. Kling, *A Field of Divine Wonders: The New Divinity and Village Revivals in Northwestern Connecticut, 1792–1822* (University Park: Pennsylvania State University Press, 1993); Douglas Sweeney, *Nathaniel William Taylor* (New York: Oxford University Press, 2002), 21–45.

5 Students drew maps: Like most academies in the early republic, Bradford relied for its support on private donations and tuition. The best treatment of these academies and their significance is Mary Kelley, *Learning to Stand and Speak: Women, Education, and Public Life in America's Republic* (Chapel Hill: University of North Carolina Press, 2006). See also Martha Tomhave Blauvelt, *The Work of the Heart: Young Women and Emotion, 1780–1830* (Charlottesville: University of Virginia Press, 2007), 50–81, 146–55; Nancy Cott, *The Bonds of Womanhood: "Woman's Sphere" in New England, 1780–1835* (New Haven, Conn.: Yale University Press, 1977), 113–18; Catherine E. Kelly, *In the New England Fashion: Reshaping Women's Lives in the Nineteenth Century* (Ithaca, N.Y.: Cornell University Press, 1999), 70–76. On Bradford Academy, see E. A. Barrows, *A Memorial of Bradford Academy* (Boston: Congregational S.S. and Publishing Society, 1870), and Jean Sarah Pond, *Bradford: A New England Academy* (Bradford, Mass.: Bradford Alumni Association, 1930).

6 He cherished "higher hopes": "On Preparing Pious Young Women for the Instruction and Government of Schools," *MH,* Feb. 1819; Levi Parsons to Lucretia Parsons, May 1, 1814, Levi Parsons Letters,

Middlebury College Archives; Isaac Bird to Josiah Brewer, Feb. 12, 1828, IBP.

9 They would have taught: Walter Harris, *A Discourse Delivered to the Members of the Female Cent Society in Bedford, New Hampshire, June 18, 1814* (Concord, 1814), 3–10; Sampler of Lucy Hackett and Anon., *Memoir of Miss Sally Ladd* (n.p., n.d.), both at New Hampshire Historical Society; Robert, *American Women in Mission,* 15–16, 99. On Emily Dickinson's resistance to the revivals at her academy, see Amanda Porterfield, *Mary Lyon and the Mount Holyoke Missionaries* (New York: Oxford University Press, 1997), 50. On the cultural significance of these pious memoirs, see Mary P. Ryan, *Cradle of the Middle Class: The Family in Oneida County, New York, 1790–1865* (New York: Cambridge University Press, 1981), 87–88.

10 The examples set by Mary: Barrows, *Memorial of Bradford Academy,* 77–80; Pond, *Bradford,* 128; "Boarding School at Manepy," *MH,* May 1824; Robert, *American Women in Mission,* 7–8, 43–46.

11 After Ann settled in Beirut: Ann Parker Bird to Gridley, Feb. 10, 1827, ABC 16.5, microfilm reel 502.

13 From those perches Newell: Leonard Woods, *A Sermon Preached at Haverhill (Mass.) in Remembrance of Mrs. Harriet Newell . . . to Which Are Added Memoirs of Her Life,* 5th ed. (Boston, 1815), 12–13, 21, 28, 166, 177–78, 185, 188–90, 192–93, 196, 200–201; *MH,* June 1825; *Memoir of Miss Sally Ladd;* Robert, *American Women in Mission,* 40–42; Jonathan Allen, "The Farewell Sermon" (1812), in *Pioneers in Mission: The Early Missionary Ordination Sermons, Charges, and Instructions,* ed. R. Pierce Beaver (Grand Rapids: William B. Eerdmans, 1966), 277. The term "moral radicals" comes from Larissa MacFarquhar, *Strangers Drowning: Impossible Idealism, Drastic Choices, and the Urge to Help* (New York: Penguin, 2016). By one count, of the 134 graduates of Andover Theological Seminary who served in foreign missions between 1812 and 1858, 34 died in the field. Mortality rates among their wives and children ran higher still (Rufus Anderson, *Memorial Volume of the First Fifty Years of the American Board of Commissioners for Foreign Missions* [Boston, 1861], 275). Martha might also have had some personal acquaintance with another missionary wife, Philomela Thurston Newell Garrett. In 1818, the then-fourteen-year-old Mar-

tha would have been fascinated to learn that her onetime Bradford neighbor, despite knowing Harriet Newell's fate and having never met her widowed husband, Samuel, sailed to Bombay and married him. When he died three years later, Philomela remained in India and married another American missionary. The Records of the First Congregational Church of Dunbarton, 1789–1877, at the New Hampshire Historical Society show Philomela Thurston and her parents on the membership rolls prior to their moving to Bedford, New Hampshire. Some women in the mission field continued to command celebrity status well into the twentieth century, as I am reliably informed by Grant Wacker and several other distinguished historians of religion whom he interviewed on my behalf; they include Edith Blumhofer, Joel Carpenter, Elizabeth Flowers, Lydia Hoyle, Mandy McMichael, and William Svelmoe.

15 They enjoyed an especially: "Extracts from the Journal of Mrs. Nichols," *MH,* June 1819; the other accounts appear in *MH,* April, May, June, and Aug. 1821; Abigail Goodell to Elizabeth Dodd, Nov. 14, 1823, William Goodell Papers, Library of Congress. According to Ann Judson, the viceroy himself treated her and her husband "with much more familiarity and respect than are the natives of the country." Ann Hasseltine Judson, *A Particular Relation of the American Baptist Mission to the Burman Empire* (Washington, D.C., 1823), 35, 44. Abigail's experiences would have become widely known because of the common practice of families passing around and even publishing letters received from all foreign missionaries.

16 It was exactly that readership: Daniel Morton, *Religious Exercises of Miss Laura Chipman* (Middlebury, Vt., 1818), 9; Rufus Anderson journal, ABC 30, vol. 4, Aug. 5, 1815, and vol. 5, Jan. 30 and Feb. 2, 1816. A pioneering study of women missionaries is Barbara Welter, " 'She Hath Done What She Could': Women's Missionary Careers in Nineteenth-Century America," in *Women in American Religion,* ed. Janet Wilson James (Philadelphia: University of Pennsylvania Press, 1980), 111–25. On missionary memoirs, see Ashley E. Moreshead, " 'Beyond All Ambitious Motives': Missionary Memoirs and the Cultivation of Early American Evangelical Heroines," *Journal of the Early Republic* 38, no. 1 (Spring 2018): 37–60; Mary Kupiec Cayton,

"Canonizing Harriet Newell: Women, the Evangelical Press, and the Foreign Mission Movement in New England, 1800–1840," in *Competing Kingdoms: Women, Mission, Nation, and the American Protestant Empire, 1812–1960,* ed. Barbara Reeves-Ellington, Kathryn Kish Sklar, and Connie A. Shemo (Durham, N.C.: Duke University Press, 2010), 69–93; Joan Jacobs Brumberg, *Mission for Life: The Story of the Family of Adoniram Judson* (New York: Free Press, 1980), 76–77. Scholars estimate literacy in northern New England at 90 percent for men and 80 percent for women. Joel Perlman, Silvana R. Siddali, and Keith Whitescarver, "Literacy, Schooling, and Teaching Among New England Women," *History of Education Quarterly* 37 (1997): 117–39.

17 Had there been a guide: Brumberg, *Mission for Life,* 56–59. As Amanda Porterfield observes, "Judson's life promoted a more aggressive and self-possessed image of female piety" than did the memoirs of earlier evangelical women, suggesting "a widespread but cautiously promoted eagerness for adventure, work, and self-mastery among antebellum Protestant women" (*Mary Lyon and the Mount Holyoke Missionaries,* 56, 59). Her view accords with Nancy Cott's estimate that "if the popular sales of the published memoirs of missionaries are any guide, that model of religious commitment, which proposed a submission of the self that was simultaneously a pronounced form of self-assertion, had wide appeal." *Bonds of Womanhood,* 141.

18 Standing out, garnering praise: Mary Kelley's *Learning to Stand and Speak* advances the important argument that female academies formed a subjectivity in which the rights and obligations of citizenship were fundamental to their students' sense of self. On ambition and academies, see Jason Opal, *Beyond the Farm: National Ambitions in Rural New England* (Philadelphia: University of Pennsylvania Press, 2008), 96–125, and Blauvelt, *Work of the Heart,* 62–70. I have argued elsewhere that young evangelicals of both sexes torn by their conflicting aspirations for selflessness and fame found plausible deniability for their ambition in missionary careers. Christine Leigh Heyrman, *American Apostles: When Evangelicals Entered the World of Islam* (New York: Hill and Wang, 2015), 32.

18 But he was then in his mid-forties: William Parker moved his family to Dunbarton between 1805 and 1810, leaving his parents behind

in Bradford. Appraisers calculated the worth of his real estate at $5,500.00 and his personal estate at $2,402.05, which in today's dollars would amount to about $74,900 and $32,687, respectively. But charges against the estate, mainly debts owed his neighbors, nearly equaled the value of his personal property (Inventory and Administration of William Parker's Estate, New Hampshire County Probate Records, 1660–1973, Probate Records, 1815–1818, 25:144–46, 598–99). For more information about the village, see Caleb Stark, *History of the Town of Dunbarton, Merrimack County, New Hampshire* (Concord: G. Parker Lyon, 1860). For the narrow range of employments open to young women in the early republic, see Cott, *Bonds of Womanhood*, 19–62.

19 While launching her three: The census of 1820 shows two persons engaged in agriculture in the widow Martha Parker's household, most likely her eldest surviving son, William, and a hired man; the census also notes one person engaged in commerce, a probable reference to her taking in lodgers. For other evidence that she kept a boarding-house, see no. 26 Gridley's Statement, ABC 74, which alludes to Elisha Jenney lodging at the Parker home. For the Parker-Mills marriage, see *Farmer's Cabinet* (Amherst, N.H.), Feb. 24, 1821. Emily entered Bradford Academy in 1818 (aged eighteen) and left in 1821, which suggests that she might also have served as an assistant teacher; Martha spent a single year as a student there in 1822 (also at the age of eighteen). Possibly her time at school was short because her sister Ann had left by the end of 1822, which might have raised Martha's tuition. Unlike her two eldest sisters, Martha spent a year at most in the academy. Perhaps Ann and Emily had homeschooled their younger sister during long winters in Dunbarton, when Bradford's "female department" shut down (*Semi-centennial Catalogue of the Officers and Students of Bradford Academy, 1803–1853* [Cambridge, Mass.: Metcalf, 1853], 3, 50, 61, 63). Between 1825 and 1860, about one-fourth of all native-born New England women taught school for some years of their lives, usually those prior to marriage (Lee Virginia Chambers-Schiller, *Liberty, a Better Husband: Single Women in America: The Generations of 1780–1840* [New Haven, Conn.: Yale University Press, 1984], 32). The great majority taught in common schools rather than academies.

19 Her new acquaintances: James Kimball to Isaac Bird, May 28, 1823, IBP; Pond, *Bradford,* 100; *New-Bedford Mercury,* April 18, 1823, and Feb. 25, 1825.

21 Or did suddenly becoming: John Farmer, "Descriptive and Historical Account of Boscawen, New Hampshire," *Collections of the Massachusetts Historical Society,* 2nd ser., 10 (1823): 71–76; *New Hampshire Repository* (Concord), April 5, 1824; *New Hampshire Observer* (Concord), March 21, April 23, June 6, May 2 and 9, 1825; Kelley, *Learning to Stand and Speak,* 66–111. The Parker sisters' school was a little pricier than most academies in New Hampshire, with tuition running $3.50 per quarter and board an additional dollar a week. The Adams Female Academy in Derry, New Hampshire, superintended by Zilpah Grant, a fervent evangelical who influenced Mount Holyoke's founder, Mary Lyon, offered an equally ambitious curriculum to a larger student body, and that institution probably served as a model for the Parker sisters.

22 Indeed, by involving: For an astute discussion of these themes and the close linkage between ideals of womanhood validating collective activism and the evolution of evangelical voluntary associations, see Anne M. Boylan, *The Origins of Women's Activism: New York and Boston, 1797–1840* (Chapel Hill: University of North Carolina Press, 2002), 7–9, 16–37. See also Martha Tomhave Blauvelt, "Women and Revivalism," in *Women and Religion in America: The Nineteenth Century,* ed. Rosemary R. Reuther and Rosemary Skinner Keller (New York: Harper & Row, 1981), 1–9; Ruth Bloch, "American Feminine Ideals in Transition: The Rise of the Moral Mother, 1785–1815," *Feminist Studies* 4 (June 1978): 101–26; Ruth Bloch, "The Gendered Meanings of Virtue in Revolutionary America," *Signs* 15 (Autumn 1987): 37–58; Cott, *Bonds of Womanhood,* 146–48; Catherine A. Brekus, *Strangers and Pilgrims: Female Preaching in America, 1740–1845* (Chapel Hill: University of North Carolina Press, 1998), 146–54; Barbara Leslie Epstein, *The Politics of Domesticity: Women, Evangelism, and Temperance in Nineteenth-Century America* (Middletown, Conn.: Wesleyan University Press, 1981), 77–85; Lori D. Ginzberg, *Women and the Work of Benevolence: Morality, Politics, and Class in the Nineteenth-Century United States* (New Haven, Conn.: Yale University Press, 1990), 5,

11–13; Mary Kelley, *Private Woman, Public Stage: Literary Domesticity in Nineteenth-Century America* (1984; Chapel Hill: University of North Carolina Press, 2002), xi–xiii; Jan Lewis, "The Republican Wife: Virtue and Seduction in the Early Republic," *William and Mary Quarterly,* 3rd ser., 44 (Oct. 1987): 689–721; Barbara Welter, "The Feminization of Religion in Nineteenth-Century America," in *Clio's Consciousness Raised,* ed. Lois Banner and Mary Hartman (New York: Octagon, 1973), 135–57; Amanda Porterfield, *Female Piety in Puritan New England: The Emergence of Religious Humanism* (New York: Oxford University Press, 1992), esp. 153–56.

23 Accordingly, James did a favor: James Kimball to Isaac and Ann Bird, March 3, 1823, IBP; no. 25 Kimball to Gridley, Aug. 15, 1826, ABC 74; JEN, 44. The fullest biographical treatment of Gridley appears in Leonard Woods, *Memoirs of American Missionaries* (Boston: Pierce and Parker, 1833), 127–34; see also Franklin Bowditch Dexter, *Biographical Notices of Graduates of Yale College* (New Haven, Conn.: issued as a supplement to the obituary record, 1913), 49–50.

25 Though hardly immune: JEN, 21–22, 27–34; no. 6 Extracts from Gridley's letter, Jan. 14, 1825, no. 7 Evarts to Gridley, March 2, 1825, and [unnumbered] Leonard Woods to Gridley, Nov. 3, 1827, all in ABC 74; James Kimball to Ann and Isaac Bird, Sept. 28, 1826, IBP. Both Gridley and Brewer belonged to the Brethren by 1821; for a membership list, see the Papers of the Brethren in the archives of the Andover-Newton Theological Society's library. Evarts learned of Fisk's death on April 10, 1826 (Evarts to Bird and Goodell, June 29, 1826, ABC 1.01, vol. 6). Thereafter the American Board evidently planned to partner William Goodell with Gridley, the latter to serve as an explorer missionary in Armenia.

25 And the sooner his son: Estate of Elijah Gridley, 1822, no. 1182, Farmington, Connecticut, Probate Packets, 1769–1880, microfilmed from State Library, Hartford, Conn., by the Family History Center. Elijah's real property amounted to about $330,000 in today's money; his total estate came to $469,000. The continuity of the male line remained a concern—even an obsession—among Elijah's descendants. The gravestone of his younger son, Elijah Omri Gridley (1802–1862), identifies him as "last relict in the male line of the ancient family in Farmington

of that name" (www.billiongraves.com). I am indebted to Bruce Mann of Harvard Law School for helping me to understand the will's provisions.

26 She, yielding at last: No. 9 Gridley to Evarts, Dec. 7, 1825; JEN, 42–44, 100. As late as mid-March 1826, the Prudential Committee was still pressing Gridley not to take a wife (Rufus Anderson to Isaac Bird and William Goodell, March 18, 1826, ABC 1.01, vol. 6). For descriptions of Gridley, see JEN, 27; Rufus Anderson to William Jowett, April 13, 1827, and Anderson to Daniel Temple, June 21, 1827, both in ABC 1.01, vol. 8. Because of James Kimball's friendship with Gridley, it's possible that Martha became acquainted with the latter before he made romantic overtures to her. But Kimball dated the beginning of the couple's formal courtship to the fall of 1825. JEN, 100.

27 No sooner had they wed: Leonard Woods to Samuel Worcester, n.d. 1817, ABC 6, Candidate Department, vol. 1, no. 56; see also Evarts to Worcester, Aug. 14, 1815, and June 18, 1816, ABC 11, vol. 1, microfilm copy; Robert, *American Women in Mission*, 10, 18–24; Jennifer Thigpen, *Island Queens and Missionary Wives: How Gender and Empire Remade Hawai'i and the Pacific World* (Chapel Hill: University of North Carolina Press, 2014), 41–43. For young ministers assisting future missionaries in recruiting marriage partners, see E. D. G. Prime, *Forty Years in the Turkish Empire; or, Memoirs of Rev. William Goodell* (1876), 52–59.

27 Emily, in turn, believed: No. 27 Tenney's Statement, 13, ABC 74; James Kimball to Ann and Isaac Bird, May 18, 1823, IBP. On love-based marriage and its relationship to the rise of individualism and the culture of sensibility, see Anya Jabour, *Marriage in the Early Republic: Elizabeth and William Wirt and the Companionate Ideal* (Baltimore: Johns Hopkins University Press, 1998), 2–3, 8–9; Timothy Kenslea, *The Sedgwicks in Love: Courtship, Engagement, and Marriage in the Early Republic* (Hanover, N.H.: University Press of New England, 2006), 43; Lucia McMahon, "'While Our Souls Together Blend': Narrating a Romantic Readership in the Early Republic," in *An Emotional History of the United States,* ed. Peter N. Stearns and Jan Lewis (New York: New York University Press, 1998), 67–68, 81; Anthony Giddens, *The Transformation of Intimacy: Sexuality, Love, and Eroti-*

cism in Modern Societies (Stanford, Calif.: Stanford University Press, 1992), 26; Blauvelt, *Work of the Heart,* 86.

28 Then again, understanding: Woods, *Memoirs of Mrs. Harriet Newell,* 179; Edward Hooker, *Memoir of Mrs. Sarah Lanman Smith,* 2nd ed. (Boston: Perkins and Marvin, 1840), 296, 298. For a thoughtful exploration of marriages among the earliest cohort of American missionaries, see Emily Conroy-Krutz, "The Forgotten Wife: Roxana Nott and Missionary Marriage in Bombay," *Early American Studies* 16, no. 1 (Winter 2018): 64–90. Dana Robert and Patricia Grimshaw have emphasized that women who agreed to such marriages had long hoped for a career in missions and found in such unions a way to fulfill their vocational ambitions (Robert, *American Women in Mission,* 18–24; Patricia Grimshaw, *Paths of Duty: American Missionary Wives in Nineteenth-Century Hawaii* [Honolulu: University of Hawaii Press, 1989], 6–23). David Brooks has written about present-day couples who view marriage as "a binding moral project" in "Three Views of Marriage," *New York Times,* Feb. 23, 2016. *Mariage blanc* was a rarity among missionary couples, but the regular appearance of children reveals nothing about whether or for how long love came to figure in these unions.

30 What more could Madam Mills: No. 35 Gridley to Martha Parker, Sept. 8, 1826, and [unnumbered] Leonard Woods to Gridley, Nov. 3, 1827, both in ABC 74.

32 "I sometimes think": Extract of a letter from Martha Parker dated Aug. 13, 1826, in no. 33 Continued Tenney Narrative, 14, and no. 25 James Kimball to Gridley, Aug. 15, 1826, both in ABC 74.

CHAPTER TWO: THE REDEEMER'S CHILDREN

34 Yes, she would see him: No. 30 Extracts from Miss Parker's letters to Sarah Tenney, ABC 74.

36 Tittle-tattle from so obscure: No. 21 Tenney to Evarts, no. 10 Anonymous to Evarts, June 12, 1826, no. 11 Evarts to William Gould, June 17, 1826, no. 12 Gould to Evarts, June 19, 1826, no. 13 Evarts to Gould, June 24, 1826, no. 15 Gould to Evarts, July 1, 1826, all in ABC 74; JEN, 39–40, 42–43, 46; Evarts to Isaac Bird and William Goodell, June 29,

1826, ABC 1.01, vol. 6; Justus W. French to Samuel Worcester, n.d. [ca. 1817–1829], ABC 6, Candidate Department, vol. 1. What dampened Evarts's enthusiasm for Gridley's "going out" single was the death of Pliny Fisk, news of which reached Evarts during his southern tour. Without the veteran Fisk's guidance, any novice missionary would have had great difficulty navigating the Levant.

39 Even unconverted, Martha: No. 27 Tenney's Statement, 16, ABC 74; Ann Parker Bird to Gridley, Feb. 10, 1827, ABC 16.5, microfilm reel 502; Tenney to Bezaliel Smith, Nov. 3, 1825, Rauner Library, Dartmouth College, cited in Kelly, *In the New England Fashion,* 198; Isaac Bird's Journal, Jan. 13, 1829, IBP. Decades of intermarriage had turned the Merrimack Valley into a tangled cousinry that stretched from Massachusetts into New Hampshire. A shirttail connection might also have linked Thomas to the Kimball clan.

40 Can we ever know?: Tenney improbably professed to have written this portion of his narrative (no. 27 Tenney's Statement, ABC 74), only to explain himself to Martha's friends after she broke their engagement— which took place early in 1826—and "without any intimation having been made to him, that objections could be preferred against her to the Committee" (JEN, 109). It's far more likely that what prompted him to write the statement was receiving Evarts's inquiries and complying with Bennet Tyler's request to answer them (no. 20 Tyler to Evarts, July 21, 1826, ABC 74). On the history of emotions, see "AHR Conversation: The Historical Study of the Emotions," *American Historical Review* 117 (2012): 1487–531; William Reddy, *The Navigation of Feeling: A Framework for the History of Emotions* (Cambridge, U.K.: Cambridge University Press, 2001); Barbara H. Rosenwein, *Generations of Feeling: A History of Emotions, 600–1700* (Cambridge, U.K.: Cambridge University Press, 2016).

40 The answer this time came: No. 27 Tenney's Statement, 1, ABC 74. Young women sometimes put off their suitors, either refusing to respond immediately to a proposal or rejecting it outright as a way of testing men's affection. Doubtless Thomas hoped that Martha was among them. On this practice, see Blauvelt, *Work of the Heart,* 83, 108–9.

42 Thomas felt sure: No. 27 Tenney's Statement, 2–4, ABC 74; Ann

Parker Bird to Gridley, Feb. 20, 1827, ABC 16.5, microfilm reel 502.

42 Whatever he said stopped: JEN, 43–44.

43 Thomas crawled back: No. 27 Tenney's Statement, 4–6, ABC 74. Elisha's stay at the Parker home dates to December 1825, a month before Dartmouth's usual winter recess. Most Dartmouth students received permission to extend their winter vacation to three months or more for the purpose of teaching school (Jonathan Fox Worcester, *A Memorial of the Class of 1827, Dartmouth College,* 2nd ed. [Hanover, N.H., 1869], 76). Elisha's father, Levi Jenney, had amassed an estate worth nearly $700,000 in today's money at his death in 1850. His assets included shares in a cotton factory and more than twenty vessels (see the probate records for Levi Jenney, 1850 and 1865, Bristol County Probate Records, Commonwealth of Massachusetts, 1690–1881, Family History Center, microfilm roll 16). By contrast, William Parker's estate even before administration amounted to less than $110,000 in today's money. Elisha claimed that Martha had chosen a rich man over him by getting engaged to Elnathan, possibly because Elnathan stood to come into his patrimony sooner than did Elisha or perhaps because Levi Jenney came into his considerable fortune in the decades after 1826.

44 The missionary had renewed: No. 27 Tenney Statement, 7–9, ABC 74; JEN, 100.

46 Even a minister's wife: No. 27 Tenney's Statement, 10–12, ABC 74.

46 She would regret it: Ibid., 12–15, and #26 Gridley's Statement, ABC 74.

47 Reconciled to the will: No. 27 Tenney's Statement, 15–16, ABC 74.

48 Then, out of the blue: No. 26 Gridley's Statement, and No. 27 Tenney's Statement, 16–17, both in ABC 74.

49 Indeed, the immersion: For the eighteenth century's elevation of sensibility, see John Brewer, *A Sentimental Murder: Love and Madness in the Eighteenth Century* (New York: Farrar, Straus and Giroux, 2004); G. J. Barker-Benfield, *The Culture of Sensibility: Sex and Society in Eighteenth-Century Britain* (Chicago: University of Chicago Press, 1996); Andrew Burstein, *Sentimental Democracy: The Evolution of America's Romantic Self-Image* (New York: Hill and Wang, 1999); Sarah Knott, *Sensibility and the American Revolution* (Chapel Hill: University of North Carolina Press, 2009).

50 Each, too, favored: No. 27 Tenney's Statement, 9, ABC 74. On the penchant of academy alumnae to refer to themselves in the third person, see Blauvelt, *Work of the Heart,* 31.

51 In all those ways: No. 27 Tenney's Statement, 13, 15, ABC 74; James and Emily Kimball to Ann and Isaac Bird, Sept. 28, 1826, IBP. Northerners typically exhibited greater restraint under revival preaching than did Southerners. Camp meetings pitched in Kentucky backwoods clearings built to a crescendo of ecstatic responses among some in attendance—swooning and dancing, barking and "jerking"—as they plumbed the depths of their sinfulness and sought the assurance of salvation. By contrast, those attending a New Hampshire revival might allow themselves only an occasional sob of relief or groan of remorse. But even if they did not rattle the meetinghouse rafters, Yankee preachers still put audiences in touch with their feelings and beckoned their expression. For an eyewitness description of early-nineteenth-century revivals among New England Presbyterians and Congregationalists, see Bennet Tyler, *Memoir of the Life and Character of the Rev. Asahel Nettleton, D.D.,* 4th ed. (Boston: Doctrinal Tract and Book Society, 1852). For a discussion of the foreign missions movement as a link between evangelicalism and sensibility, see Heyrman, *American Apostles,* 33. Ruth Bloch has pointed up evangelicalism's sacralization of the emotions as one source of a new conception of romantic love among the middle and upper classes in the early republic ("Changing Conceptions of Sexuality and Romance in Eighteenth-Century America," *William and Mary Quarterly* 60 [Jan. 2003]: 13–42). On the "new emotional standards for intimate relationships" that individualism and the cult of sensibility encouraged, see McMahon, "'While Our Souls Together Blend,'" 67. For an illuminating discussion of the ways in which religious seriousness encouraged friends "to lay bare their souls," see Shelby M. Balik, "'Dear Christian Friends': Charity Bryant, Sylvia Drake, and the Making of a Spiritual Network," *Journal of Social History* 50, no. 4 (Summer 2017): 630–54. For an analysis of the influence of revival emotionalism on antebellum sentimentalism, see Claudia Stokes, *The Altar at Home: Sentimental Literature and Nineteenth-Century American Religion* (Philadelphia: University of Pennsylvania Press, 2014), 21–47. On the con-

nection between revivalism and romanticism, see Perry Miller, *The Life of the Mind in America: From the American Revolution to the Civil War* (New York: Harcourt Brace, 1965), 60–61, and Ralph H. Gabriel, "Evangelical Religion and Popular Romanticism in Early Nineteenth Century America," *Church History* 19, no. 1 (March 1950): 34–47.

54 Veterans of today's digital dating: Ann Parker Bird to Gridley, Feb. 10, 1827, ABC 16.5, microfilm reel 502; James Kimball to Isaac Bird, May 28, 1823, IBP; Records, First Congregational Church of Dunbarton, 1789–1877, entries for July 4, 1816, and May 9, 1824, New Hampshire Historical Society; no. 27 Tenney's Statement, 13, ABC 74. No record exists of the date that Ann joined the church; Emily joined at sixteen, and another Parker sister, Marianne, joined at seventeen. What would have heightened Martha's concerns about her eternal fate was the New Divinity's emphasis on "immediate repentance." In pulpit appeals targeting the young, their preachers taught that the longer they took converting, the less likely they were to find divine forgiveness. Kling, *Field of Divine Wonders*, 196–97; Sweeney, *Nathaniel William Taylor*, 33.

57 But the possibility that Thomas: JEN, 24. On sexuality, see Ellen K. Rothman, *Hands and Hearts: A History of Courtship in America* (New York: Basic Books, 1984), 23–25, 45–49, 50–51; Daniel Scott Smith and Michael S. Hindus, "Premarital Pregnancy in America, 1640–1971: An Overview and Interpretation," *Journal of Interdisciplinary History* 5 (1974–1975): 537–70; Laurel Thatcher Ulrich, *A Midwife's Tale: The Life of Martha Ballard, Based on Her Diary, 1785–1812* (New York: Knopf, 1990), 156–58. Ulrich finds that some families condoned premarital sex but others did not. All agreed that marriage should certainly follow and that fathers as well as mothers were responsible for children born out of wedlock. New Divinity culture sanctioned mixed gatherings at singing schools and sleigh rides. It shunned dancing parties or balls but permitted young men to visit the homes of young women and allowed courting couples, even if not yet engaged, to sit together in the parlor late at night without parental supervision. Patricia Cline Cohen points out that rates of prebridal pregnancy among New Englanders in the late eighteenth century ranged from 30 to 40 percent, so its incidence was declining by the 1820s,

marking the increased cultural value put on virginity, enforced by the belief in women's "passionlessness." *The Murder of Helen Jewett: The Life and Death of a Prostitute in Nineteenth-Century New York* (New York: Alfred A. Knopf, 1998), 226–29.

58 Should anyone try: Aaron Bigelow, *A Sketch of Courtship Between Aaron Bigelow and Susan Griggs* (Boston: printed for the author, 1814). Their intimacies included intercourse, because at one point Susan feared being pregnant and wondered if they had "done right to do as we had done before marriage."

59 She promised to withdraw: No. 33 Continued Tenney Narrative, 2–3, ABC 74; Isaac Bird to Jeremiah Evarts, Jan. 20, 1829, ABC 16.6, vol. 2, microfilm reel 514.

CHAPTER THREE: PATRIARCHS UNDER PRESSURE

66 Between Joseph and Julius Caesar: No. 18 Tyler to Evarts, July 13, 1826, no. 19 Evarts to Tyler, July 18, 1826, no. 20 Tyler to Evarts, July 21, 1826, all in ABC 74; JEN, 58. On Tyler's career, see Nahum Gale, *A Memoir of the Reverend Bennet Tyler* (Boston: J. E. Tilton, 1860), 40, 46, 127, 131–33; Baxter Perry Smith, *History of Dartmouth College* (Boston: Houghton, Osgood, 1878), 132–38; Wilder Dwight Quid, *The Story of Dartmouth* (Boston: Little, Brown, 1914), 115–19, 125, 131–36. For the location of "the Missionary Rooms," see Rufus Anderson to Bird and Goodell, March 18, 1826, and Anderson to Daniel Temple, March 24, 1826, both in ABC 1.01, vol. 6.

68 He added that President Tyler: JEN, 57; no. 21 Tenney to Evarts, July n.d., 1826, ABC 74.

72 The same qualities that made: No. 26 Gridley's Statement, no. 25 James Kimball to Gridley, Aug. 15, 1826, both in ABC 74; JEN, 75–76. Elnathan's statement has Martha agreeing twice to marry Thomas but breaking it off both times within a few days; other sources mention only a single formal engagement.

73 Whatever the case, Evarts: No. 23 Evarts to Tenney, Aug. 8, 1826, ABC 74; JEN, 69.

75 "They take only": No. 22 Woods to Evarts, Aug. 8, 1826, ABC 74; JEN, 63, 64, 66, 67, 72; Baker, *Reminiscences of Woods,* 131; Woods,

Memoirs of Mrs. Harriet of Newell, 20. Medieval and early modern scholars have done pioneering work on the relationship between spiritually gifted women and their male hagiographers; see especially Jodi Bilinkoff, *Related Lives: Confessors and Their Female Penitents, 1450–1750* (Ithaca, N.Y.: Cornell University Press, 2005); John W. Coakley, *Women, Men, and Spiritual Power: Female Saints and Their Male Collaborators* (New York: Columbia University Press, 2006); and Catherine M. Mooney, ed., *Gendered Voices: Medieval Saints and Their Interpreters* (Philadelphia: University of Pennsylvania Press, 1999).

77   During his tours of the South: Worcester to Mrs. Sarah Bonney, Feb. 15, 1817, Worcester to Miss Sarah Vaill, Dec. 2, 1818, Samuel Worcester, Letterbooks, ABC 1.01, vol. 2, ABC; Parsons to Fisk, Oct. 23, 1817, ABC, microfilm reel 502; Evarts to Battelle, Feb. 9, 1822, ABC 8.2.13, and Battelle to Evarts, ABC 10, vol. 3, Jan. 5 and 29, 1822, ABC; Evarts to Worcester, April 21, 1817, Evarts to Worcester, Feb. 19, March 4, and April 16, 1818, all in ABC 11, vol. 1, microfilm. Trust my colleague Anne Boylan to know that Evarts's wife served as an officer in the Female Society for Promoting Christianity Among the Jews, which sponsored an American Board missionary in the Mediterranean. Besides Boylan's definitive *Origins of Women's Activism,* the secondary literature on women's voluntary societies includes Barbara J. Berg, *The Remembered Gate: Origins of American Feminism* (New York: Oxford University Press, 1978); Cott, *Bonds of Womanhood,* 142–59; Bruce Dorsey, *Reforming Men and Women: Gender in the Antebellum City* (Ithaca, N.Y.: Cornell University Press, 2002); Ginzberg, *Women and the Work of Benevolence,* esp. 14–17, 25–26, 34–35, 33–66; Nancy Hewitt, *Women's Activism and Social Change: Rochester, New York, 1822–1872* (Ithaca, N.Y.: Cornell University Press, 1983); Kelly, *In the New England Fashion,* 199–203; Carolyn J. Lawes, *Women and Reform in a New England Community, 1815–1860* (Lexington: University Press of Kentucky, 2000); Mary Ryan, *Women in Public: Between Banners and Ballots, 1825–1880* (Baltimore: Johns Hopkins University Press, 1990). By the mid-1820s, the American Board "had grown to the point that its ambitions constantly threatened to outrun its resources," according to John A. Andrew, making the fund-raising work of women all the more important. *From Revivals to Removal:*

Jeremiah Evarts, the Cherokee Nation, and the Search for the Soul of America (Athens: University of Georgia Press, 1992), 130, 165.

78 Only a few letters: No. 25 Kimball to Gridley, Aug. 15, 1826, ABC 74; JEN, 65, 86.

79 Bad enough if she lost: JEN, 65–66, 71. Besides serving on the American Board's Prudential Committee, Tyler had a son who became a missionary to the Zulus of South Africa. Gale, *Memoir of Tyler,* 97, 128–29.

80 The power of this notion: There is a rich literature treating the emergence of the doctrine of "separate spheres." My thinking about its origins within the evangelical movement owes a great deal to Rosemarie Zagarri's emphasis on the doctrine arising in reaction to women's more extensive involvement in politics in the early republic and serving as a way to justify their exclusion from the electorate (*Revolutionary Backlash: Women and Politics in the Early Republic* [Philadelphia: University of Pennsylvania Press, 2007], 115–73). Many scholars have called attention to the evangelical movement's pivotal role in placing limits on women's engagement with politics, beginning with Barbara Welter, "The Cult of True Womanhood, 1820–1860," *American Quarterly* (Summer 1966): 151–74. Ellen DuBois agrees, observing that ministers "controlled women's moral energies and kept pietistic activism from becoming political activism" (*Feminism and Suffrage: The Emergence of an Independent Women's Movement in America, 1848–1869* [Ithaca, N.Y.: Cornell University Press, 1978], 33–34). Nancy Cott argues that women's benevolent and reform organizations accorded women just enough in the way of self-worth to keep them within a clerically defined compass. She adds that even though evangelicals "fostered women's emergence as social actors," those roles were "based on female responsibility rather than on human rights" (*Bonds of Womanhood,* 140–41, 156–59). Lori Ginzberg takes a similar view, positing that by the 1820s evangelical Protestantism served as a justification for limiting women's standing and authority in political debate by emphasizing that because of their having special responsibilities of a religious nature, wives and mothers would be diminished by attaining full political rights (see her *Women and the Work of Benevolence,* 17, 25–26, 34–35, and her more recent study, *Untidy Origins: A Story of Wom-*

en's Rights in Antebellum New York [Chapel Hill: University of North Carolina Press, 2005]). Other interpretations construe evangelicalism's influence on women's status and scope as more ambiguous, improving them in some ways, diminishing them in others. Ruth Bloch writes that "it provided ideological justification and incentive for the contraction of female activity into the preoccupations of motherhood" but also "broke with tradition by attributing to women strong moral authority and granting them an important field of special expertise" ("American Feminine Ideals in Transition"). Similarly, David Kling notes that New Divinity evangelicalism "at once reinforced the cult of domesticity as well as challenged it" (*Field of Divine Wonders,* 206–7, 220, 222–23). In her study of voluntary associations, Anne Boylan contends that such organizations "gave energetic women a place to exercise voice and decision-making power," even as their members "adopted a complementary rather than equal model of gender relations," one "predicated on male supremacy" (*Origins of Women's Activism,* 7–8). Other studies emphasizing the ways in which evangelical belief and practice could empower women include Joanna Bowen Gillespie, "The Clear Leanings of Providence: Pious Memoirs and the Problems of Self-Realization for Women in the Early Nineteenth Century," *Journal of the Early Republic* 5 (Summer 1985): 197–221, and Catherine Brekus, *Strangers and Pilgrims,* 117–54, 274–75. For discussions of the growing awareness of the power exerted by voluntary associations, see Johann N. Neem, *Creating a Nation of Joiners: Democracy and Civil Society in Early National Massachusetts* (Cambridge, Mass.: Harvard University Press, 2008); Maartje Janse, "'Association Is a Mighty Engine': Mass Organization and the Machine Metaphor, 1825–1840," in *Organizing Democracy: Reflections on the Rise of Political Organization in the Nineteenth Century,* ed. Henk te Velde and Maartje Janse (Basingstoke, U.K.: Palgrave Macmillan, 2016), 32–33.

CHAPTER FOUR: SATISFACTION

84 Perhaps she availed herself: No. 24 Tenney to Evarts, Aug. 12, 1826, and no. 25 Kimball to Gridley, Aug. 15, 1826, both in ABC 74; JEN,

77; Benjamin Hale Correspondence, Sept. 17 and 24, Oct. 9, 1827, Rauner Library; John King Lord, *A History of Dartmouth College, 1815–1909* (Concord, N.H.: Rumford Press, 1913), 48–49; Worcester, *Memorial of the Class of 1827*, 79–80. Estimates put Hanover's population at just over six hundred in the 1820s.

86 Making their acquaintance: For a striking parallel in the early modern period illustrating the Catholic clergy's often ambivalent response to spiritually gifted women, see Jodi Bilinkoff, "Navigating the Waves (of Devotion): Toward a Gendered Analysis of Early Modern Catholicism," in *Crossing Boundaries: Attending to Early Modern Women*, ed. Jane Donawerth and Adele Seeff (Newark: University of Delaware Press, 2000), 161–72.

87 It answered to his aggrievement: JEN, 54, 89; no. 26 Gridley's Statement, and no. 24 Tenney to Evarts, Aug. 12, 1826, both in ABC 74; John D. Kingsbury, *Sketch of the Reverend Silas Aiken* (Cambridge, Mass.: Welch, Bigelow, 1870).

89 Would the poor fellow: Bird to Gridley, Feb. 16, 1827, ABC 16.5, reel 502; Worcester, *Memorial of the Class of 1827*, 82; Shelby Balik, *Rally the Scattered Believers: Northern New England's Religious Geography* (Bloomington: Indiana University Press, 2014), 129. Newspapers in the 1820s in the United States routinely carried stories about breach of promise suits, and cases involving actual seduction abounded in the courts. Patricia Cline Cohen finds that between 1815 and 1830 "courts increasingly entertained cases of jilted brides and desolate or pregnant lovers and began to award fairly hefty damages, typically from five hundred to two thousand dollars," thus "compensating women and their families for loss of reputation, emotional damage, and lowered marital chances." *Murder of Helen Jewett*, 200, 209.

92 "I know not what": Benjamin Hale to Caroline Hale, Sept. 17, 1827, Hale Correspondence; Barrows, *Memorial of Bradford Academy*, 69; Brumberg, *Mission for Life*, 58; no. 26 Gridley's Statement; Evarts to Worcester, Dec. 22, 1820, ABC 11, vol. 1, microfilm; Anderson to Evarts, June 17, 1822, ABC 11, vol. 1, microfilm; Rufus Anderson, *Memoir of Catharine Brown, a Christian Indian of the Cherokee Nation* (Boston: Armstrong, Crocker, and Brewster, 1825); Woods, *Memoirs of*

Mrs. Harriet Newell, 30. Some evangelical ministers expressed ambivalence about women's involvement in all benevolent and reform activism; see Berg, *Remembered Gate*, 150–52.

93 Instead, they reveled in: Zagarri, *Revolutionary Backlash*, 82–186; Jean Harvey Baker, "Public Women and Partisan Politics, 1840–1860," in *A Political Nation: New Directions in Mid-Nineteenth-Century American Political History*, ed. Gary W. Gallagher and Rachel A. Sheldon (Charlottesville: University of Virginia Press, 2012), 65–81.

94 Even more irksome: Ann Parker Bird and Isaac Bird to Jeremiah Evarts, April 3, 1827, ABC 16.5, reel 502; JEN, 51.

I am indebted to Thomas Calvin Carter for tracking down this telling information about the Gould family. For their information, see www.findagrave.com.

95 In other words, what the three: Dartmouth College Society of Inquiry Records, 1821–1872, April 1, May 6, Nov. 4, 1822, April 7, July 7, 1823, June 6, 1824, April 4, Aug. 1, 1825, Rauner Library. The model for Dartmouth's Society of Inquiry, founded in 1821, was similar groups at Yale, Princeton, and Andover Theological Seminary.

97 The best that could be said: No. 33 Continued Tenney Narrative, 2–4, and no. 27 Tenney's Statement, 10–14, both in ABC 74; JEN, 76.

98 In awe of Ann Judson: James Kimball to Ann and Isaac Bird, March 3 and May 18, 1823, IBP.

98 And both William and James: No. 25 Kimball to Gridley, Aug. 15, 1826, ABC 74.

99 Had the tutor freely: JEN, 48.

102 "Our mothers and": Clergymen at the New Lebanon conference divided over whether women should be allowed to pray aloud in social meetings. A growing number of more liberal Congregationalists and Presbyterians were allowing women to testify and exhort at prayer meetings. Catherine Brekus has detected clues that even female preaching began to spread into mainline churches during the late 1820s and the 1830s (Brekus, *Strangers and Pilgrims*, 271–79; Balik, *Rally the Scattered Believers*, 122–23). For the involvement of women in Finney's revivals, see Charles Hambrick-Stowe, *Charles Finney and the Spirit of American Evangelicalism* (Grand Rapids, Mich.: William B. Eerdmans Publishing Company, 1986), 50–57, 60–61, 68–73;

Nancy A. Hardesty, *Your Daughters Shall Prophesy: Revivalism and Feminism in the Age of Finney* (Brooklyn: Carlson, 1991), 79–93, 156–58; Ryan, *Cradle of the Middle Class,* 92–104; William McLoughlin, *Modern Revivalism: Charles Grandison Finney to Billy Graham* (New York: Ronald, Press Co., 1959), 27. For the opposition to women's participation, see John Frost to Charles Finney, April 21, 1827, Finney Papers, Oberlin College Archives, cited in Hewitt, *Women's Activism and Social Change,* 72; Tyler, *Memoir of Nettleton,* 213–14, 243; William B. Sprague, *Lectures on Revivals of Religion* (Glasgow: William Collins, 1832), lxxxvii, 326, 438–39. Leonard Woods also opposed women speaking in church but tried to make light of his opposition. Baker, *Reminiscences of Woods,* 130.

103 So, too, did the complaint: Heyrman, *American Apostles,* 69; Harriette Newell Woods Baker, *Reminiscences and Records of My Father, Rev. Leonard Woods, D.D., of Andover* (Boston: Alfred Mudge & Son, 1887), 109–10. For Catharine Beecher, see "An Address to the Protestant Clergy of the United States," in *The Evils Suffered by American Women and Children* (New York: Harper & Brothers, 1847), 33. For anti-Catholicism on both sides of the Atlantic, see Ryan K. Smith, *Gothic Arches, Latin Crosses: Anti-Catholicism and American Church Designs in the Nineteenth Century* (Chapel Hill: University of North Carolina Press, 2006); Jon Gjerde, *Catholicism and the Shaping of Nineteenth-Century America,* ed. S. Deborah Kang (New York: Cambridge University Press, 2012); Jenny Franchot, *Roads to Rome: The Antebellum Protestant Encounter with Catholicism* (Berkeley: University of California Press, 1994); John Wolffe, "Anti-Catholicism and Evangelical Identity in Britain and the United States, 1830–1860," in *Evangelicalism: Comparative Studies of Popular Protestantism in North America, the British Isles, and Beyond, 1700–1990,* ed. Mark A. Noll, David W. Bebbington, and George A. Rawlyk (New York: Oxford University Press, 1994), 179–97; John Wolffe, "A Transatlantic Perspective: Protestants and National Identities in Mid-Nineteenth-Century Britain and the United States," in *Protestantism and National Identity: Britain and Ireland, c. 1650–c. 1850,* ed. Tony Claydon and Ian McBride (Cambridge, U.K.: Cambridge University Press, 1998), 291–309. For the appeal of the Virgin Mary to antebellum Protestant

women, see Elizabeth Hayes Alvarez, *The Valiant Woman: The Virgin Mary in Nineteenth-Century American Culture* (Chapel Hill: University of North Carolina Press, 2016). Perhaps not coincidentally, this young woman who delighted in dressing as a nun became the mother of Elizabeth Stuart Phelps Ward, a postbellum women's rights activist.

103 Small wonder, resonating: For the ways in which rumors flourish by answering to a culture's fears and preoccupations, see Gregory Evans Dowd, *Groundless Rumors, Legends, and Hoaxes on the Early American Frontier* (Baltimore: Johns Hopkins University Press, 2015); James E. Lewis Jr., *The Burr Conspiracy: Uncovering the Story of an Early American Crisis* (Princeton, N.J.: Princeton University Press, 2017).

CHAPTER FIVE: A COQUETTE?

106 What held her back: No. 33 Continued Tenney Narrative, 16, Extract of a letter from Martha Parker to Sarah Tenney, Aug. 2, 1826, in no. 33 Continued Tenney Narrative, 8, both in ABC 74.

107 No wonder, then, that: Extract of a letter from Martha Parker to Thomas Tenney, Aug. 13, 1826, in no. 33 Continued Tenney Narrative, 41, ABC 74; Records, First Congregational Church of Dunbarton, 1789–1877, entries for Oct. 31, 1824, Dec. 17, 1826, April 22, 1827, March 2 and 5, 1835, New Hampshire Historical Society. On church affiliation in northern New England, see Balik, *Rally the Scattered Believers*, 116–18.

108 Martha could easily end up: Gridley to Isaac and Ann Bird, n.d., as cited in Bird to Evarts, Jan. 20, 1829, ABC, reel 514. Many young women in the early republic postponed their marriages after becoming engaged, some because they enjoyed their brief period of empowerment, others to see if the man would remain constant in his affection, still others because they feared abandoning the security of the parental household or their responsibilities to their families. Blauvelt, *Work of the Heart*, 108–9; Kelly, *In the New England Fashion*, 107–10; Rothman, *Hands and Hearts*, 71–74.

109 If she regained Thomas's good graces: No. 26 Gridley's Statement, ABC 74.

111 That should be satisfaction: Extract of a letter from Martha Parker to

Thomas Tenney, July 30, 1826, and Extract of a letter from Martha Parker to Sarah Tenney, Aug. 2, 1826, in no. 33 Continued Tenney Narrative, 5–8, ABC 74.

111 She credited Thomas: Note how closely Martha channeled Thomas's declaration at Townshend, in which he described discerning in their broken engagement "the design of God," a recognition that made him regard his years of heartbreak as "one of the most profitable occurrences of my life." Their drawing on religion as a resource brings to mind Robert Darnton's observation that ordinary people "think with things, or with anything else that their culture makes available to them, such as stories or ceremonies." *The Great Cat Massacre and Other Episodes in French Cultural History* (New York: Basic Books, 1984), 4.

112 All in all, it was: No. 33 Continued Tenney Narrative, 6, ABC 74.

113 Most encouraging of all: JEN, 85.

113 He told the president: No. 33 Continued Tenney Narrative, 4, ABC 74.

114 "if she feels as she ought": Ibid., 9–11.

115 Intellectually, he had rejected: Douglas L. Wilson, *Honor's Voice: The Transformation of Abraham Lincoln* (New York: Knopf, 1998), 215–92.

116 It was a world: Harriet Beecher Stowe, *The Minister's Wooing* (1859; New York: Penguin Books, 1999), 294, 302–3, 308. Stowe's story unfolds in late-eighteenth-century Newport, Rhode Island.

117 Ah, there would be no need: No. 33 Continued Tenney Narrative, 11–13, ABC 74. Thomas asked Tyler to write to Walter Harris or to Martha herself expressing his views of her engagement to Gridley being "null and void," but Tyler declined, thinking "it important, that Mr. Gridley, Martha and the P[rudential]. Com. should know my feelings [his willingness to marry Martha himself] before any decision was made."

118 Or recalled by her faith: No. 26 Gridley's Statement, ABC 74.

119 Still, she added: Martha Parker to Thomas Tenney, Aug. 13, 1826, in no. 33 Continued Tenney Narrative, 13–16, ABC 74.

120 No, the truth: Martha Parker to Sarah Tenney, Aug. 2, 1826, 8, in no. 33 Continued Tenney Narrative, 17–18, ABC 74. Martha's statement to Evarts also admits to her being "governed by proud feelings"

when she broke her engagement to Tenney (no. 28 Parker to Evarts, Aug. 29, 1826, ABC 74). Thomas consistently emphasized that Martha had rejected him for reasons that were untrue. In his version, she told Emily Parker Kimball that she didn't love him, and her sister objected to the engagement on those grounds. But Martha told Evarts during his visit to Dunbarton that Emily had objected to the engagement for other reasons (no. 29 Conversation Between Mr. Evarts and Miss Parker, ABC 74). Martha didn't disclose to Evarts what Emily's actual objections were—or he did not see fit to mention them. It's possible that Martha was shading the truth to protect herself and/or that Emily's strongest reservations about the engagement were so unflattering to Thomas—fundamental concerns about his character—that Martha didn't wish to disclose them. For his part, Elnathan believed that Thomas had somehow manipulated Emily into saying that "had she known all the circumstances" of Martha's relationship with Thomas, "she should have desired the connexion." In other words, he charged that Thomas made out Martha to be a liar, when in fact she was only trying to shield her sister. No. 26 Gridley's Statement, ABC 74.

121 And if that great man: Thomas Tenney to Martha Parker, Aug. 10, 1826, 13, in no. 33 Continued Tenney Narrative, ABC 74. Martha was writing love letters to Elnathan during the same weeks, as both Thomas and Evarts acknowledged. But Thomas believed because her letters to Elnathan were scrutinized by friends, Martha felt obliged to express "stronger attachment" than she felt. In fact, Thomas was explaining away the ardor of Martha's correspondence. According to Evarts, her letters to Elnathan "manifested a strong attachment" and contained "some expressions which appeared inconsistent" with her profession of love for Thomas. JEN, 107.

122 In her way, if not in ours: Virginia Woolf described one fictional heroine as an "organism that has been under the shadow of the rock these million years—feels the light fall on it, and sees coming her way a piece of strange food—knowledge, adventure, art. And she reaches out for it . . . and has to devise some entirely new combination of her resources, so highly developed for other purposes, so as to absorb the new into the old without disturbing the infinitely intricate and elabo-

rate balance of the whole." *A Room of One's Own* (1929; New York: Harcourt, 1989), 85.

122 When they parted: Gridley to Isaac and Ann Bird, Jan. 20, 1829, ABC 16.6, vol. 2, microfilm reel 514; JEN, 88–89.

123 Martha had led Elnathan: No. 27 Tenney's Statement, 2–3, 7, and no. 26 Gridley's Statement, both in ABC 74. Martha owned up to Thomas about her role in prompting his proposals, but she appears not to have disclosed that information to Elnathan or even the Kimballs. See extract of a letter from Martha Parker to Thomas Tenney, July 30, 1826, in no. 33 Continued Tenney Narrative, 5, ABC 74.

124 Elnathan responded similarly: No. 27 Tenney's Statement, 10, and no. 35 Gridley to Parker, Sept. 8, 1826, both in ABC 74. On Edwardsean Calvinists conceiving of their religious community as "a radically new kind of society, standing apart from the ways of the world," see Sweeney, *Nathaniel William Taylor*, 33.

125 They were using the novel: *The Coquette* owes its enduring popularity—and its status in the literary canon—to the tantalizing ambiguity of Foster's message. For years scholars have debated whether the novel is emancipatory or constraining. In Cathy Davidson's view, Eliza is a proto-feminist rebel, and the novel reveals the "fundamental injustices" of "patriarchal culture" by dramatizing that women have no sure choices or real freedom. Laura Korobkin and Thomas Joudrey have challenged that view, arguing that Foster offers conservative critiques of undisciplined individualism and materialism. Cathy N. Davidson, *Revolution and the Word: The Rise of the Novel in America* (New York: Oxford University Press, 1986), 140–50; Thomas J. Joudrey, "Maintaining Stability: Fancy and Passion in *The Coquette*," *New England Quarterly* 86, no. 1 (March 2013): 60–88; Laura Korobkin, " 'Can Your Volatile Daughter Ever Acquire Your Wisdom?': Luxury and False Ideals in *The Coquette*," *Early American Literature* 41, no. 1 (2006): 79–107.

125 It was an identification: Extract of a letter from Parker to Tenney, July 30, 1826, in no. 33 Continued Tenney Narrative, 5, ABC 74.

126 The novel appears to have made: Hannah Webster Foster, *The Coquette* (1797; New York: Oxford University Press, 1986), 2, 20, 53.

127 Now even Elnathan: On the power of novels to authorize emotion and serve as scripts for real lives, see Blauvelt, *Work of the Heart,* 24–26, 66. For an analysis of the ways in which different classes used seduction literature as a script, see Cohen, *Murder of Helen Jewett,* 404–5. See also Cynthia A. Kierner's comments on the uses of sentimental novels as "paradigms of interpretation" that helped the wider public to make sense of a scandal (*Scandal at Bizarre: Rumor and Reputation in Jefferson's America* [New York: Palgrave Macmillan, 2004], 63–89). Robert Darnton describes a change in the quality of reading in late-eighteenth-century France that he identified with Rousseau, one that "taught readers to 'digest' books so thoroughly that literature became absorbed in life. The Rousseauistic readers fell in love, married, and raised children by steeping themselves in print." Darnton also notes that this style of reading "showed the influence of the intense, personal religiosity of his Calvinist heritage. His public probably applied an old style of religious reading to new material, notably the novel" (*Great Cat Massacre,* 251). For other work on reader response, see Mary Kelley, "Reading Women/Women Reading: The Making of Learned Women in Antebellum America," *Journal of American History* 83 (Sept. 1996): 401–24; Cathy N. Davidson, "The Novel as Subversive Activity: Women Reading, Women Writing," in *Beyond the American Revolution: Explorations in the History of American Radicalism,* ed. Alfred F. Young (DeKalb: Northern Illinois University Press, 1993), 283–316; James L. Machor, ed., *Readers in History: Nineteenth-Century American Literature and the Contexts of Response* (Baltimore: Johns Hopkins University Press, 1993).

129 If, in the judgment: JEN, 85, 91. Some literary critics interpret *The Coquette* as a novel of sexual inversion that dramatizes what happens when a woman tries to act like a man. Gillian Brown, for example, contends that the coquette assumes the role of the rake, arranging courtships to suit her pleasure ("Consent, Coquetry, and Consequences," *American Literary History* 9, no. 4 [Winter 1997]: 625–52). My colleague Anne Boylan suggested to me that Martha Parker was behaving like a man by getting engaged and breaking it off—the same offense for which female moral reform societies sought to punish men who used promises of marriage to seduce women. Natalie Zemon

Davis observes that the trope of a woman behaving like a man often found expression in the popular culture of early modern Europe. It functioned as a "multivalent image," one with potentially subversive effects that could "widen behavioral options for women," "yield criticism of the established order," and even encourage "the unruly woman to keep up the fight." *Society and Culture in Early Modern France* (Stanford, Calif.: Stanford University Press, 1975), 124–51.

CHAPTER SIX: YOU BELONG TO ME

130 Maybe it was also Elnathan: Kimball to Gridley, Sept. 3, 1826, ABC 74; JEN, 104.

132 When Martha replied: For Evarts's stay in Dunbarton, see JEN, 90, 91, 95, 97, 99, 101, 105, 114, and no. 29 Conversation Between Mr. Evarts and Miss Parker, ABC 74. Evarts had hoped to meet with James Kimball, but a letter arranging their encounter reached him too late. Kimball to Gridley, Sept. 3, 1826, ABC 74.

132 No, he warned Woods: Evarts left Dunbarton on the evening of August 25 and lodged overnight in Concord, New Hampshire, some several miles distant. JEN, 102; no. 31 Woods to Evarts, Aug. 29, 1826, ABC 74.

136 She would have felt particularly: Gridley to Woods, Jan. 16, 1827, ABC 16.5, microfilm reel 502; JEN, 103; no. 28 Parker to Evarts, Aug. 29, 1826, ABC 74; Gridley to Ann and Isaac Bird, Jan. 20, 1829, ABC 16.6, vol. 2, microfilm reel 514. It's not clear from whom Elnathan learned about Tyler's trip to Dunbarton and his threats about adultery; a member of the Prudential Committee could have made that disclosure, or it might have reached him directly through Martha or secondhand from James and Emily Kimball.

138 And on September 2: No. 31 Woods to Evarts, Aug. 29, 1826, no. 32 Woods to Evarts, Sept. 1, 1826, no. 34 Meetings of the Prudential Committee, Aug. 30, 1826, all in ABC 74; JEN, 103–7, 114.

138 And lately there had: Besides Evarts, the Prudential Committee included the lawyers and judges William Reed and Samuel Hubbard as well as the Reverend Warren Fay, pastor of the First Congregational Church in Charlestown, Massachusetts. Some years after the Pru-

dential Committee's decision, Rufus Anderson weighed in with the opinion that its members had decided to accept Martha's resignation because they were unable to "conscientiously take the ground of her defence and justify themselves to the community which had already begun to utter the voice of censure." Anderson to William Jowett, Feb. 20, 1829, ABC 16.5, microfilm reel 502.

140 He also asked her: John Demos, *The Heathen School: A Story of Hope and Betrayal in the Age of the Early Republic* (New York: Knopf, 2014), 146–95, 221–27; Andrew, *From Revivals to Removal,* 86–87, 133–37; Heyrman, *American Apostles,* 32–33; Leonard Woods, *A Sermon Delivered at the Tabernacle in Salem* (Boston, 1812), 11–13; JEN, 116–17; Evarts to Parker, Sept. 4, 1826, ABC 1.01, vol. 6, 275–76.

142 "Few indeed, can fill": No. 35 Gridley to Parker, Sept. 8, 1826, ABC 74. For pondering the many possible readings of Elnathan's letter, I am particularly indebted to Dr. Lisa Keamy.

145 A tempest in a teapot: Homan Hallock to Evarts, March 26 and Sept. 20, 1826, Rev. William A. Hallock to Anderson, Sept. 26, 1826, all in ABC 10, vol. 8.

146 Together, the two men worked: Heyrman, *American Apostles,* 122–26; Gridley to Anderson, Jan. 31, 1827, ABC 16.6, vol. 3, microfilm reel 515; Daniel Temple to Evarts, Dec. 20, 1827, ABC 16.6, vol. 2, microfilm reel 514.

150 That's what Leonard Woods: Gridley to Woods, Jan. 16 and June 1, 1827, both in ABC 16.5, microfilm reel 502; JEN, 21–23, 31–32. In response to Elnathan's charges, Evarts replied that the Prudential Committee "had not the slightest idea that you sailed, while suffering under a desire of immediately forming a new connexion." But even if they had, "such a connexion would have appeared to us highly imprudent, and would doubtless have exposed yourself and the cause to much reproach and ridicule." Evarts to Gridley, May 10, 1827, ABC 1.01, vol. 8, 108–11.

151 Here was hardly the sort: Noah Porter to Gridley, June 30, 1827, and Statement of facts and confession of Martha T. Parker to the Church of Christ in Dunbarton, both n.d., ABC 74; Gridley to Woods, Jan. 16 and June 1, 1827, ABC 16.5, microfilm reel 502. Isaac Bird wrote to Gridley in Smyrna, "You will doubtless have received let-

ters from Sister M. since we have," and even asked him to send them along to Beirut (Bird to Gridley, June 27, 1827, ABC 16.5, microfilm reel 502). In Gridley's desk at Smyrna, there were a number of letters from Martha, but the latest is dated July 9, 1826. Josiah Brewer gave those letters to the American Board on his return to Boston (Catalogue of Mr. Gridley's Papers Retained by the Committee, July 27, 1818, ABC 74). Martha's letters to Elnathan written during the month of August 1826 have been lost. They might have been in his Smyrna desk, and Evarts speculated that he either returned those letters to her or sent them to some of the missionaries in the Levant. Either Evarts or Brewer might have done the same with any of her letters that Elnathan received at Malta or Smyrna (JEN, 107). Rufus Anderson gave a different account, stating that he returned Martha's letters in Gridley's desk to Thomas Tenney on October 27, 1831. Catalogue of Mr. Gridley's Papers.

CHAPTER SEVEN: LIKE A VIRGIN

153 "It was because I loved her": Bird's Journal, Feb. 10, 1827, IBP. The extract of Gridley's letter to the Birds, Dec. 10, 1826, appears in Isaac Bird to Evarts, Jan. 20, 1829, ABC 16.6, vol. 2, microfilm reel 514.

154 Climb into the hills: Descriptions of early-nineteenth-century Beirut appear in George Robinson, *Three Years in the East: Syria*, 2 vols. (London: Henry Colburn, 1837), 2:1–7, and James Silk Buckingham, *Travels Among the Arab Tribes* (London: Longman, Hurst, Rees, Orme, Brown, and Green, 1825), 438–46; see also Ussama Makdisi, *Artillery of Heaven: American Missionaries and the Failed Conversion of the Middle East* (Ithaca, N.Y.: Cornell University Press, 2008), 89–91. My colleague Steven Sidebotham, a classical archaeologist, offered the following interpretation of the artifact described in Buckingham's account in an email communication of November 2017: "The written description of the relief suggests what one would typically find in ancient Attica (area around Athens) from the fifth century B.C. and somewhat later and would have been absolutely typical of a tombstone. The deceased would be the one seated and the male would, likely, have been her husband or some other relative." He adds that

it's odd to find such an artifact in Beirut: "And, unless one could see a drawing or photo, my identification and dating cannot be considered secure. Perhaps this relief is an ancient copy made in the Levant mimicking tombstones from Attica? That part of the Levant certainly copied fifth century B.C. and later Attic/Athenian coinage. So, why not tombstones as well?" Professor Sidebotham consulted with two philologists, Rodney Ast and Julia Lougovaya, both of Heidelberg, to translate the inscription on this artifact.

158 A love match: Ann Parker Bird to Gridley, Feb. 10, 1827, ABC 16.5, microfilm reel 502; Goodell and Bird to Evarts, Jan. 2, 1827, reel 515. The "Miss Cleaves" in question was either Almira (from Bradford) or Nancy (from Beverly), both of whom attended Bradford Academy in 1821 (Catalogue of Bradford Academy, 1803–1853, 60). The reference to women friends writing to Ann about the scandal appears in Daniel Temple to Isaac Bird and William Goodell, Nov. 30, 1826, American Missionaries in the Near East and Malta, 1822–1865, Rauner Library. For Rufus Anderson's earliest years, see Rufus Anderson Journal, ABC 30, vol. 4, and Heyrman, *American Apostles,* 31; for his career at the American Board, see Paul William Harris, *Nothing but Christ: Rufus Anderson and the Ideology of Protestant Foreign Missions* (New York: Oxford University Press, 1999).

160 Far from restraining her: No. 26 Gridley's Statement, ABC 74; JEN, 76; "Report of the Woman's Rights Convention, July 19–20, 1848," reprinted in *Women's Rights Emerges Within the Antislavery Movement, 1830–1870,* ed. Kathryn Kish Sklar (Boston: Bedford/St. Martin's, 2000), 172–79. Evangelically inspired organizations to combat the double standard of sexual behavior began to organize in 1834 with the founding of the Female Moral Reform Society in New York City; see Carroll Smith-Rosenberg, "Beauty, the Beast, and the Militant Woman: A Case Study in Sex Roles and Social Stress in Jacksonian America," *American Quarterly* 23, no. 4 (1971): 562–84.

163 No wonder the blasted hopes: Goodell to Evarts, Feb. 15, 1827, and Goodell and Bird to Evarts, Jan. 2, 1827, both in ABC 16.5, microfilm reel 502. For Goodell's boyhood, see his *The Old and the New* (New York: M. W. Dodd, 1853), xiii–xiv, and for his role in recruiting missionary wives, see Prime, *Forty Years in the Turkish Empire,* 14–42, 55–59.

164 Protestants had nothing: Heyrman, *American Apostles,* 98–99, 205, 252, 322n3; Fisk to Temple, July 5, 1825, ABC 16.5, microfilm reel 502.

166 For all four members: Abigail Davis Goodell attended Byfield Academy in Maine; she and her husband established schools for more than one hundred girls in Ottoman Syria and later the Female Boarding School in Constantinople in 1845. See Abigail Goodell to Elizabeth Dodd, Nov. 14, 1823, Goodell Papers; Goodell to Evarts, Feb. 15, 1827, ABC, microfilm reel 502; William Goodell's Journal at Beirut, Feb. 21, March 18, and April 27, 1824, ABC 16.6, vol. 2, microfilm reel 514; Goodell, *The Old and the New,* 66–67, 89–109; Prime, *Forty Years in the Turkish Empire,* 82, 93, 189–90. For Ann Parker Bird's educational work in Syria, see Isaac Bird, *Bible Work in Bible Lands* (Philadelphia: Presbyterian Board of Publication, 1872), 136, 268–69. Elnathan's views of the ideal missionary matched those of the Goodells. "The time is past in which missionaries are to be going from place to place," Elnathan wrote to Rufus Anderson, "they must come down to a station, and there establish a character, before much can be effected." Gridley to Anderson, Nov. 16, 1826, ABC 16.6, vol. 3, microfilm reel 515.

167 Just as Josiah Brewer: Goodell to Evarts, Feb. 15, 1827 (see installment for Feb. 19), and Ann Bird to Gridley, Feb. 10, 1827 (see installment for Feb. 19), both in ABC 16.5, microfilm reel 502.

169 Instead, his silence on the subject: JEN, 10–11; William Goodell, "A Brief Memoir of Gregory Wortabet from His Birth to the Present Time, Relating Both to His Soul and Body, His Thoughts and Actions, Written by Himself," trans. William Goodell, ABC 16.6, vol. 3, microfilm reel 515. For William's dealings with his Armenian translators, see Goodell to Henry Hill, Dec. 31, 1825, Goodell to Evarts, Jan. 17 and Feb. 2, 1825, Jan. 3, June 19, Sept. 15, and Nov. 27, 1826, and April 3 and May 3, 1827, Goodell to Anderson, Feb. 13, 1827, Sept. 29, 1829, all in ABC 16.6, vol. 2, microfilm reel 514. William had been a member of the Brethren while studying at Andover Theological Seminary, by which time that secret society had abandoned its rule concerning lifelong celibacy. "Convents" was the term for Armenian monasteries.

170 Worst of all, ministers: JEN, 18; Fisk to Temple, Bird, and Goodell, Oct. 1, 1823, and Fisk to Evarts, June 21, 1825, both in ABC 16.5,

microfilm reel 502; Fisk to Bird, March 18, 1825, American Missionaries in the Near East and Malta, 1822–1865, Rauner Library.

171 After Parsons's death: Heyrman, *American Apostles,* 85–86; Daniel O. Morton, *Memoir of Levi Parsons: First Missionary to Palestine from the United States,* 2nd ed. (Burlington, Vt.: Chauncy Goodrich, 1830), 158–60; Parsons to Fisk, Oct. 23, 1817, and Dec. 10, 1818, ABC, 16.5, microfilm reel 502. On romantic friendships, see especially Richard Godbeer, *The Overflowing of Friendship: Love Between Men and the Creation of the American Republic* (Baltimore: Johns Hopkins University Press, 2009); see also Caleb Crain, *American Sympathy: Men, Friendship, and Literature in the New Nation* (New Haven, Conn.: Yale University Press, 2001); Carroll Smith-Rosenberg, "The Female World of Love and Ritual: Relations Between Women in Nineteenth-Century America," in *Disorderly Conduct: Visions of Gender in Victorian America* (New York: Knopf, 1985), 53–76; Anthony Rotundo, *American Manhood: Transformations in Masculinity from the Revolution to the Modern Era* (New York: Basic Books, 1993); Donald Yacavone, "'Surpassing the Love of Women': Victorian Manhood and the Language of Fraternal Love," in *A Shared Experience: Men, Women, and the History of Gender,* ed. Laura McCall and Donald Yacavone (New York: New York University Press, 2001); John D'Emilio and Estelle B. Freedman, *Intimate Matters: A History of Sexuality in America* (New York: Harper & Row, 1988), 121–30. For laws concerning sodomy, see Geoffrey R. Stone, *Sex and the Constitution: Sex, Religion, and Law from America's Origins to the Twenty-First Century* (New York: Liveright, 2017), 212–13. On the persecution of gay men in Britain, see Robert Morrison, *The Regency Years: During Which Jane Austen Writes, Napoleon Fights, Byron Makes Love, and Britain Becomes Modern* (New York: W. W. Norton, 2019), 156–73.

172 At the time of this writing: Goodell to Anderson, June 2, 1828, ABC 16.6, vol. 2, microfilm reel 514.

173 It also raises the possibility: Christine Leigh Heyrman, *Southern Cross: The Beginnings of the Bible Belt* (New York: A. A. Knopf, 1997), 146–49. A broad consensus has emerged that the Enlightenment propelled fundamental changes in the practice and understanding of sexuality,

and some scholars posit a veritable sexual revolution on both sides of the Atlantic during the eighteenth century. Younger people embraced more permissive attitudes toward premarital sex, same-sex romantic friendships blossomed, and marriages based on affection came to govern the expectations among the middle class. See Faramerz Dabhoiwala, *The Origins of Sex: A History of the First Sexual Revolution* (London: Penguin, 2013); Richard Godbeer, *The Sexual Revolution in Early America* (Baltimore: Johns Hopkins University Press, 2002); Kirsten Fischer, *Suspect Relations: Sex, Race, and Resistance in Colonial North Carolina* (Chapel Hill: University of North Carolina Press, 2001); Clare A. Lyons, *Sex Among the Rabble: An Intimate History of Gender and Power in the Age of Revolution, Philadelphia, 1730–1830* (Philadelphia: University of Pennsylvania Press, 2006). Rachel Hope Cleves has produced some of the most thoughtful work on long-term, same-sex loving partnerships in the early republic and the acceptance of such unions by the wider community; see *Charity and Sylvia: A Same-Sex Marriage in Early America* (New York: Oxford University Press, 2014) and her review essay "A Field of Possibilities: Erotic Variations in Early America," *William and Mary Quarterly*, 3rd ser., 70, no. 3 (July 2013): 581–90. For the evangelical affinities and religious practices of the couple, see Balik, " 'Dear Christian Friends.' "

175 True, he had "sinned": Gridley to Harris, draft, June 2, 1827, ABC 16.5, microfilm reel 502. There is no indication of whether Gridley posted and Harris received that letter.

175 Once back in America: Temple to Anderson, June 17, 1827, ABC 16.6, vol. 2, microfilm reel 514; Gridley to Woods, June 1, 1827, and the draft of that letter also dated June 1, 1827, ABC 16.5, microfilm reel 502; Anderson to Isaac Bird and Goodell, March 18, 1826, ABC 1.01, vol. 6.

176 What did it mean: For Elnathan's time in Smyrna, see Gridley to Rufus Anderson, Dec. 28, 1826, Jan. 18 and 31, March 18, 1827; for Caesarea, see Gridley to Anderson, June 25 and July 27, 1827; for an allusion to his success as a fund-raiser, see Brewer to Gridley, April 23, 1837; on his death, see Josiah Brewer's Journal, March 29, 1828, all in ABC 16.6, vol. 3, microfilm reel 515.

CHAPTER EIGHT: THE BUTTERFLY

180 Notwithstanding their differences: James and Emily Kimball to Ann and Isaac Bird, Sept. 28, 1826, Jan. 18, 1827, and Sept. 16, 1828, IBP; Emily Kimball to Evarts, Nov. 28, 1827, ABC 10, vol. 9 (J–K).

183 If the members of: Isaac Bird to Evarts, Jan. 20, 1829, ABC 16.6, vol. 2, microfilm reel 514; Evarts to Ann and Isaac Bird, Oct. 7, 1826, and Ann and Isaac Bird to Evarts, April 13, 1827, both in ABC 16.5, microfilm reel 502; JEN, 48. Bird's account of his Maronite convert led *The Missionary Herald* from February to October 1827. Makdisi, *Artillery of Heaven*, 148–49.

185 She "certainly gave": Temple to Anderson, Jan. 15, 1828, ABC 16.6, vol. 2, microfilm reel 514; no. 36 Report of Rufus Anderson, Boston, Nov. 23, 1827, ABC 74; Anderson to Jowett, April 13, 1827, and Anderson to Gridley, April 14, 1827, both in ABC 1.01, vol. 8; JEN, 107; Thomas Tenney to Isaac and Ann Bird, Nov. 8, 1827, unnumbered, ABC 74. Rufus later wrote to Thomas, thanking him for his letter to the Birds, which would "conduce to the great end we have in view." Anderson to Thomas Tenney, Nov. 30, 1827, ABC 1.01, vol. 7.

187 Martha Parker had deserved: JEN, 3, 6–24. Evarts accurately claimed that the board had asked only some men, those who had volunteered for dangerous postings abroad and in the United States, to refrain from marrying for a period of two to six years. That said, he was quick to add that some men had found that they could give "greater service" to the church by staying single and chaste, mentioning in the same flattering breath both Saint Paul and Bennet Tyler's friend Asahel Nettleton. Indeed, Evarts claimed, celibacy was "unfavorable to purity of life" only in the "Romish" religion because it kept people from reading the Bible and mired them in "the miserable delusions of pardons and indulgences."

188 Perhaps he had, but: JEN, 36–39, 41–46, 50–56, 67, 77–78, 83, 90; Evarts made mention of Elnathan's death before writing all of those passages. Note, too, that the Prudential Committee did not permit Elnathan to see letters concerning Martha written by Gould and Tyler (JEN, 86–87). Elnathan also gave Evarts "several original letters from Miss Parker," none of which found their way into the documentary

record (JEN, 87). Nor did the letter that Elisha Jenney had written to Thomas while Martha and Elnathan were in Fairhaven (no. 27 Tenney's Statement, 16, ABC 74). Evarts's narrative also lowballed the size of Elijah Gridley's estate and admitted that he had made no effort to meet with James Kimball—who would have given him a narrative of events distinctly different from Thomas's version—during his trip to New Hampshire. JEN, 33–35, 103–4.

189 Yet Evarts did not include: JEN, 89–91, 94–95, 108, 113–15.

190 Certainly not without the advice: Ibid., 58, 62–63, 102–6, 114. Missing was any mention of the fact that Martha had expressed her preference for Elnathan to Evarts and then, according to Tyler, only a few days later, said that she favored Thomas.

190 Instead, as Martha, now: Ibid., 96–98.

192 This chipping away: No. 27 Tenney's Statement, 4–9, ABC 74; Isaac Bird's Journal, Jan. 13, 1829, IBP; JEN, 97–100, 116–21. While at Dunbarton, Evarts interviewed Martha Parker Mills about the engagement, taking as dispositive her recollection that the couple had said nothing about its being conditional. Thomas's professed willingness to break off with a future fiancée if Martha changed her mind could have been an allusion to the possibility of his becoming engaged to Emily.

193 That made her letter: JEN, 99–100; no. 28 Martha Parker to Evarts, Aug. 29, 1826, ABC 74. Evarts insisted that he and the rest of the Prudential Committee did not learn that the specific reason Martha had broken her engagement to Thomas was to marry Elnathan until a year after the latter had left America. Put another way, Evarts was denying that the Prudential Committee had punished Martha for her ambition. But Evarts also acknowledged at the time of their decision that the Prudential Committee considered it "possible, though not probable, that Martha would marry Gridley if he remained in America."

194 To do so as quickly as possible: Evarts to Gridley, May 10, 1827, ABC 1.01, vol. 8, 108–11; Ann Bird to Gridley, May 1, 1827, ABC 16.5, microfilm reel 502. See also Evarts to Josiah Brewer, ABC 1.01, vol. 6, 216–18.

194 Evarts figured as one: The "William Penn" essays appeared in the *National Intelligencer* between August and December 1829; Evarts made the case that treaty law should prevent both the federal and the

state governments from interfering with indigenous nations. Evarts hoped that the board's missions would make the Native people into sedentary farmers, and the mounting demands for removal imperiled his vision (Andrew, *From Revivals to Removal*, 133–268). For Evarts's leadership of the Sabbatarian movement, see Richard R. John, "Taking Sabbatarianism Seriously: The Postal System, the Sabbath, and the Transformation of American Political Culture," *Journal of the Early Republic* 10, no. 4 (1990): 517–64; Richard R. John, *Spreading the News: The American Postal System from Franklin to Morse* (Cambridge, Mass.: Harvard University Press, 1995), 186–88. Evarts died in May 1831.

195 Evarts himself came under: For attacks on Evarts's compensation and fundraising, see Andrew, *From Revivals to Removal*, 144. For Channing's concerns, see William Ellery Channing, "Associations," *Christian Examiner*, Sept. 1829, 106, cited in Andrew, *From Revivals to Removal*, 254, and William Ellery Channing, "Remarks on the Disposition Which Now Prevails to Form Associations and to Accomplish All Objects by Organized Masses" (1829), in *The Works of William E. Channing*, 6 vols. (Boston: American Unitarian Association, 1841), 1:281–332.

On evangelicals' intensifying efforts to shape the social order and the mounting opposition in the United States, see James Bratt, "Religious Anti-revivalism in Antebellum America," *Journal of the Early Republic* 24, no. 1 (2004): 65–106; John, "Taking Sabbatarianism Seriously"; Daniel Walker Howe, "The Evangelical Movement and Political Culture in the North During the Second Party System," *Journal of American History* 77, no. 4 (March 1991): 1216–39; Neem, *Creating a Nation of Joiners*. For recent and imaginative work on this subject by Maartje Janse, see " 'Anti Societies Are Now All the Rage': Jokes, Criticism, and Violence in Response to the Transformation of American Reform, 1825–1835," *Journal of the Early Republic* 36, no. 2 (2016): 247–82; " 'Association Is a Mighty Engine' "; and "A Dangerous Type of Politics? Politics and Religion in Early Mass Organizations: The Anglo-American World, c. 1830," in *Political Religion Beyond Totalitarianism: The Sacralization of Politics in the Age of Democracy*, ed. Joost Augusteijn, Patrick Dassen, and Maartje Janse (Basingstoke: Palgrave Macmillan, 2013). For evangelical domination of print media, see Candy Gunther Brown, *The Word in the World: Evangelical Writing, Publishing, and Reading in America, 1789–1880* (Chapel Hill: University of North Carolina Press, 2004); David Paul Nord, *Faith in Reading: Religious Publishing and the Birth of Mass Media in America* (New York: Oxford University Press, 2004); Peter J. Wosh, *Spreading the Word: The Bible Business in Nineteenth-Century America* (Ithaca, N.Y.: Cornell University Press, 1994).

197 Constant newspaper coverage: On Frances Wright, see Lori D. Ginzberg, "'The Hearts of Your Readers Will Shudder': Fanny Wright, Infidelity, and American Freethought," *American Quarterly* 46, no. 2 (1994): 195–226. Royall was a Quaker in youth, but she attended no church regularly as an adult. Her beliefs inclined toward liberal Christianity, and after a visit to the Convent of the Visitation in Georgetown in 1826, she also expressed admiration for Catholics (Anne Royall, *Sketches of History, Life, and Manners in the United States* [New Haven, Conn.: printed for the author, 1826], 179–81, 227, 240, 301–3, 324, 336–37). For her early attacks on evangelicals, see *New York Telescope*, June 23, 1827, 4; *Ariel*, Aug. 25, 1827, 1, 9. For her fully developed indictment of missionary societies, see *The Black Book; or, A Continuation of Travels in the United States*, 2 vols. (Washington, D.C.: printed for the author, 1828), 1:163–247, 326–28. For contemporary descriptions of Royall, see *Boston Lyceum*, April 15, 1827, 209; *Literary Cadet and Saturday Evening Bulletin* (Providence), July 28, 1827, 2; *Hallowell (Maine) Gazette*, Aug. 23, 1827, 2; *New England Galaxy and U.S. Literary Advertiser* (Boston), Sept. 15, 1826, 3; *American Advocate* (Hallowell, Maine), Oct. 6, 1827, 3. For biographies of Royall, see Elizabeth J. Clapp, *A Notorious Woman: Anne Royall in Jacksonian America* (Charlottesville: University of Virginia Press, 2016), esp. 91, 103–24; Jeff Biggers, *The Trials of a Scold: The Incredible True Story of the Writer Anne Royall* (New York: St. Martin's Press, 2017), 80–110.

199 American evangelicals had: Gridley to Woods, June 1, 1827, ABC 16.5, microfilm reel 502; Evarts to Thomas Tenney, Nov. 18, 1828, ABC 1.01, vol. 9; Evarts to Anderson, Nov. 28, 1828, quoted in Clifton Jackson Phillips, *Protestant America and the Pagan World: The First Half Century of the American Board of Commissioners for Foreign Missions, 1810–1860* (Cambridge, Mass.: Harvard University Press, 1969), 142; see also

Ebenezer C. Tracy, *Memoir of the Life of Jeremiah Evarts, Esq.* (Boston: Croker and Brewster, 1845), 292–93.

199 Well, one of them—the man: Bird to Brewer, Feb. 12, 1828, IBP.

201 On April 29, 1828, the Birds: Isaac Bird's Journal, March 23 and 26 and Dec. 24, 1826, Jan. 14 and 25, March 6, 1827, April 9, 1828, all in ABC 16.6, vol. 2, microfilm reel 514; virtually all Bird's entries for late 1826 to early 1827 describe the harassment of their schoolteachers, parents forbidden to send children to missionary schools, and servants forced to resign. See also Isaac Bird's Journal, Feb. 6–7, May 24, Aug. 4–6, 1827 ("Disturbance at Ehden"), Jan. 11, April 28, 1828, IBP; Goodell to Evarts, April 8, 1826, Goodell to Anderson, May 15, 1826, Goodell to Evarts, May 3, 1827, Goodell to unidentified correspondent, Aug. 20, 1827, Goodell to Evarts, Nov. 7, 1827, Goodell to Evarts, Nov. 27, 1827, Goodell to Anderson, April 3, 1828, all in ABC 16.6, microfilm reel 514; Smith to Anderson, Feb. 1, 1828, and Smith to Evarts, June 19, 1828, ABC 16.6, vol. 3, microfilm reel 515; Prime, *Forty Years in the Turkish Empire,* 87–93, 98–99, 101–3; James A. Field Jr., *From Gibraltar to the Middle East: America and the Mediterranean World, 1776–1882* (Princeton, N.J.: Princeton University Press, 1969), 99–100; Michael B. Oren, *Power, Faith, and Fantasy: America in the Middle East, 1776 to the Present* (New York: W. W. Norton, 2007), 114; Makdisi, *Artillery of Heaven,* 103–37. The great European powers feared that Greece's secession from Ottoman rule would inaugurate the Ottoman Empire's total disintegration and trigger a war over the pieces. The Sublime Porte sent a fleet to southern Greece, where French, British, and Russian gunboats intercepted the flotilla in October 1827 and sank three-quarters of the sultan's ships. This defeat at Navarino emboldened the Greeks in their quest for independence and inaugurated the very scramble for Ottoman lands that the rest of Europe had hoped to avoid.

202 Elnathan was dead: "Memorandum of the Mediterranean Missionaries," July 11, 1829, addressed to Anderson, ABC 16.6, vol. 3, microfilm reel 515; Isaac Bird's Journal, Jan. 12–14, 1829, IBP; Goodell to Evarts, Jan. 17, 1829, Isaac Bird to Evarts, Jan. 20, 1829, both in ABC 16.6, microfilm reel 514; Anderson to Evarts, Feb. 20, 1829, ABC 16.5, microfilm reel 502. As for Josiah Brewer, the missionaries dismissed

him as a malcontent who, "even before coming out," "had conceived a prejudice against the Committee and had become distrustful of their more serious declarations."

203 Indeed, as Eli Smith: No. 24 Anderson to David Greene, Feb. 14, 1829, ABC 16.5, microfilm reel 502; Isaac Bird to Evarts, Jan. 20, 1829, IBP.

204 "Tho he was never": Kimball to Ann and Isaac Bird, Jan. 12, 1830, American Missionaries in the Near East and Malta, 1822–1865, Rauner Library. A few months later, James reported to Isaac Bird that he had been conversing with Rufus Anderson, who said "you had become tired of thinking on that unpleasant subject and were glad to be relieved[.] It had probably better be dropped *entirely*. Sister M. appears to enjoy herself and Mr. Tenney [torn] useful." Kimball to Bird, Nov. 2, 1830, IBP.

CHAPTER NINE: THE SORCERER'S APPRENTICE

207 "Mary Irving" disappeared: For the westward course of the Tenney family and biographical information on Mary Eliza, see M. J. Tenney, *The Tenney Family; or, The Descendants of Thomas Tenney of Rowley* (Concord, N.H.: Rumford Press, 1904), 256, 456. Ann and Isaac Bird returned to America in 1836; they ran a school in Hartford, Connecticut, between 1846 and 1869. On *The National Era,* see Stanley Harrold, *Gamaliel Bailey and Antislavery Union* (Kent, Ohio: Kent State University Press, 1986), 81–166. Moderate abolitionists supported by the Tappan brothers—those who broke with Garrisonians over their radical views on women's rights—published the magazine. Mary Eliza Tenney might have become connected with Bailey through either Betsy Mix Cowles or one of her aunts, Marianne Parker Dascomb, who became the head of the Female Department at Oberlin College. On the use of pseudonyms by many antebellum women writers, see Kelley, *Private Woman, Public Stage,* 29–30, 126–37.

208 Doing history keeps us: The most eloquent statement of this caution comes from Robert Darnton, who writes that people in the past "do not think the way we do. And if we want to understand their way of thinking, we should set out with the idea of capturing otherness. . . . We constantly need to be shaken out of a false sense of familiarity

with the past, to be administered doses of culture shock." *Great Cat Massacre*, 4.

209 Disguised as male, the hero: The Tenneys and their three younger children moved to Wisconsin in 1847. Dates appended to her poems place Mary Eliza there in the summer of 1848, but by 1850 she was living in the household of Ann and Isaac Bird and teaching in their Hartford school (U.S. Census of 1850). Most likely she remained with them until 1852, when she received additional training at Bradford Academy. I could not track down her whereabouts in 1853 and 1854, but she appears to have been somewhere unfamiliar enough to inspire a poem about homesickness ("The Exile's Wish in Winter," *National Era*, April 7, 1853, 53). During that period she also wrote a short story, "First Marriage in the Family," about the eldest daughter marrying a missionary and going off to India with him (*National Era*, May 19, 1853, 77). For a sampling of her other contributions to *The National Era* on various topics, see the following: on Indian massacres, "An Incident of Border Life in Maine," March 29, 1849, 49, and "The Masquerade of S—— Fort: A Story of the French and Indian War," Sept. 5, 1850, 141; on anti-Catholicism, "Agatha: The Power of Education," Oct. 31, 1850, 190; on opposition to Mormonism and spiritualism, "The 'Spirits' of the Age," June 6, 1850, 89; the grandmother cited in "Arachne: A Chapter on Needles and Needlework," April 18, 1850; "Bessie Lindsay; or, The Hoyden Tamed," Oct. 3 and 10, 1850, 157 and 161; "The Return: A Leaf from Life's Volume," March 1, 1849; on her success as a contributor, April 17, 1851, 62. On her unwillingness to marry, "Home," Nov. 17, 1853. For her correspondence from Tokat, see Aug. 7, 1856, 125; Sept. 4, 1856, 141; Sept. 3, 1857, 141; Dec. 31, 1857; April 8, 1858, 53; April 15, 1858, 57.

210 By the end of the nineteenth century: As in earlier decades, these single women and the growing ranks of missionary wives drew inspiration from the memoirs that made some into celebrity heroines. Succeeding Harriet Atwood Newell and Ann Hasseltine Judson, the new marquee players of missionary drama in the 1830s and 1840s were Judith Lathrop Grant in Persia and Sarah Lanman Smith in Syria. Composed by evangelical ministers, those memoirs fixed both women in the popular imagination as martyrs to the missionary cause, Grant claimed by

disease and Smith by shipwreck. See William W. Campbell, *A Memoir of Mrs. Judith S. Grant* (New York: J. Winchester, 1842); and Edward Hooker, *Memoir of Mrs. Sarah Lanman Smith* (Boston: Perkins and Marvin, 1839). For the preponderance of single women in the mission field, see Chambers-Schiller, *Liberty, a Better Husband,* 87–88; Robert, *American Women in Mission,* 89, 104–9, 114–16, 120, 123; Jane Hunter, *The Gospel of Gentility: American Women Missionaries in Turn-of-the-Century China* (New Haven, Conn.: Yale University Press, 1984), 11–14; Reeves-Ellington, Sklar, and Shemo, *Competing Kingdoms,* 2.

212 How it must have galled him: Isaac Bird to Rev. S. L. Pomroy, April 27 and May 26, 1855, Mary E. Tenney to Pomroy, July 21, 1855, Ann Parker Bird to Pomroy, Aug. 3, 1855, Joel Hawes to Pomroy, Aug. 1, 1855, all in Candidate Department, ABC 6, vol. 22. The founder of the female academy in Thibodaux, Louisiana, where Mary Eliza taught, was Shubael Tenney, a first cousin to both Ann Parker Bird and Martha Parker Tenney; he was more distantly related to Thomas Tenney. Daniel Tenney, Thomas's younger brother, was a trustee of the female academy in Oxford, Ohio, which became the Western College for Women, now part of Miami University.

214 His fellow evangelicals: Justin Perkins, "Journal of a Visit to America, 1842–1843," 235–36, 348–50, 435–48, 453, 460–62, 464–70, 474, 489–91, Justin Perkins Papers, Frost Library, Amherst College; Thomas Laurie, *Woman and Her Saviour in Persia* (Boston: Congregational Publishing Society, 1863). Despite the variant spellings of their surnames, Fidelia Fiske was a cousin of Pliny Fisk. It appears to have become common practice for the heads of missions, like Perkins, to use their personal prestige and renown to recruit both male missionaries and female teachers. William and Abigail Goodell spent two years back in the United States between 1851 and 1853, possibly with that object, among others, in mind. Indeed, it's possible that Mary Eliza's availability became known to the head of the Tokat mission through the Goodells' influence. Prime, *Forty Years in the Turkish Empire,* 354–59.

214 But if that was a lost: Rosemarie Zagarri offers a compelling argument that the foreign missions movement helped to blunt feminism by focusing the attention of American women on the status of women

in the benighted non-Protestant world. In that way, she contends, missionary discourse "affirmed the structure of America's own existing gender hierarchy." "The Significance of the 'Global Turn' for the Early American Republic," *Journal of the Early Republic* 31, no. 1 (Spring 2011): 1–37.

215 They got plenty of opportunities: As Anne Boylan notes, some antebellum women "oriented their organizational careers around family roles, or pursued voluntary labor in ways that never let it *appear* to conflict with family needs." Ironically, "as they did, they helped create and entrench a new gender system based on masculine superiority and feminine subordination." *Origins of Women's Activism,* 8–9, 31–32, 53–93.

215 To the contrary, the most: The most careful profile of the social and religious backgrounds of women involved in the variety of antebellum benevolence and reform activism appears in Boylan, *Origins of Women's Activism,* 2–4, 47–51; Anne M. Boylan, "Women in Groups: An Analysis of Women's Benevolent Organizations in New York and Boston, 1797–1840," *Journal of American History* 74 (Dec. 1984): 195–236; Hewitt, *Women's Activism and Social Change,* esp. 18–23, 36, 54, 69, 78, 124–25; see also Sally G. McMillen, *Seneca Falls and the Origins of the Women's Rights Movement* (New York: Oxford University Press, 2008). As these studies suggest, some women from evangelical backgrounds numbered among the earliest feminist leaders, a group that included Antoinette Brown (who later embraced Universalism), Lucy Stone, and Paulina Wright Davis, but women from Quaker and Unitarian backgrounds predominated. What's less clear is the precise connection between evangelical affiliation and the resistance to feminist activism. Hewitt suggests a link between the conversion experience's emphasis on submission and "the subordination of bourgeois womanhood," which prompted such women to seek approval from their husbands, male ministers, and Jesus. *Women's Activism and Social Change,* 124–25.

Scholars generally agree that a backlash against women seeking influence outside the household gained strength within the evangelical movement and elsewhere in the United States after about 1830. See Carroll Smith-Rosenberg, "Women and Religious Revivals: Antiritualism, Liminality, and the Emergence of the American Bourgeoisie," in *The Evangelical Tradition in America,* ed. Leonard I. Sweet (Macon, Ga.: Mercer University Press, 1984), 199–231; Brekus, *Strangers and Pilgrims,* 271–301; and Cott, *Bonds of Womanhood,* 154–59. Rosemarie Zagarri traces a similar reaction against women's involvement in politics to this period; see *Revolutionary Backlash,* 82–186.

216 For all their prominence: Cowles taught school for several years before enrolling at Oberlin, as did Mary Eliza Tenney before attending Bradford Academy. Cowles served as preceptress of the Female Department at Grand River Institute from 1843 to 1848; Thomas Tenney arrived as principal in 1842. During the 1830s, she organized the largest women's antislavery society in the nation. Her subsequent work in support of women's rights focused on improving educational and employment opportunities for women, not securing them the vote. See Linda L. Geary, *Balanced in the Wind: A Biography of Betsey Mix Cowles* (Lewisburg, Pa.: Bucknell University Press, 1989), 46–89, and Stacey M. Robertson, *Betsy Mix Cowles: Champion of Equality* (Boulder, Colo.: Westview Press, 2014), 6–7, 14–17, 42, 52–110. Julie Roy Jeffrey has criticized "the tendency to classify some women abolitionists as radical and others as conservative, usually based upon their attitude toward feminism." To most antebellum women, the formal political power sought by feminists seemed an unattainable goal— perhaps even an undesirable objective, given the low esteem in which politics was held by both sexes. *The Great Silent Army of Abolitionism: Ordinary Women in the Antislavery Movement* (Chapel Hill: University of North Carolina Press, 1998), 6–8, 136–37.

219 She specifically condemned: Susan Zaeske, *Signatures of Citizenship: Petitioning, Antislavery, and Women's Political Identity* (Chapel Hill: University of North Carolina Press, 2003), 9, 24–26, 147, 164, 166; Kathryn Kish Sklar, *Catharine Beecher: A Study in American Domesticity* (New Haven, Conn.: Yale University Press, 1973), 63–104; Mary Hershberger, "Mobilizing Women, Anticipating Abolition: The Struggle Against Indian Removal in the 1830s," *Journal of American History* 86, no. 1 (June 1999): 15–40. Susan Zaeske notes that Beecher relented and signed a petition in the 1850s objecting to the repeal of the Missouri Compromise, by which time such limited activism on the part

of women met with general acceptance. The reaction against Beecher's efforts to claim leadership of the revival is not surprising. Catherine Brekus notes the declining number by the 1830s of female preachers in churches and sects that had once allowed the practice, noting that women who might have become preachers instead became Sunday school teachers, religious writers, and especially home and foreign missionaries. *Strangers and Pilgrims,* 274–79, 281, 284–98, 300–301.

220 This message from the pulpit: Boylan, *Origins of Women's Activism,* 32–37; Sklar, *Women's Rights Emerges Within the Antislavery Movement,* 18–19, 32; Catharine E. Beecher, *Essay on Slavery and Abolitionism, with Reference to the Duty of American Females* (Philadelphia: Perkins, 1837); Angelina Grimké to Theodore Dwight Weld and John Greenleaf Whittier, Aug. 20, 1837, Weld-Grimké Letters, 1:427, both cited in Sklar, *Women's Rights Emerges Within the Antislavery Movement,* 131–33. In her letter, Angelina Grimké wrote, "If it can be fairly established that women *can lecture,* then why may they not preach, and if *they* can preach, then woe! woe be unto the Clerical Domination which now rules the world under the various names of General Assemblies, Congregational Associations, etc. . . . As there were *prophetesses* as well as prophets, so there *ought* to be now *female* as well as male ministers."

221 Could it be that the attacks: For another antebellum spiritual challenger to patriarchy, see Paul Johnson and Sean Wilentz, *The Kingdom of Matthias: A Story of Sex and Salvation in 19th-Century America* (New York: Oxford University Press, 1994).

221 But much to Child's disappointment: Lydia Maria Child, *Liberator,* July 23, 1841, cited in Aileen S. Kraditor, *Means and Ends in American Abolitionism: Garrison and His Critics on Strategy and Tactics, 1834–1850* (New York: Pantheon, 1967), 47. For Child's religious views, which mingled Unitarianism with Swedenborgianism, see Deborah Pickman Clifford, *Crusader for Freedom: A Life of Lydia Maria Child* (Boston: Beacon Press, 1992), 32–33, 36–38, 204–5, 217–19; Carolyn L. Karcher, *The First Woman in the Republic: A Cultural Biography of Lydia Maria Child* (Durham, N.C.: Duke University Press, 1994), 13–15, 356, 374–83, 402.

Index

Page numbers in *italics* refer to illustrations.